While traveling in the Cana
Karın, of Cornwall ın the L
dreamlike to them. They were in the restaurant of the hotel where they were staying, about to have their evening meal, when in walked a man who was the spitting image of Mike's best friend, Colin, who had died a couple of years earlier.

Mike and his wife glanced at each other and both of them said, "Doesn't he look like Colin?"

Mike had known Colin for thirty years and found it unsettling when this man sat down quite near the table where he and his wife were sitting. "In a way, I wanted to find an excuse to talk to him, but then I felt I shouldn't. I couldn't, however, stop looking at him. When the waiter came over to the man, it was if I were dreaming. Colin had a habit of putting two fingers of his right hand in his top pocket when he was slightly nervy. This is exactly what his doppelganger did as he placed his order for a drink."

After a few days, Colin's double left and Mike felt almost relieved. But when he and Karin were at Tenerife Airport to fly back to England, the man was there, waiting for the same flight they were taking. "This particular flight was heading for Bristol, where Colin was born, an airport we don't normally return to when returning home."

First edition

THE SYNCHRONICITY HIGHWAY

EXPLORING COINCIDENCE, THE PARANORMAL, & ALIEN CONTACT

BY
TRISH MacGREGOR & ROB MacGREGOR

PANTA REI

Other Books by Trish MacGregor

Black Moon
Black Water
Category Five
Cold As Death
Dark Fields
Esperanza
Fevered
Ghost Key
Hidden Lake
High Strangeness
In Shadow
Lagoon
Out of Sight
Tango Key
The Hanged Man

Other Books by Rob MacGregor

YOUNG ADULT NOVELS

Double Heart
Hawk Moon
Prophecy Rock

ADULT NOVELS

Time Catcher
Romancing the Raven
Crystal Skull
Indiana Jones and the Last Crusade
–The Peril at Delphi
–Dance of the Giants
–The Seven Veils
–The Genesis Deluge
–The Unicorn's Legacy
–The Interior World
Peter Benchley's Amazon: Ghost
JUST/IN TIME with Billy Dee Williams
PSI/NET with Billy Dee Williams

Other Books by Trish MacGregor & Rob MacGregor

Aliens in the Backyard: UFO Encounters, Abductions, & Synchronicity

The 7 Secrets of Synchronicity: Your Guide to Finding Meaning in Signs Big and Small

Synchronicity and the Other Side: Your Guide to Meaningful Connections with the Afterlife

This one is for our daughter, Megan,
with much love always
We would also like to thank everyone who contributed stories.
Your experiences have expanded our collective knowledge of
synchronicity, the paranormal, and alien contact.

Table of Contents

Introduction
—Wonderland
—Unlocking the Message
—A Zen Koan

PART ONE: THE HIGHWAY

Chapter 1: The Synchro Travelers
—Where's Your Focus?
—A Deeper Reality
—Interconnected
—Across Town
—Common Travel Synchros
—Traits of a Synchro Traveler

Chapter 2: Guises of the Trickster
—The Archetype
—Snowden and the Red Panda
—Trickster as a Mirror
—Just Chill
—Playing with Irony
—As the Crow Flies
—A Skeptic's Take on Synchronicity

Chapter 3: Colossal Coincidences
—The Titanic
—JFK-Lincoln
—Tecumseh's Curse
—Aurora/Sandy Hook
—Intertwined Storms
—9-11
—Global Consciousness Project
—Movies & 9-11
—Making Sense of It

Chapter 4: Critter Coincidences
—The Swallows & the Skydive
—Crows & Blackbirds
—Doves & Owls
—Grey Wolf in Delaware
—Those Mice
—Oscar the Cat
—Ladybugs
—Flies
—The Swan & the Cormorant
—Things to Keep in Mind

Chapter 5: Names & Dates
—Tocayos
—Tale of Richard Parker
—The Red Balloon
—More Doppelgangers
—Matching Tales
—Pseudonyms
—Harry Who?
—The Unsinkable Hugh Williams
—In the Name of Murder
—Birthdates

Chapter 6: Love & Synchronicity
—Angie's Story
—Timer
—Renee and Tennerin
—Synchronicity & Alchemy
—Full Circle
—How She Said Good-Bye

Chapter 7: Synchronicity & Healing
—The Legacy of Brugh Joy
—Mass Beliefs
—Homeopathy & Medical Intuitives
—Spirit Healer
—Carol & Chase Bowman
—A Secondhand Furniture Store
—A Healing Meditation

PART TWO: THE INNER WAY

Chapter 8: Spirits Speak
—Hank & Judy
—Seeking Contact
—A Meditation to Initiate Spirit Contact
—Ancient Origins
—The Aztec Mirror
—Raymond Moody's Psychomanteum
—Voices of the Dead
—The Medium Way
—Esther Hicks and the Bird
—A Spirit Request
—Straight Pins at Castillo de San Marcos

Chapter 9: Telepathy
—Identical Twins
—E-mail Telepathy
—Telepathy with Partners
—Telepathic Friends & Siblings
—Telepathy with Strangers
—Telepathy with Pets
—Telepathy with a Dolphin

Chapter 10: Psychokinesis
—Pauli & Jung
—Uri Geller
—PEAR: Princeton Engineering Anomalies Research
—Jung & Rhine
—Power of the Collective Mind
—Your Pauli Effect

Chapter 11: Precognition
—Free Will or Predestination?
—A Shaman's Predictions
—Impulses, Precognition, and Premonitions
—The Koi Pond
—Precognition in Dreams & Altered States
—Romania?
—Adele & John Lilly
—The Drowning
—Lost Checkbook
—The Dream Post-It

Chapter 12: Clairvoyance
—ESP Trainer
—Remote Viewing
—The Missing Man in Tokyo
—Renie Wiley, Adam Walsh and Christie Luna

Chapter 13: Remote Views: Connecting with Joe McMoneagle

PART THREE: THE SKYWAY

Chapter 14: The Abduction Scenario
—Encounter in Germany
—On the Fence
—Montreal Abductee
—Primed for Contact
—Darren's Story
—A Lifelong Abductee
—The Divide

Chapter 15: Xperiencers, Synchronicity & Encounters

Chapter 16: UFOs and the Paranormal
—Blown Open
—Precognition & Encounters
—Psychokinesis & Encounters
—Synchronicity & the Origami Ball
—Telepathy and Encounters
—Paranormal Abilities or Advanced Technology?

Chapter 17: UFOs and the Dead
—The Photo
—Exit 33
—The Quebec Connection
—High-Pitched Screeching
—Orange Lights
—Illuminated Cloud
—What's It Mean?
—The Spirit Connection

Chapter 18: A Close Encounter with Whitley Strieber

Chapter 19: The Fearless Journey

Introduction
WONDERLAND

When we started a blog on synchronicity or meaningful coincidence in February 2009, we had no idea it would result in a book—much less four books on the topic. But once you're on the synchronicity highway, you're traveling through a realm that often seems as magical and strange as Alice's Wonderland. You feel connected to something larger than yourself and your immediate world. Your perceptions change, you see and experience yourself and life differently. You become immersed in a mystery that often defies reason and logic. Your worldview can be turned inside out like a dirty sock.

Numerous exit ramps exist on this highway and each one of them holds a deeper mystery, a different kind of logic, a kind of quantum weirdness. Explore any of them and no telling what you might uncover—astounding odds, tricksters, messengers from the unknown, the unseen, and the seemingly miraculous. And always, you're peeling away the intricate layers of this phenomenon, decoding and deciphering it. Sometimes, the significance of a particular synchronicity may be as elusive as a ghost; other times it's glaringly obvious, so in your face you can't dismiss it as random.

On the synchronicity highway, your guidance system lies in your awareness, curiosity, feelings, intentions, and beliefs. It lies *within*. Once you trust that inner guidance, synchronicities seem to pop up everywhere. They are signposts, friends, allies that guide and direct you, warn you, clarify and confirm your decisions, laugh at you and with you.

Carl Jung, the Swiss psychiatrist who coined the term, defined synchronicity as the coming together of inner and outer events in way that is meaningful to the observer and can't be explained by cause and effect. Let's say you think in passing about a former friend, roommate, lover, someone you haven't heard from in years. Awhile later, you log onto Facebook and find a friend request from that individual. That's the simplest kind of synchro: no cause and effect is involved and it's meaningful to you.

Now imagine this. Your cat just died and as you're digging a grave for your beloved pet, you've got the car radio on in the background and Peter Gabriel's song *Digging in the Dirt* comes on. What are the odds that out of all the music on planet Earth, this particular song happens to come on just as it does, capturing the essence of what you're doing? Meanwhile, a friend calls interrupting you and greets you with a phrase that you haven't heard for a long time. "Hey, dig this…" Not quite as simple, right? In fact, this seizes your attention so completely that your life pivots in a flash.

Jung included extrasensory perception under the broad umbrella of synchronicity. This stance is sometimes controversial. Some people feel that calling ESP an aspect of synchronicity suggests that accurate, psychically obtained information is merely coincidental. But Jung was simply saying that telepathy, precognition, mediumship, clairvoyance and other psychic abilities work outside of cause or effect.

If, for instance, a psychic with no previous knowledge of events in your life predicts that you will receive a surprise sum of money in the near future and two days later, an unexpected check arrives in the mail, that's precognition. But it also fits under synchronicity because cause and effect weren't involved. The psychic didn't tell anyone to send you a check and had no logical reason to expect you would receive one. So an inner experience—the psychic's prediction—and an outer event—the receipt of a check—came together outside of cause and effect and undoubtedly was meaningful.

Synchronicity is an equal opportunity experience. It isn't bound or limited by the color of your skin, your religious and spiritual beliefs, your gender, profession, marital status, age, fame or lack of it. It doesn't care how much money you have, what your politics are, whether you're educated or not. It isn't limited by time or space.

Your awareness and receptivity to the phenomenon creates an atmosphere that invites synchronicity to occur. In some situations and environments synchronicities flourish. They are threaded throughout mass events like natural and manmade disasters. They occur in travel and creative endeavors, in social movements and popular culture, and they sometimes proliferate during and after UFO encounters. During intensely emotional periods and when are lives are in transition, synchronicity is usually right there with us.

It could be that the synchronicity highway never ends, that innumerable tangents exist off an infinite number of exits. Perhaps it's similar to the "interstate" that author and consciousness researcher Robert Monroe talked about when he referred to the route that opens to us when we die. But we don't have to die to experience and explore synchronicity. In fact, meaningful coincidence may act as a kind of interface between life and death, between our consciousness as humans and our larger consciousness after death.

Synchronicity spans the spectrum from the simple to the complex and can involve virtually anything. In *The Synchronicity Highway*, you'll find synchros that involve everything from numbers, music, and books to spirits and aliens. Some synchros unfold over time—months or even years—and others are complete within seconds. Either way, we're invited into direct experience with who we are.

UNLOCKING THE MESSAGE

Some of the people you'll meet in this book have experienced synchronicities so powerful that their consciousness was blown open. That was the case for Darren of Australia, who experienced the cat burial in conjunction with the Peter Gabriel song. Not long after that experience, he started a blog on synchronicity and has been researching it ever since.

When the meaning of a synchro isn't immediately obvious, be patient. It will reveal itself, it always does. In the spring of 2013, it seemed that whenever Trish noticed the time, it was 4:44. She took note of the repeating cluster, but didn't have any idea what it meant. During the weeks this was occurring, we heard from a TV consultant who was interested in our book, *Aliens in the Backyard: UFO Encounters, Abductions & Synchronicity,* and wanted to talk with us about how the book might translate for TV. During our conversation with him, he told us he kept seeing the same numbers over and over on his digital clock, on the microwave oven, in his car, on random mailboxes. He wondered what it meant. The numbers? 4-4-4.

He intuitively knew the repeating clusters were significant, but didn't understand the significance. But right then, Trish understood that her 4-4-4 clusters were about connecting with him. In numerology, 4-4-4 equals 12 and when those numbers are added together, you get 3. Interestingly, three parties were involved in the discussion—the authors, the consultant, and a production company. Trish stopped seeing the clusters after the production company bowed out of the discussions.

You run into all types of people on this highway. Some of them will join you for a time on your mutual journey, then will head down a particular exit ramp and fall out of your experience. Others will openly share their insights and your understanding of synchronicity is deepened because of the interaction. Then there are the few who declare that synchronicity should make you afraid, very afraid, and you must turn away from it. It's the devil's work. This type is countered by those who believe synchronicity is God's work. Then there are the egomaniacs who insist they have the answers, the truth, and you must believe what they believe about synchronicity or fall by the wayside.

The bottom line is that on the synchronicity highway, we're all seekers and our collective experiences help us to understand the phenomenon.

A ZEN KOAN

Synchronicity is subjective, dependent on the perspective of the observer. If you don't recognize a coincidence as meaningful, it's not synchronicity. It's just a coincidence. It's like the familiar Zen koan: if a tree falls in a forest and no one is around to hear it, does it make a sound?

Synchronicity doesn't exist unless you recognize that coincidences can have meaning. Angela, a writer, e-mailed us after she read *Aliens in the Backyard* and addressed this very thing:

"I had no previous idea what synchronicity was or that such a concept had actually been defined and documented. The more I thought about it, the more I've realized I've had probably hundreds of these meaningful coincidences throughout my whole adult life, but the prominent skeptic in me always dismissed them as random and meaningless.

"Now I know better. I've started paying attention to them, and they are accelerating. Good things are starting to happen for me professionally and personally. Your writing and research into synchronicity has turned some of what I've believed on its ear, but in a good way."

Synchronicity exists along the border between the seen and the unseen, the known and the unknown, life and death. It can be that twilight zone Rod Serling brought to us in the 1960s or the archetypal place George Lucas brought us to with the *Star War* sagas and with Indiana Jones. It seems to be an intricate component of human consciousness and yet it may also be the bridge to a greater consciousness.

We see The Synchronicity Highway as a direct route to understanding that an underlying web of reality exists where everything and everyone is connected. Synchronicity is the most conscious aspect of this web, the glue that binds, linking our everyday reality with a deeper reality.

Part One:
THE HIGHWAY

"Synchronicity is an ever present reality for those who have eyes to see."
—Carl Jung

Chapter 1
THE SYNCHRO TRAVELERS

When you venture forth on a journey, a trek that takes you out of your normal routines and concerns, your consciousness has greater freedom to explore. Your comfort zones are gone, your kitchen, your bed and your pillows are memories. You're in new, unfamiliar territory and must confront who you are.

"Often I go to some distant region of the world to be reminded of who I really am," wrote Michael Crichton in *Travels*. "Stripped of your ordinary surroundings, your friends, your daily routines, your refrigerator full of your food, your closet full of your clothes—with all of this taken away, you are forced into direct experience. Such direct experience inevitably makes you aware of who it is that is having the experience. That's not always comfortable, but it is always invigorating."

If you're traveling in a rigid fashion, getting from one place to another, taking care of business and leaving little or no room for changes, then you probably won't have many chance encounters or unusual coincidences. However, if you're willing to allow variations in your travel plans and approach each moment of your journey as an opportunity, stay alert to and remain in the present moment, it's more likely that synchronicity will become your most trusted traveling companion. You'll constantly be in the groove, in the flow, in the right place at the right time, with the right people. You'll become a magnet for positive experiences on the synchronicity highway.

One of the first curiosities you might discover is that what you concentrate on has a way of manifesting itself more quickly than it might in your ordinary life. So if you focus on what irritates you—the long security lines, the flight delays, the cramped seats in the plane—then more of the same could continue throughout your journey until you change your attitude.

Travelers are a diverse bunch, but they usually have three things in common: a destination, a specified time frame, and a resolve to enjoy the journey, leaving room for variations in plans. Beyond that, they come in several broad types:

The first type takes a guided tour or combines business with pleasure. The schedule is fixed for most of the trip. Only minimal decisions must be made, so surprises aren't expected and there are usually fewer opportunities for meaningful coincidence to serve as a guide. Synchronicities, however, are likely to come into play when plans are altered by unexpected events. Perhaps a tour bus breaks down, forcing you to take a taxi back to your hotel. You share the taxi with a stranger who gives you an idea for a side trip to fill the rest of your day. On the side trip, you meet someone from your hometown who will play an important role in your life. While the original incident—the breakdown—was probably an annoyance, it created an opportunity that not only changed your travel plans, but perhaps changed your life as well.

The second type of traveler has general plans, a direction, goals, but is not tied to a schedule or a guided tour. He plays the trip by ear, leaving himself open to synchronicity. In essence, he begins and ends his day on the synchronicity highway. This style of travel is more challenging, but amazing coincidences, such as encountering an old friend, play important roles.

The third type is rarer—she takes off with her ATM card and a backpack without any distinct time frame or plans beyond an original destination that will serve as a starting point. Possibly she is on a quest of self-discovery. She's willing to follow a new path on a whim. Perhaps she's offered a temporary job and decides to take it. Or she ends up in a hospital after a minor accident and meets someone who becomes a romantic partner and changes her life. Synchronicity is her best friend, her compass.

One person, of course, might experience all three types of travel over a period of time, if not on the same journey, as needs and priorities change. For Hilary Carter, the change from one type to the other occurred over the course of six years. In the fall of 2004, she and a friend visited a small country church in an English village. The church had been built on the site of a Benedictine Priory that dated back to the thirteenth century. As they pulled up outside the church, her friend pointed at the speedometer. It showed the car had reached exactly 111,100 miles. The trip meter displayed 111 and the time was exactly 11:11 on November 11 (11-11).

"It was frightening. All those elevens! It was too much for my rational mind to handle." But she knew it meant something. "Looking back, I can see that day was a pivotal moment in my life. I knew I had experienced something exceptional."

She didn't have any idea *what it meant,* but was intrigued enough to begin researching 11, 111 and 11:11. She discovered she wasn't the only person in the world experiencing the 11:11 phenomenon.

Carl Jung considered numbers to be archetypal and believed that when you experience clusters of a particular number, it has become active within your psyche. It apparently stays active until you *get the message.* The message of 11:11 seems to be about evolution in consciousness, that you're being ushered into a greater reality, the flow of universal energy. It can also act as a warning and as confirmation.

Hilary went on to write a book, *The 11:11 Code,* and as part of her research, undertook a journey along the 11th parallel line of latitude in India. So she started out as a second type of traveler and ended up as that rarest of creative travelers, one on a quest. The nature of her travel synchronicities along the 11th parallel were radically different from those she had experienced before. "My journey ended in Kozhikode, Kerala. That night I met a German publisher at an Ayurvedic Temple. I told him about my book, *The 11:11 Code,* and he couldn't believe it because his son was born on November 11 at 11 a.m.!"

It was as if the 11:11 synchronicities she experienced six years earlier had come full circle. These synchros tend to multiply. For instance, as Rob was editing this chapter, he noticed that the above sentence appeared at the top of page 11 on his computer. He mentioned that to Trish, who was reading the galley proofs of her novel, *Apparition,* and she noted that she was on page 111.

WHERE'S YOUR FOCUS?

Before you embark on your next trip, train yourself to notice where you place your attention throughout the course of a given day. Is your attention often on what you can't control? Do you fret a lot about what hasn't happened yet? Do you gnaw away at something that happened in the past, struggling to piece things together? We all do it. The trick is to bring your attention back to a positive place in the here and now.

Granted, it's not always an easy thing to do. We are so easily swept up in the minutia of our own lives that we lose sight of the bigger picture. But with practice, we can train our minds to remain in the present moment and once it becomes second nature, we quickly adjust our perspective and notice synchronicities that we might've otherwise overlooked. We also might find that we are experiencing synchronicities more frequently.

When you find your thoughts straying, here are a couple of techniques for bringing yourself back into alignment quickly and easily:

–Whether you're in a crowded airport or on the street of an unfamiliar city, bring your attention into alignment by focusing on your breathing. Be conscious of each inhalation and exhalation. Feel the air moving into and throughout your body, energizing you.

–Look around. Find something to appreciate. It doesn't matter what it is—the pattern the light makes as it falls across the floor, the sound of the wind through trees. The act of appreciating brings your attention to where you are *right now.*

–Awaken your senses through a good meal, the touch of a soft fabric against your skin, the scent of food, perfume, something that puts you in a pleasant frame of mind.

–Get lost in a riveting book.

The better you get at this, the easier it becomes to pay close attention to your surroundings when you're traveling. As it becomes your normal way of being, your awareness of meaningful coincidence will be heightened and you'll become more proficient at reading the signs and symbols that appear in your life. One of the most interesting stories we ran across addresses what can happen when you ignore or dismiss these signs and symbols.

In Robert Moss's book, *The Three "Only" Things, Tapping the Power of Dreams, Coincidence, and Imagination,* he relates a harrowing personal story. Shortly before the stock market crash of 1987, Moss was in the restroom of a plane and accidently dropped a wallet into the toilet. It contained his credit card and checks from a brokerage account he had at the time. He rescued the wallet just before it swirled down the toilet. "Had this been a dream, I might have written a one-liner like: If you're not careful, your stock market investments will go down the toilet."

At the time, he wasn't fully aware of synchronicity. "I didn't harvest the message, neglected to take the appropriate action to limit the risk to my brokerage account—and saw a large percentage of my net worth go down the toilet." Now he recommends interpreting a synchronicity or any event that includes signs and symbols—*wallet, toilet, brokerage account*—as if it's a dream. "…incidents in waking life speak to us exactly like dream symbols."

A DEEPER REALITY

While traveling in the Canary Islands, Mike Perry and his wife, Karin, of Cornwall in the U.K., experienced an event that seemed dreamlike to them. Mike blogs about synchronicity at www.67notout.com so he is particularly aware of anomalies that point to a deeper reality.

They were in the restaurant of the hotel where they were staying, about to have their evening meal, when in walked a man who was the spitting image of Mike's best friend, Colin, who had died a couple of years earlier. Mike and his wife glanced at each other and both of them said, "Doesn't he look like Colin?"

Mike had known Colin for thirty years and found it unsettling when this man sat down quite near the table where he and his wife were located. "In a way, I wanted to find an excuse to talk to him, but then I felt I shouldn't. I couldn't, however, stop looking at him. When the waiter came over to the man, it was if I were dreaming. Colin had a habit of putting two fingers of his right hand in his top pocket when he was slightly nervy. This is exactly what his doppelgänger did as he placed his order for a drink."

After a few days, Colin's double left and Mike felt almost relieved. But when he and Karin were at Tenerife Airport to fly back to England, the man was there, waiting for the same flight they were taking. "This particular flight was heading for Bristol, where Colin was born, an airport we don't normally return to when returning home."

The connection to Colin's birthplace was like a giant exclamation point at the end of his and Karin's trip. Perhaps, for Mike, the synchronicity was also a reminder that he could connect with a deeper reality anywhere, at any time.

Some travel synchros are like mirrors, reflecting your immediate surroundings and circumstances in bizarre ways. That was the case for us years ago on a trip to Venezuela, where Trish was born and raised. We visited the Gran Sabana, one of the most fascinating wilderness regions of the planet. Our adventure among the soaring buttes, waterfalls and forest went by too quickly and we soon found ourselves back in Caracas.

At the airport, we headed to customs, where we were surrounded by guards with machine guns. Colombian drug dealers had begun using Caracas to export cocaine and the government was cracking down. The guards were particularly interested in the man in front of us, a tall, middle-aged Venezuelan in a dark, three-piece suit who carried a briefcase. They told him to open it up. Slowly, the man unlatched the briefcase and the guards leaned forward to see what was inside. The tension was thick and tight, the air seemed to heat up. What would they do if the briefcase was filled with packets of cocaine? What would the man do?

We were directly behind the man and had a good view. Surprisingly, there was only one item in the briefcase, a paperback book, *Fevered,* one of Trish's novels, that she'd written under a pseudonym, Alison Drake. The man had no idea the author was standing behind him and we were too stunned by the synchronicity to tell him.

And seriously, what are the odds that we would be standing in line behind this guy, in the airport of Trish's birthplace, that the guards would order him to open the briefcase right then, and that the only item in it was one of her novels? Then there was the title of the novel, a perfect reflection of the atmosphere around us—the feverish search by armed guards for drug smugglers.

In essence, the synchronicity provided a window to the mystery of a deeper reality that connects everyone and everything.

INTERCONNECTED

Lauren Raines is an artist and sculptor who lives in Tucson, Arizona. In the summer of 2013, she drove across the country to the East Coast to participate in a series of art festivals. She always experiences powerful synchronicities when she travels and this trip was no exception.

An acquaintance she hadn't heard from in years e-mailed her when she was on the road about an amazing, bright and talkative little boy she met in Brooklyn this summer while she was doing face painting at an outdoor festival. She painted his face, and was delighted at how charming he was. She got to talking to the boy's father as well.

Lauren's acquaintance told the man she had participated in the New

York Renaissance Fair and he said his wife's mother had done it for a while as well. At this point, the acquaintance realized she was painting the face of Lauren's grandson. "Once more," said Lauren, "I'm blessed to remember that, no matter what goes on at the surfaces of our lives, we're all really connected, a part of each other, at the roots."

Again what are the odds? When you think about the orchestration required for this synchronicity to have occurred, it's mind-blowing. Out of all the people who live in Brooklyn—2.533 million as of 2011—how did this little boy and his father just *happen* to stop for face painting with a woman who *just happened* to know the boy's grandmother? As author Robert Hopcke said, "There are no accidents."

ACROSS TOWN

You don't have to travel to some far-flung port of call to experience a meaningful coincidence. A trip across town can just as easily create the atmosphere in which synchronicity flourishes.

In 2009, Isabella Dove, a European expatriate, was living in Bangkok, a city of ten million.

She had recently bought a USB air card with a SIM card from her mobile service provider that enabled her to access WiFi anywhere with a laptop or notebook computer. A few days later, she sat down at a local Starbucks and, eager to try her new purchase, brought out her USB modem.

A young Thai man walked in just then and searched for an electrical outlet, but there weren't any more available. So Isabella waved him over to her table. He smiled, sat down, opened his notebook and glanced at her USB card. He asked her if she liked it and she said that she did.

"I'm the one who designed it," he said. "I work for the company producing these USBs. We're now designing a WiFi version of it."

"We had a nice conversation," Isabella recalled. "I offered ideas on how to make his product better. Only 10,000 of these USB air cards were produced and sold. There are loads of service providers in Thailand and only one has these USBs. So, with ten million residents in the city, what are the odds?"

Synchros like this one often come about when you're feeling excited and enthusiastic about something, filled with wonderment and appreciation. It's as if your positive, heightened emotions act as a hub, a magnet, that attracts a kind of magic.

Metaphysical teachers often address the importance of appreciation. Author and publisher Louise Hay notes that before she even gets out of bed in the morning, she sets the tone for her day by spending ten minutes just being thankful for "all the good" in her life. She even thanks her bed for her good night's sleep! It sounds like a simple thing to do. But how many of us leap out of bed in the morning, rushed for time before we've even had breakfast, dreading a commute through traffic or a confrontation with the boss? It's part of why we take vacations!

If you commute to work, use that time to appreciate "all the good" in your life, as Hay does. By doing this, you're nurturing an inner atmosphere conducive to synchronicity.

It seems this is what Mike Clelland, an author and blogger, was doing one morning in Manhattan, in the mid-80s, when he was in his early twenties.

"It was a lovely summer morning. I got on the subway in lower Manhattan on my way to an office job uptown. This was the E train, and I got on, as usual, at Spring Street. The next stop was West 4th Street, and when the doors opened a very pretty young woman got on the train. I don't understand why, but for some reason I literally thought she was an angel. I was convinced she was somehow delivering some mystical message to me. Maybe I died, and she was escorting me to the great beyond? Maybe this was the subway to heaven? I was thunderstruck, and it was extremely strange."

It's obvious that Mike was in a state of mind that invites synchronicity: *a lovely summer morning, a pretty young woman...*

Even today, he can recall exactly was this woman looked like and what she was wearing—short blonde hair, simple white summer sun dress, white cotton "boating" shoes, low top and clean. "No socks and unshaven legs. She folded the *New York Times* in the proper way that only the savvy New Yorker knows."

Mike recalls that she was smiling as she read the paper, that she stood, never sat down, and never looked at him. The woman got off at 34th street.

At the time, Mike was living with his girlfriend, Catherine, in a little apartment in SoHo. "When I got home that evening I told her about this weirdly profound event. She didn't understand how intense it was. She actually got kind of angry at me—and that was typical of her. She simply saw it as me ogling, and immediately I felt defensive."

A few months later, Mike and Catherine were on a busy street in Greenwich Village. It was a cold day, a Saturday, and they were squabbling about something. "Then Catherine suddenly blurted out, 'What are we doing? We shouldn't be together! I'm not your type, *she's* your type!' And she pointed to this random woman on the sidewalk... *And it was her!* The angel from the subway. And she was wearing the *same* shoes!"

COMMON TRAVEL SYNCHROS

Travel synchronicities are as varied and different as the people who experience them. They can be mind-blowing game-changers or just curious oddities that hint at some deeper order in the universe. They can involve virtually anyone, anywhere, at any time. They happen more frequently when you're aware of them and are receptive to their occurrence. They also tend to manifest themselves more often when you request them in much the same way you might request having a dream that will provide insight into a personal concern.

We've compiled a list of some of the most common travel synchronicities. As you move along through your journeys, add to this list, and ultimately create your own travel synchronicity MO. After all, each of us gravitates toward people, situations, and events that inflame our passions, push our buttons, and speak to us on an intuitive level. What seizes us may leave you as flat as day-old Coke. So use this list merely as a guideline.

1. *Places.* You need a certain kind of information and it's provided in an unusual and synchronistic manner. Perhaps you're looking for a particular restaurant in an unfamiliar city and suddenly a bus drives by with the name and address of that restaurant written on the side. Or you hear a song or open a book that provides the information.

2. *People.* While traveling in a place you've never been before, you and your family reminisce about the neighbors you used to have. You fell out of touch years ago and wonder what happened to them. A few hours later, you're at a restaurant and your former neighbors walk in.

3. *Numbers.* You're driving out of state, on your way home, and notice that the same number clusters keep appearing—on your restaurant tab, your gasoline bill, the car clock, your exit off the interstate. You know it's

significant but don't fully understand it until you arrive home and find a check for that amount in your mailbox.

4. *Dreams*. You have a series of dreams about a place you've never been. The dreams are shockingly vivid and you're able to research them and find the location. Sensing the importance of these dreams, you follow an urge to travel to this place. While there, you pursue other synchronicities and end up meeting your soul mate. Or you land the ideal job. Or you realize you absolutely must live in this place. Permanently.

5. *Six degrees of separation*. You keep running into the same people on your trip. Strangers. They notice this oddity, too, and before long, you introduce yourselves. Even though you are all from different parts of the world, you discover you have mutual friends. Or you decide to travel with these people and inadvertently are led to a place that is the locus of your soul.

6. *Challenges*. A travel challenge or issue is reflected in something you've read or seen before, during, or immediately after you confront the challenge/issue.

7. *Game-changer*. This type of synchro, especially when it occurs during travel, can alter your life or your worldview and the impact is powerful and long-term. For example, it could be a seemingly random meeting with a person who changes your life—he or she becomes your life partner or business partner.

That was the case for us years ago when we were working as freelance travel writers. Through contacts we'd made in the travel industry we had gotten offers to join travel agents on 'fam trips,' which are free or low-cost trips to destinations with the intent of familiarizing the agents with the city or region.

We were on one such trip to Nashville when we sat next to a Miami travel agent from Colombia. When he found out we were travel writers, that Trish had been born and raised in Venezuela and was fluent in Spanish, he proposed that we lead groups of travel writers to South American destinations. He was well-connected with people in the South American travel industry and before long, we—sponsored by Avianca Airlines—were leading trips to the Amazon and Andes and Caribbean beach destinations on the northern coast of the continent. We not only traveled free, but were being paid to do so.

Once you understand that every experience, situation, encounter, and event holds clues to some vital part of your *life's journey*, your immediate journey is enriched. Once you're on the synchronicity highway, you're exactly where you're supposed to be all of the time.

A good example of number 6 in the above list happened to us in Peru, when we were leading one of those travel writer tours in the mid-1980s. At the time, the tourism industries in Peru and Colombia were suffering from bad press as a result of the drug trade and various terrorists groups. The idea was that through travel articles published in American newspapers and magazines, Americans might conclude that these countries were safe for tourists.

The itinerary on this particular trip took us from Miami to Bogotá, Colombia and then to Leticia, Colombia, where we boarded the *Rio Amazona* for a 350-mile trip to Iquitos, Peru, the mouth of the Amazon. The *Rio Amazona* was no *QEII*. However, as a former rubber-hauling vessel that had been refurbished for passengers, it had a wonderful open deck that provided fantastic views of the jungle. Its sister ship was the vessel used in Werner Herzog's 1982 film *Fitzcarraldo*.

The movie star Klaus Kinski brilliantly captures the challenges of would-be rubber baron Brian Sweeney Fitzgerald, an Irishman known in Peru as Fitzcarraldo. In one scene, Fitzcarraldo wants to pull a steamship over a jungle-covered hill in order to reach a tributary that provided access to rich rubber territory. We watched the film as a preparation for the travel tours, so were surprised to discover our boat's connection to the one used in the movie.

The boat stopped frequently for side trips on wooden skiffs with our bilingual guides, most of whom were the sons of Rivereños—Amazonian fishermen. These young men understood the river, the jungle, its moods, risks, and beauty. So one afternoon when the boat hit a sandbar, we saw concern on the faces of the crew members and immediately knew we were in trouble. It was too early in the dry season for the river to drop so low. The owner of the boat, an American who had lived in Peru for years, tried to down play the problem, assuring us that the crew would find a way to free the vessel. But we could see he was apprehensive.

Meanwhile, below the deck, passengers were watching a video of

Fitzcarraldo, which had begun before the boat hit the sandbar. We joined the others and were astonished that the scene showed our sister vessel being dragged through the jungle to the nearby tributary. We looked at each other, shocked not only by the synchronicity, but by how none of the other passengers seemed to connect the parallel worlds of the movie and our situation.

Fitzcarraldo had been chosen from two boxes of videos, but even if it had been the only movie on board, what were the odds that the scene of a stranded boat would be playing just as the same thing was happening to us? Besides that, the boat in the movie was virtually identical to the one on which we were traveling.

A short time after the movie ended, the crew managed to maneuver the boat into deeper water and we continued our trip. We commented that it was fortunate that we didn't have to drag the boat, like in the celluloid version of events. "That would only happen in movies," one of our fellow passengers remarked.

Maybe true, but the real-life version of our experience with its startling synchronicities seemed stranger than fiction.

TRAITS OF A SYNCHRO TRAVELER

You're primed and ready for whatever unfolds. All synchro travelers are adventurous types, but not in the traditional sense of the word. While you might want to climb Mount Everest just because it's there or attempt to sail solo across the Atlantic, it's more likely that you're simply on vacation and your adventurous spirit surfaces in other ways.

When writer Nancy Atkinson traveled to Hawaii for a break from Nevada's gelid winter, she wasn't thinking about much of anything except enjoying the beach, the weather, the sunlight and beauty. But she was open to new experiences and alert for synchronicities.

During the course of the vacation, an opportunity surfaced to buy a waterfront condo on the island of Maui with another couple she and her husband had known for years. It was in a unique location, the price was right, but the condo was on a *leasehold*, where the owner of the land can actually take back the property without owing the condo owner anything. For Nancy, this provision was nearly a deal breaker.

But one of the people involved in the deal was a developmental attorney and he discovered that the condo board was in negotiation with the owners of the land to buy the property. At that point the value of the condos would jump and their investment would probably escalate.

Just after Nancy and her husband had agreed to go ahead with the deal, a blog friend in Amsterdam sent Nancy a quote that astonished her. The friend quoted Alan Cohen, author of *Chicken Soup for the Soul*: "It takes a lot of courage to release the familiar and seemingly secure, to embrace the new. But there is no real security in what is no longer meaningful. There is more security in the adventurous and exciting, for in movement there is life, and in change there is power. You expect the unexpected. You encourage it, welcome it, embrace it."

The friend didn't have any inkling of what was going on with the condo, but as soon as Nancy read the e-mail she felt certain that the synchronicity indicated she and her husband had made the right decision. As it turned out, she was right. They not only made a good investment, but spend a few weeks in the condo every year enjoying Maui.

The trick with this trait is that the synchronicity may not come in the form that you expect. In 2006, we visited Aruba for a windsurfing vacation. We stayed at a wonderful spot, The Boardwalk, where we had a one-bedroom apartment, a full kitchen, wireless Internet. Trish found a booklet on the history of The Boardwalk and the land on which it sat and asked Julie, one of the owners, if she could get a copy of it. Trish explained that she was a writer and wanted to set part of her next novel on Aruba. Julia made her a copy of the material.

Some months later, Trish e-mailed Julia the cover of her novel, *Kill Time*, in which Aruba and The Boardwalk played prominent roles. Julia reacted so strongly to the title that Trish, worried about a lawsuit, went back through the manuscript and changed the name of the hotel. All of this occurred a few months after Natalee Holloway, 17, had disappeared during a school trip to the island and was feared dead. The media coverage of this case damaged Aruba's image as a safe tourist location. A young local man, Joran van der Sloot, whose father was a judge in Aruba, was arrested twice for the murder—and released.

A year passed. Julia had now read *Kill Time* and realized it was a time travel novel, not about serial killers, and that Aruba was portrayed positively. She apologized for her reaction and offered us a free week at a cottage on the edge of a desert preserve. We changed the dates twice because of other commitments, but finally decided on the week of June 7-14, 2010.

We bought our tickets in March. Between then and June, Joran van der

Sloot was accused of killing a young Peruvian woman and fled to Chile. A few days before we arrived in Aruba, van der Sloot was arrested for the homicide of the Peruvian woman, *five years to the day* of his release from an Aruban jail.

As we arrived in Aruba, the story was receiving widespread attention in the U.S. and in Aruba. Ironically, the issue leading to our trip was being played out again to an international audience. The synchronicity had come full circle.

Turn travel snafus to your advantage. This one boils down to an adage you probably heard first from your parents or grandparents: *there's always a silver lining.* Of course, when a volcano in Iceland blows, cancelling thousands of flights worldwide for days on end and you can't get home, a silver lining seems preposterous. When you miss the last bus out to wherever or your car dies in the middle of traffic, it's a challenge to pivot your attention away from your irritation and dismay. But if you can do it, then synchronicities flow your way.

Use the tools of your inner world to help you navigate. Dreams, impressions, hunches, psychic experiences: all are part of your inner geography and help you to make your way through life. But these same tools can be used effectively in physical travel, to make your journey richer, more meaningful. And the voice of this inner world is synchronicity.

During a trip to Australia, Jane Clifford, a healer from Wales, had plenty of time for daily meditations intended to attract everything she needed. One day while in Sydney she decided she wanted some decorative baskets for storage. "On the day I set out to buy some, I stepped out of the house and there on the pavement next door were lovely baskets of the type and size I needed. In Australia, whatever is put out to be collected can be taken away and used by anyone who wants it. A wonderful form of instant recycling." And a great synchro.

She continued her meditative work and it wasn't long before more magic unfolded. She had set out to explore Manley Island but neglected to bring along shorts or swimwear or a beach towel. While she was walking on the beach, she stopped and asked a stranger if there was a charity shop nearby. The stranger happened to be British and was from the same area where Jane had been born.

Even though the woman didn't know of any such shops, Jane started walking with her. Her destination was the post office and there, right next to it, was a huge charity shop. "She was astonished because she had never seen it before. It turned out the shop had just opened two days before," Jane said. "If I had not walked with her for a few hundred yards I wouldn't have found it."

After enjoying the beach, Jane stepped into an ethnic gift shop looking for something with a lizard on it to give her son. Unable to find anything, she asked the young man who was reading a book behind the counter. He looked up from the book, an astonished expression on his face. He explained that she'd spoken the very words he had just read.

"He showed me the sentence in which an older woman turned her head and said the exact same words to a young man."

Take risks. Many definitions of risk are negative. They include words like endanger, hazard, jeopardize, menace, exposure, liability. But the kind of risk we're talking about here occurs when you step outside your comfort zone. This is when you're most likely to experience synchronicities.

Let's say that your annual vacation is always spent at a resort somewhere. So the kind of risk you might take would be to hike the Appalachian Trail, join a photo safari in Africa, or hitchhike across the country. If you've never left the borders of your own country, then a risk would be to venture to some far flung corner of the world where the culture is vastly different. Or perhaps you, like George Clooney in *Up in the Air,* travel so frequently that being in transit is your comfort zone. For you, then, a risk would be to stay close to home, where the streets of your neighborhood may be as foreign to you as the streets of Marrakesh are to someone traveling overseas for the first time.

The beauty of taking such a risk, whatever it might be for you, is that unconscious elements of your personality, your psyche, are integrated into your consciousness and you are forever changed.

Chapter 2
GUISES OF THE TRICKSTER

THE ARCHETYPE

Several years ago, Darren of Brisbane, Australia placed an order at a novelty shop for a set of cards called, "500 Things You Have to Do Once in a Lifetime." The subtitle read "Reinvent Your Life." Darren bought them with the hope that the cards might help him set some goals when he was away from the monotonous job he'd held for more than two decades.

When the deck arrived, he found fifty double-sided cards with five suggestions on each side. The middle suggestion on either side appeared in bold type, so you naturally focus on that suggestion when you look at a card. Darren shuffled the deck and flipped over a card. His eyes went immediately to the bold-faced words: DRIVE A FORKLIFT TRUCK. Ironically, that was his job. He had been driving forklift trucks for twenty-three years.

First of all, it's strange that one of the 500 things you should try once in a lifetime would be to drive a forklift. But what are the odds that a forklift driver would select that choice on his first try? One rule that pervades all synchronicity is that *like attracts like*. It was as if the trickster had deadpanned: *Here's one you can try Monday.*

Darren recognized it as a cosmic joke, but knew that the deeper message went right to the heart of his dilemma: Did he want to spend the next twenty-three years driving a forklift?

This kind of in-your-face trickster synchronicity seems to be driven by what Carl Jung called the archetypal Self, which pushes us to expand our boundaries, overcome our limitations, and to sense in the deeper parts of ourselves how we are unique. Sometimes, in order to do that, we must leave what is familiar and safe—a relationship, a place, a job. And if we don't do it willingly, events do it for us.

Not too long after Darren pulled this card, he was laid off from his job.

His decision to change his life's path was made for him. But it was also made at an unconscious level. He was ready to move on.

As George Feuerstein points out in his book, *Holy Madness: The Shock Tactics and Radical Teachings of Crazy-Wise Adepts, Holy Fools and Rascal Gurus,* trickster stories always have a deeper significance. "The trickster reminds us of truths that we generally choose to forget—perhaps because we vaguely sense that there is a trickster in each of us who protests and wants to rid himself of the myriad cultural forms that keep our spontaneity carefully contained."

As an archetype, the trickster is found in mythology, dreams, fantasies, folklore, legends, hallucinations, movies, and even in divination systems. In the tarot, for instance, card zero, The Fool, can be seen as a trickster. The Fool indicates beginnings, innocence, a playful mischievousness, an eagerness to embrace whatever comes your way. But suppose what's headed your way is something you don't see, like a truck in your blind spot, barreling toward you at a hundred miles an hour? Are you going to embrace *that?* That's how trickster synchronicities sometimes feel when they catch you unaware, sneaking along behind you like thieves up to no good.

If you've ever visited archaeological sites in the American Southwest and have wandered through Anasazi ruins, you've probably seen petroglyphs of Kokopelli, the humpbacked flutist. The Anasazi, Hopi, and Zuni considered him the deity of music, dance, replenishment, and mischief. He's one face of the trickster. His counterpart in Norwegian mythology is Loki, who isn't quite as benign as Kokopelli. Loki, the son of a pair of giants, enjoyed stirring up trouble among the gods. He could shape shift, change his gender, and was often a boisterous bully.

In Native American lore, Coyote is often depicted as a trickster. His more familiar counterpart is Wile E. Coyote, a cartoon character who always came up with bizarre and ridiculous way to pursue his prey. Trickster can also be a clown—the court jester type of clown—who makes us laugh at ourselves. Or he can be a prankster every bit as annoying as some kid in elementary school who hides the teacher's chalk or pours molasses inside your backpack just because he can.

In Australian Aboriginal mythology, Crow is not only a trickster, but also a hero and ancestral being who supposedly brought fire to mankind. Crow's brother, Raven, another guise of the trickster, is believed to convey messages between the living and the dead and is linked with birth and rebirth as well as shamanic magic.

Trickster can be a darker figure, too, serving what Jung called the Shadow, those unexpressed parts of our personalities. In fact, the dark trickster is a favorite figure in American movies—Joker in the Batman franchise, particularly as played by Heath Ledger in *The Dark Knight*, is the paragon of this archetype. A more subtle version was played by Meryl Streep in the 2004 version of *The Manchurian Candidate*. She played Eleanor Shaw, a powerful congresswoman who used her son's reputation as a war hero to enhance her own political clout.

Jung saw this kind of trickster as an expression of an "earlier, rudimentary type of consciousness." In *The Archetypes and the Collective Unconscious*, he wrote: "He is both subhuman and superhuman, a bestial and divine being, whose chief and most alarming characteristic is his unconsciousness…"

The dark trickster is ever present in American politics and often appears with media stories that reach a tipping point and spill over into collective consciousness. This trickster may address some undercurrent of energy in society that relates to a belief prevalent in the twenty-first century.

If you're a politician who lies, cheats, steals, starts wars without just cause, caters to the very bankers who caused the recession in 2007-2008, it seems much can be forgiven. But in the U.S., if you're a politician involved in a sex scandal, your best bet is to resign and hope that you can make a comeback somewhere up the road. For Congressman Anthony Weiner, the dark trickster eclipsed any opportunity for a comeback.

Weiner served as a Congressman of New York's ninth congressional district from January 1999 to June of 2011. His politics were progressive, he appeared frequently on progressive cable shows to talk against Gitmo—the American off-shore prison for terrorists—and George W. Bush, about the financial meltdown, the mortgage crisis, all of the talking points that are near and dear to the hearts of progressives. Then in 2011, the photo of a man's "bulging, underwear-clad groin" (Wikipedia's description) appeared on Weiner's Twitter account. From the onset, he denied that he'd posted it and said his Twitter account had been hacked. But when more photos emerged showing Weiner bare-chested in his congressional office, he came clean. Yes, he had sexted with several women, but insisted he'd never met any of them, had never had sex with any of them. On June 23, 2011, Weiner resigned.

Here are the synchros:

His name, of course.

One of the women 'involved' with Weiner was deemed by her high school newspaper as "Most Likely to Be Involved in a Tabloid Scandal." At the time of the Weiner scandal, she was a 21-year-old college student in Washington state.

Weiner's wife, Huma Abedin, is a longtime aide to Hilary Clinton, whose husband was involved in a sex scandal with Monica Lewinsky.

Late-night shows and social media held 'Weiner roasts,' that included an old advertising jingle from the 1960s that began: *I wish I were an Oscar Mayer Weiner....*

On May 21, 2013, through a You Tube video, Weiner announced that he would run for mayor of New York City in 2013. By late summer, another more recent sexting scandal emerged. Weiner was accused of sexting with a 22-year-old woman over a period of six months, using the name Carlos Danger. The story was released on a website called *The Dirty*. The *Danger* handle and the name of the website are two more synchros to add to the Weiner fiasco.

Weiner held a hasty press conference, the media was all over the story, and the former Congressman's poll numbers began to plummet. The message of this dark trickster synchronicity addresses America's strange obsession about politicians and sex. Clinton was impeached because of the Lewinksy scandal, but was allowed to remain in office. Once he was out of office, he went on to become one of the most powerful statesmen in the world. As did his wife. The masses ultimately forgave Clinton for his indiscretions.

Mark Sanford was governor of South Carolina from 2002 to January 2011. But for a week in June 2009, his whereabouts were unknown to the public, his wife, and to the State Enforcement Division, which provided security for him. He was missing in action and it became a nationwide news item. Before his disappearance, Sanford told his staff he would be hiking the Appalachian Trail.

Upon his return, that was his story until a reporter intercepted him at Atlanta's airport where he had arrived on a flight from Argentina. Within a few hours, Sanford held a news conference and admitted that he'd been unfaithful to his wife, that he'd spent a week in Argentina with his soul mate.

His admission ultimately led to censure. His wife divorced him, and he became engaged to his mistress. When his term as governor ended, he left politics, but returned two years later and won a congressional seat for South Carolina. Apparently, he was also forgiven.

As one MSNBC commentator put it, Sanford can be forgiven because he is now engaged to his soul mate, the woman who was his mistress. *True love prevails.* Never mind that it broke up his marriage and nearly ruined his career. True love is true love, right?

The Weiner sexting scandals, on the other hand, were creepy and sleazy, but he apparently never met any of the women in person. When it comes to American politicians and sex, says the dark trickster, we are a collective of schizophrenics, skating on thin ice.

SNOWDEN AND THE RED PANDA

On May 20, 2013, Edward Snowden, an outside contractor for the National Security Agency, left Hawaii and flew to Hong Kong with four laptops filled with classified information on the NSA's massive national and international spying program. On June 1, journalists Glenn Greenwald and Ewen MacAskill from the U.K's *The Guardian* met with Snowden and conducted interviews with him. On June 5-6, *The Guardian* and the *Washington Post* broke the story on the Foreign Intelligence Surveillance Act (FISA) and the PRISM program, and a media feeding frenzy quickly followed.

The revelations about the extensive surveillance programs carried out by the U.S. government on its own people as well as on foreign countries—including countries that are allies of the United States—sent politicians into a fury. When Snowden revealed his identity on June 9, the entire drama ratcheted upward. Suddenly, the whistleblower—or, depending on where you fall in the political spectrum—the traitor—had a face, a name, a history.

On June 10, Snowden left his hotel in Hong Kong and on June 23, fled Hong Kong for Moscow. And there, with a Wikileaks attorney, he began requesting asylum and continued to release information about the surveillance programs. The U.S. revoked his passport.

Here's where the trickster comes in.

On the day that Snowden fled Hong Kong—which is now part of China—a red panda named Rusty escaped from the National Zoo in Washington, D.C. Fortunately for the zoo—and Rusty—the panda was captured about fourteen blocks from his exhibit. How he escaped was a mystery since no security cameras faced the panda's cage. But zoo officials think he climbed out on a branch of a tree in his cage.

On Monday, June 24, MSNBC's Rachel Maddow led off her news show with the story about Rusty the panda. She then shifted seamlessly into the latest story on Snowden, and his efforts to evade the long arm of the U.S. justice system as he fled from his temporary refuge in Hong Kong to Russia. Maddow recognized the synchronicity in the dual escapes—although didn't call it that.

But there's another layer to this trickster synchro. Red pandas are native to southwestern China and the Himalayas. We tend to think of pandas and China as intertwined. But a *red* panda makes the creature sound even more at home in China. So a red panda makes a mysterious escape as Snowden, the whistle blower who has exposed the secrets of the 'thought police,' flees China under mysterious conditions.

And it wasn't just any zoo from which Rusty escaped—it was the National Zoo in the nation's capital and the zookeepers began an all out search for the rogue creature. Similarly, the Justice Department issued an arrest warrant, charging Snowden with espionage, and called on foreign countries to capture and extradite him. But Snowden turned up in the transit zone of the Moscow airport where he stayed for several weeks until the Russian government granted him temporary asylum.

TRICKSTER AS A MIRROR

Trickster is a paradox, a riddle that we chew at like the proverbial dog and his bone. He confuses and delights us, enrages and puzzles us, and we usually can't ignore him. Even when he isn't creating chaos, when he's simply acting as a mirror that faithfully reflects our thoughts, focus, or environment, he seizes our attention.

Over the Thanksgiving holidays in 2012, our daughter brought out a board game we'd never heard of—Apples to Apples. There were five of us—our family of three, a friend named Rob, and our nine-year-old neighbor, Maddie. The game is simple: each player chooses seven cards from the red pile. There's also a green pile and when it's your turn you select a card from the green pack and the other players must select one of their seven cards that closely fits the word on the green card.

Let's say you choose a green card entitled *SMOOTH—even, level, flat.*

Each of the other players must play a card they hold that best describes *smooth*. Perhaps the choices are: watermelon, pond scum, killer whales, and Robert Di Niro. The person who has chosen the green card must decide which card best describes the word or phrase on the green card. The game is over when one player wins eight rounds.

When it was Trish's turn, she drew a green card that read, *alien abduction*. She burst out laughing and said, "That's a trickster synchro!" The reason: Before sitting down to play the game, she'd been working on an abduction chapter in our book, *Aliens in the Backyard*.

In this instance, the trickster synchronicity seemed to underscore Jung's contention that like attracts like.

JUST CHILL

Some trickster synchronicities are so benign and harmless that they simply serve to remind us not to take ourselves so seriously, that nothing is ever as dire as it seems. These types of tricksters break up tense moments, disagreements, and anxiety and as soon as they occur, we recognize them immediately.

Four sisters planned a birthday party at a local restaurant for their father, who was turning eighty-five. There were numerous details to be tended to, preparations to make. One of the husbands was supposed to order the cake from the local grocery store, with a greeting on it that read: *Happy 85*th *birthday, Dad.*

But when the husband arrived at the store, the little Asian woman who decorated the cake informed him the words wouldn't fit across the top of the cake.

"Well, can you write it on the plate or something?" he asked.

The Asian woman said that would work and told him to return in thirty minutes. He did some shopping but became increasingly anxious about the time. So when he picked up the cake, now boxed, he didn't check it. He set the cake carefully on the passenger seat and sped toward the restaurant where the festivities were being held.

His wife and the other three sisters were worried that he was going to be late and wouldn't get to the restaurant with the cake before their father arrived. When the husband finally hurried through the door, his wife grabbed the box, set it on the table, flipped open the top.

Puzzled, she just stared at the cake. The other sisters joined her.

"Oh my God, what should we do?" one of the sisters asked anxiously.

"Nothing," said another sister. "It's too late. Here he is."

The birthday dad appeared, saw the inscription, leaned over and read it: *Happy Birthday Plate.*

"Synchronicities are the jokers in nature's pack of cards for they refuse to play by the rules and offer a hint that, in our quest for certainty about the universe, we have ignored some vital clues," wrote F. David Peat in *Synchronicity: The Bridge Between Matter and Mind.*

Synchronicity may actually be more than that. Whether the phenomenon expresses itself through the trickster or in some other form, it's like a force of nature. It's the F5 tornado that seems to sweep in out of nowhere, the Category 5 hurricane that catches everyone unaware. Even when it tiptoes into our awareness in a gentle way, we intuitively recognize that the coincidence isn't random, that it's personally significant in some way, that it may, in fact, be our closest companion on our journey through life.

PLAYING WITH IRONY

Irony is a favorite tool of the trickster and appears in many of his synchronicities. Sometimes, as in the following historical example, the irony isn't realized until another event takes place. In this case, as we look back, the irony is so blatant that we can't help but wonder how the people and circumstances could have come together.

About a year before his father was assassinated, Robert Todd Lincoln, the oldest son of Abraham and Mary Todd Lincoln, was nearly killed on a railroad platform in Jersey City, New Jersey. An impatient crowd on the platform shoved Robert toward the path of a departing train. An alert bystander saw what was happening, dropped his luggage and, with his ticket clenched between his teeth, grabbed Robert by the collar of his overcoat and yanked him to safety.

When Robert turned around to thank the man who had rescued him, he recognized him. He was one of the era's most famous actors—Edwin Booth, the brother of John Wilkes Booth, who would assassinate Abraham Lincoln, Robert's dad, on April 14, 1865.

It's almost as if the hand of destiny tapped the two families on the shoulders that day, linking them together forever in matters of life and death.

AS THE CROW FLIES

Crows, as we've said, often appear in trickster synchronicities. We learned this first hand one Sunday in April 2012, when we made what was supposed to be a drive south that would take about three and a half hours. We were headed to Sugarloaf Key, to have lunch with Trish's agent, Al Zuckerman, who also represents Rob for books that we write together, and his wife, Claire. He has a second home in the Florida Keys and we try to get down there during the winter months to see him.

We left the house around 8:30 and took the dogs over to a neighbor's place for the day, then drove to the closest turnpike entrance. However, in recent months, the entrance had been redesigned. Instead of providing access to both north and south directions, the entrance now only went north, and a new entrance provided access to the south.

As we got on the turnpike, we suddenly realized the road no longer split. Our only option was to get off at the next exit and then get on the southbound exit headed for the keys. So a few miles north, we got off and realized this exit, too, no longer featured the split highway. We were stuck moving north.

"Okay, next exit," Rob said.

By now, it was 9 a.m. and we still weren't headed south. We got off the turnpike and realized there wasn't a southbound exit here, either. Frustrated, we turned west and took the first intersection that went south. A few miles later, we finally found a turnpike entrance that would take us in the right direction.

Suddenly, a crow swept across the road in front of us, then made an abrupt U-turn, a perfect reflection of what we had just done. Crow, the trickster, had a message for us. The crow had pulled the maneuver directly in front of our car moments after we had finally found our way south.

Due to tourist traffic and our own snafus, we finally made the turnoff for Al's neighborhood and pulled into the more than five hours after we'd left home, more than half an hour late for lunch, and at 1:11, a significant cluster of numbers.

The company and lunch were great and on the trip back, we were tired and stopped frequently for restrooms, food, Cuban coffee, and pictures. We finally exited the turnpike at 7:45 that evening, nearly twelve hours after we'd left home that morning. Rob remarked: "Do you realize that the crow this morning not only reflected our immediate U-turn, but the fact that we've made a *huge* U-turn today? We drove more than 200 miles for lunch, then turned around and came home."

Granted, crows are numerous in South Florida. So are blackbirds, doves, ducks, herons, egrets, and many others. But the crow was the one that symbolized trickster behavior, and the bird's U-turn maneuver was meaningful for us.

A SKEPTIC'S TAKE ON SYNCHRONICITY

In late 2012, we came across a blog post by Michael Shermer, the founding father of the magazine *Skeptic,* and author of a number of books espousing skepticism about everything from the existence of God to pseudoscience. His blog post, though, isn't about anything so lofty. It's about a synchronicity that he dismissed as meaningless.

On the morning of Friday, November 16, 2012, Shermer left his hotel in Portland, Oregon, to get some breakfast. He noted that he could turn right or left as he exited the lobby. He turned right. At the first intersection, he could go straight, right, or left. He went left. Restaurants lined both sides of the street. Shermer chose one on the right-hand side.

The hostess asked him if he wanted to be seated near the window or next to the wall. Shermer chose the window. About halfway through his breakfast, he glanced through the window and saw a man walking by who looked familiar. The man regarded Shermer as though he recognized him. Shermer waved him into the restaurant and the man greeted Shermer by name.

"I stuttered and stammered and hemmed and hawed and finally admitted, 'I'm sorry, but I can't remember your name.' "

"He said, 'Uh, Michael, it's me, Scott Wolfman, your agent!' "

After Shermer recovered from his embarrassment, he started wondering about the odds of something like his happening. He noted that he was from southern California and Scott was from Connecticut. They had run into each other in Portland, Oregon, a city neither of them usually traveled to. Both of them were just walking around town, seeing the sights.

"We were stunned. It sure seemed like something more than a coincidence, and we both joked about how there must be some sort of scheduling god who makes these things happen."

Shermer emphasized that he and his agent were "good skeptics" and proceeded to dismantle what was a powerful synchronicity—that he and his agent, who hailed from opposite sides of the country, *just happened* to be in the same city at the same time, and *just happened* to be on the same street. He did this by considering all the other possibilities: the thousands of people he knew who didn't pass the diner; that he might have left earlier and experienced something else unusual; all the other cities to which he'd traveled and eaten in restaurants where he hadn't seen anyone he knew. The same was true for Scott, who knew thousands of people in the lecture business and might have bumped into any of them in any given city to which he traveled.

"In other words, after the fact we construct all the contingencies that had to come together in just such a way for one particular event to happen, and then we only notice and remember (and later tell stories like the above) about the events that we noticed as extraordinary, and conveniently forget to notice all the other possibilities."

But Shermer is missing the point completely. All those other possibilities *did not happen*, and just because they *might have happened* doesn't negate the synchronicity of what *did* happen.

He ended his evisceration of his own experience with: "Here's an article opening you'll never read: A remarkable thing happened to me this morning. When I went out for breakfast I didn't see a single person I know."

Shermer went to great lengths to talk about the thousands of breakfasts like this one where he didn't see a single person he knew. He claimed that what was at work in his experience was "cognitive hindsight bias… a *tendency to reconstruct the past to fit with present knowledge*. Once an event has occurred, we look back and reconstruct how it happened, why it had to happen that way and not some other way, and why we should have seen it coming all along."

The sincerity with which he ripped apart and negated his own synchronicity was stunning. He likened it to "Monday morning quarterbacking," when the results of the Sunday games are evident and it's easy to look back and say what a team should have done to improve its chances. He compared it to stock market predictions, when the pros tell you what stocks you should've bought, after the fact.

In his particular story, he said, his "hindsight bias" lay in his noticing *after the fact* all the details that had to come together in just such a way for him and Scott to run into each other. "What would have been truly and extraordinarily beyond coincidence is if I had computed ahead of time the odds of running into my lecture agent at that very time and place, and then it happened. But that's not what happened."

He emphasized that most people who are unaware of "cognitive bias" neglect to consider all the other possibilities or how the sum of these possibilities equals a certainty that something must happen. And most of the stuff that happens is not all that interesting or important so it's forgotten. "This cognitive shortcoming is, in part, the basis of a type of superstition and magical thinking that finds deep meaning in coincidence, while ignoring entirely the certainties that must happen according to the laws of nature and contingencies of history."

Really?

Two things struck us about the logic of his argument. First, according to Shermer's criteria, coincidences apparently aren't meaningful to him because of all the times when life is ordinary, when it functions on linear time and cause and effect is apparent. In other words, when coincidences aren't happening. This seems to be a strange argument; part of the magic is that such co-incidents *don't* happen all the time.

His second argument is even stranger and reveals a lack of understanding about the nature of synchronicity. Shermer says that people who believe in meaningful coincidence have a 'hindsight bias.' In other words, they figure out the synchro after it happens by retracing the events leading to it. Shermer seems to think that a real synchronicity would be one that is predicted. He's narrowing the definition of synchronicity by requiring *precognition* to be an element at play for it to be valid. It seems he's making up rules—upping the ante—in order to justify his disbelief.

If you're thinking about people who are skeptical about psychic matters and someone sends you the article about Shermer, that's synchronicity. But Shermer would require you to predict its arrival in order for the synchronicity to be significant.

The bottom line is that Shermer was bewildered, so grossly confused by the incident that he forgot the name of his literary agent. In fact, he was the one who played Monday morning quarterback and tried his best to retrofit his stunning synchro into an ordinary event.

In spite of such efforts to categorize meaningful coincidences as probability, we all have an inner means of making advantageous connections, a latent ability that someday will be considered normal.

We sent Shermer's story to Bernard Beitman, a visiting professor of psychiatry at the University of Virginia, and asked his opinion about it.

Beitman has written academic papers on coincidence and is writing a book on the topic. About Shermer's experience, he noted: "Within each of us is an internal, subconscious tracking system that helps to guide us to desirable people, ideas and things in our environments. Like lost dogs finding their way back home and migratory birds finding their winter homes, we have an ability without knowing it to create coincidences like these."

Chapter 3
COLOSSAL COINCIDENCES

When the awareness of large numbers of people is focused on a particular event—whether it's an earthquake or hurricane, terrorist attack or any high media drama—uncanny coincidences often occur. Surprisingly, they can unfold prior to the event as well as during it and even long afterward. They include pivotal historical events like the sinking of the *Titanic*, the assassinations of John F. Kennedy and Abraham Lincoln, and 9-11. More recent examples are Hurricane Sandy; the mass shootings in Aurora, Colorado, and Newtown, Connecticut; and the Boston Marathon bombings.

THE TITANIC

When the *RMS Titanic* collided with an iceberg and sank in the North Atlantic on April 15, 1912, 1,502 passengers and crew members died. The largest ship afloat at the time became the greatest peacetime maritime disaster in modern history.

Like many disasters, there were numerous synchronicities, especially premonitions, recorded. The earliest such mind-bending occurrence came in the form of a novel, *Futility, or The Wreck of the Titan,* by Morgan Roberston, published in 1898, fourteen years before the *Titanic* set out on its doomed voyage.

Robertson wrote about the maiden voyage of a transatlantic luxury liner, *Titan*. Like the *Titanic*, it was reputedly unsinkable. Yet the *Titan* struck an iceberg in the North Atlantic and sank with enormous loss of life. The stunning coincidences between the fictional *Titan* and the real *Titanic*, as well as many other synchronicities, make this story an astonishing example of a colossal coincidence.

Here's a comparison between Robertson's *Titan* and the *Titanic*:

- Both sank in the North Atlantic in the month of April.
- Both were of British nationality.
- Both were described as unsinkable.
- Both were on their maiden voyages.
- Both were the world's largest luxury liner: the *Titanic* was 882 feet long, the *Titan* was 800 feet long.
- Both had insufficient lifeboats for everyone on board: the *Titanic* had twenty lifeboats, the *Titan* had twenty-four.
- Both sank near midnight.
- Both had a capacity for 3,000 passengers: the *Titanic* had 2,228 passengers on board, the *Titan* had 3,000 passengers on board.
- The point of impact for both ships was the starboard.
- Both ships had 3 propellers: the *Titanic*'s speed at impact was 22.5 knots and the *Titan*'s speed at impact was 25 knots.

Robertson's novel wasn't the only literary effort to parallel the ill-fated *Titanic*. Six years before *Futility* was published, a journalist named W.T. Snead published a short story called *From the Old World to the New*, in which a vessel, the *Majestic*, rescued survivors of another ship that collided with an iceberg.

Six years before that, he published another short story about a steamer colliding with a ship, with high loss of life due to lack of lifeboats. Stead had added prophetically, "This is exactly what might take place and will take place if liners are sent to sea short of boats." Yet, Snead apparently didn't consider his story an omen when years later, he purchased a ticket on the *Titanic*, and went down with the ship.

Many of the synchronicities related to the *Titanic* were personal stories involving passengers. Take the case of Colonel John Weir, who was scheduled to travel on the *Titanic*. Weir woke on the morning of April 10 to find that the water pitcher on top of his dresser had unaccountably shattered, soaking his clothes. Sensing it was an omen, he considered cancelling his reservation on the Titanic until the hotel manager allayed his concerns. After reluctantly boarding the ocean liner, he couldn't shake his sense of foreboding, and told his secretary that he would get off the ship when it docked in Queenstown, Ireland. Again he was dissuaded, and went down with the ship that he'd foreseen as doomed.

Reportedly, 899 persons who initially booked passage on the *Titanic* eventually refused to board because of warnings they experienced in the forms of various omens, premonitions, dreams and precognitive events. Hundreds of others cancelled for other reasons.

One of the survivors, Elizabeth Gladys 'Millvina' Dean, was emigrating with her parents and brother to the U.S. Her father had sold his pub and planned to open a tobacconists' shop in Kansas City, Missouri, where his wife's relatives lived. They were initially scheduled to travel on another ship, but because of a coal strike were transferred to the *Titanic*.

They were passengers in the third-class quarters and her father got them out of the compartment and moving toward the lifeboats. Elizabeth was the youngest passenger aboard the ship, just nine weeks old, and was wrapped in a sack and lowered into a lifeboat with her mother and two-year-old brother. Her father didn't survive.

Elizabeth, the last of the *Titanic* survivors, passed away on May 31, 2009, *ninety-eight years to the day* of the ship's launch on May 31, 1911. It's as if the beginning and end of her life were intertwined with the *Titanic*.

Some of the incredible coincidences related to the *Titanic* are hearsay, lacking documentation. A tour guide at the Titanic Museum in Orlando told visitors a curious one, purported to be of a scientific nature. According to the guide, an unnamed man tracked the path of the iceberg that hit the Titanic. He took into account the currents, temperatures, and other factors and traced the iceberg back to the polar icecap. The date that iceberg broke free, according to his calculations, turned out to be the same day that construction on the Titanic began.

Certainly an entertaining tale, but without any statistical evidence it sounds like an urban myth from the city built by a mouse. Yet, a search for the missing evidence turned up an unrelated scientific theory about the notorious iceberg, one that also involves a colossal—and celestial—coincidence. It seems that a rare convergence of astronomical factors came into play within a single 27-hour span on January 4th, 1912, when Earth came its closest to the sun, the moon was its nearest to Earth, and the moon was full.

Writing in the April 2012 issue of *Sky & Telescope* magazine, several scientists suggested this rare positioning of the moon and sun four months before the catastrophe caused icebergs to be swept into the path of the doomed ocean liner.

All these factors contributed to abnormally high sea levels that helped dislodge grounded icebergs and sent them into the shipping lanes of the North Atlantic, the scientists maintain. "They went full speed into a region with icebergs—that's really what sank the ship, but the lunar connection may explain how an unusually large number of icebergs got into the path of the *Titanic*," wrote lead researcher Dr. Donald Olson.

The moon's perigee—its closest approach to the Earth—was closer than it had been for 1,400 years and came within six minutes of the full moon. "That's remarkable," Olson wrote. "The full moon could be any time of the month. The perigee could be any time of the month. Think of how many minutes there are in a month."

At the same time, the sun was at the Earth's perihelion, the point at which its orbit brings it closest to the sun.

The scientists initially wondered whether an abnormally high tide led to more icebergs breaking off Greenland glaciers. But to reach the *Titanic* on April 14 the icebergs would have had to move impossibly fast against prevailing currents.

A much more likely theory involved grounded and stranded icebergs. As Greenland icebergs travel south, many become stuck in shallow waters off the coasts of Labrador and Newfoundland. Normally, they stay put and can't move until their ice melts or a high enough tide frees them.

A single iceberg can become stuck multiple times during its journey southward, a process that can take several years. The unusually high tide in January would have dislodged many of the stranded icebergs and released them into the southbound ocean currents, the scientists contend. If the theory is correct, a cosmic coincidence played a major factor in the sinking of the *Titanic*.

But here's an interesting aside. The website snopes.com, a bastion of skepticism on numerous topics, reportedly tells you whether an urban legend is true—nor not. The entries on the *Titanic* are mostly negative, that these parallels are not significant all. The same is true for the parallels between JFK and Lincoln that follow. And yet, any reasonable individual can see the connections.

JFK-LINCOLN

Mass events impact mass consciousness and create an environment fertile for synchronicity. Not only do synchronicities proliferate during dramatic mass events, but synchronicity sometimes links such events with other similar occurrences. For example, the assassinations of John F. Kennedy and Abraham Lincoln are entwined with one another through names and numbers—and yet the assassinations occurred a hundred years apart.

The mysterious coincidences that link John F. Kennedy and Abraham Lincoln are among the best-known synchronicities of this type. The list of coincidences first appeared in the mass media about a year after Kennedy was killed and previously had been published earlier in a Republican newsletter. It has become part of the presidential folklore and still circulates on the Internet.

Skeptics have attempted to debunk the connections, either belittling their significance or showing other aspects of the two men's lives that bear no similarities. Yet, they can't deny the following factual links between the two presidents, and they haven't been able to randomly select two presidents and show a similar list of coincidences.

Like all coincidences, what's meaningful to one person is insignificant to another. As we've said, synchronicity only exists when a coincidence is recognized and seized by the observer as meaningful. Take a look and decide the significance of these curious coinciding events:

Abraham Lincoln was elected to Congress in 1846. John F. Kennedy was elected to Congress in 1946.

Abraham Lincoln was elected president in 1860.

John F. Kennedy was elected president in 1960.

Both defeated incumbent vice-presidents.

The names Lincoln and Kennedy each contain seven letters.

Both presidents were concerned with civil rights and made their views strongly known in '63. Lincoln signed the Emancipation Proclamation in 1862, which became law in 1863. In 1963, Kennedy presented his report to Congress on civil rights; the famous March on Washington for Jobs and Freedom took place in that same year.

When each president was in his thirties, he married a socially prominent twenty-four-year-old woman who spoke French fluently.

Both wives lost children while living in the White House.

Both Lincoln and Kennedy were second children.

Both had been boat captains.

Both were related to a U.S. senator, an attorney general, an ambassador to Great Britain, and the mayor of Boston.

Both presidents were shot in the back of the head on the Friday before a major holiday. They were seated beside their wives, neither of whom was injured.

Both presidents were accompanied by another couple when assassinated.

Both men in the other couple were wounded by the assassin.

Kennedy's secretary, Lincoln, supposedly warned him not to go to Dallas.

Both were succeeded by Southerners.

Both successors were named Johnson.

Andrew Johnson, who succeeded Lincoln, was born in 1808.

Lyndon Johnson, who succeeded Kennedy, was born in in 1908.

John Wilkes Booth was born in 1839.

Lee Harvey Oswald was born in 1939.

Both assassins were known by their three names.

Both names are comprised of fifteen letters.

Booth ran from the theater and was caught in a warehouse.

Oswald ran from a warehouse and was caught in a theater.

Booth and Oswald were both assassinated before their trials.

The stunning parallels between the two men certainly begs the question: how can it be random? How can anyone read through this list without marveling at the powerful synchronicities?

We've often wondered if Kennedy was the reincarnation of Lincoln. It might explain why both men were born during eras when civil rights was a major issue. But what about all the other parallels? Was Oswald the reincarnation of Booth? Was Jackie the reincarnation of Mary Todd? Was Lyndon Johnson the reincarnation of Andrew Johnson?

Perhaps there are events in human history that recur until we get the message. Tecumseh's cure might be one such event.

TECUMSEH'S CURSE

Tecumseh was the leader of the Shawnee and had a large Native American confederacy that opposed the U.S. during Tecumseh's War and the War of 1812. In 1810, Tecumseh met Indiana governor William Henry Harrison (who won the presidency in 1840) and demanded the rescission of land purchase treaties that the United States had forced on them. Harrison refused and in August 1810, Tecumseh led four hundred armed warriors from Prophetstown to confront Harrison at his home. The situation quickly disintegrated and eventually, Harrison ran for the presidency on his participation in the Battle of Tippecanoe, where he was viewed as the hero who defeated Tecumseh's forces.

Tecumseh's curse was supposedly: "Harrison will win next year to be the Great Chief....... He will die in his office... I who caused the Sun to darken and Red Men to give up firewater. I tell you Harrison will die. And after him, every Great Chief chosen every twenty years thereafter will die. And when each one dies, let everyone remember the death of our people."

Harrison, the first victim of Tecumseh's curse, died of pneumonia within a month of his inaugural address.

1860: Abraham Lincoln was elected, the first person to run under the Republican Party. He was assassinated on April 14, 1865.

1880: James Garfield was elected to the presidency. He took office on March 4, 1881, and less than two months later, on July 2, was shot by Charles J. Guiteau. Garfield died on September 19, 1881.

1900: William McKinley was elected to his second term as president. On September 6, 1901, McKinley was shot by Leon F. Czolgosz and died on September 14.

1920: William G. Harding was elected president. While visiting San Francisco on August 2, 1923, he died from a stroke.

1940: Franklin D. Roosevelt was elected to his third term as president. He died on April 12, 1945 of a cerebral hemorrhage. Since he was elected during one of his terms in a year that ended with a zero, he is considered part of Tecumseh's curse.

1960: John F. Kennedy was elected, the youngest president ever. He was assassinated on November 22, 1963.

1980: Ronald Reagan was elected, the oldest president ever. On March 30, 1981, John Hinckley attempted to assassinate Reagan in Washington. But quick medical attention saved him. So from 1840 to 1980, Reagan was the first president elected in a zero year to survive the curse, which is now considered to be broken.

There's an intriguing astrological component about these deaths. Until 1980, there was always a Saturn/Jupiter conjunction in an earth sign—Taurus, Virgo, or Capricorn—within a year or so of the zero-year president's election. Saturn represents authority and Jupiter symbolizes politicians. But in 1980, this conjunction occurred in an air sign, thus breaking the curse, at least from an astrological perspective.

AURORA/SANDY HOOK

On July 20, 2012, a mass shooting during a midnight screening of *The Dark Knight Rises* left twelve dead and fifty-eight injured in Aurora, Colorado. A gunman, dressed in tactical clothing, set off tear gas grenades and shot into the movie theater audience with several weapons. The sole suspect was James Eagan Holmes, who was arrested outside the cinema minutes later.

On December 14, 2012, another mass shooting occurred at Sandy Hook Elementary School when twenty-year-old Adam Lanza opened fire and killed twenty children and six adults in the village of Sandy Hook in Newtown, Connecticut. Before driving to the school, Lanza had killed his mother at their Newtown home. As first responders arrived, he committed suicide by shooting himself in the head.

Two mass murders five months and 1,800 miles apart attracted widespread attention and triggered emotional reactions that resulted in a heated debate about gun control. It's not surprising that synchronicities occurred connecting the two tragedies.

In this case, the synchronicities between the two mass killings are documented on film. Incredibly, the name Sandy Hook is written on a map seen in *The Dark Knight Rises.* As if to underscore the connection, the name Aurora also appears in the Batman movie. It can be seen on the top of a skyscraper in the backdrop of another scene.

The Aurora mass murders bridged the gap between fiction and reality. Just before the showing of *The Dark Knight Rises,* a trailer of the movie *Gangster Squad* ended with a mass shooting in a theater, in which gangsters walk through the movie screen and open fire on the crowd. Within minutes, fiction collapsed into real life as an actual gunman opened fire. It seemed so coincidental that many people in the audience initially thought the shooting was part of a promotion for the Batman movie.

Two other mass events, Hurricane Sandy and the Boston Marathon bombing on April 15, 2013, were also tied to Sandy Hook. The village of Sandy Hook was hit hard by Sandy, and the last mile of the Boston Marathon was dedicated to the twenty-six victims of Sandy Hook. The marathon is 26.2 miles long, and there were more than *26,000* runners in the marathon.

INTERTWINED STORMS

In 2012, Hurricanes Isaac and Sandy made landfall on significant anniversaries. Isaac pounded New Orleans *exactly seven years to the day* that Katrina slammed into the city, breaching the levees and flooding much of the city. In late October, Hurricane Sandy pummeled the East Coast on the twenty-first anniversary of the Perfect Storm in 1991.

The "coincidental" storms not only caused heavy damage in their paths, but also spun political turmoil. While President Bush was never able to fully recover from the damage to his administration wreaked by Katrina, the Republicans lost their footing when Isaac took a swipe at Tampa just as the GOP national convention was about to get underway. The convention was delayed for a day, but the party suffered more storm damage before election day.

The powerful storm not only shut down the Northeast and caused heavy damage on the Jersey Shore, but knocked Republican presidential candidate Mitt Romney off stride. While Romney paused in his campaigning, President Obama took charge of the disaster and toured the scenes of devastation with New Jersey governor Chris Christie, a Republican who repeatedly expressed his admiration for the president's efforts. Some pundits said that Hurricane Sandy was a turning point in the election.

9-11

Without a doubt, the dramatic and deadly terrorist attack on the World Trade Center on September 11, 2001, brought together the world's collective focus. Videos of the commercial jetliners crashing into the buildings where nearly 3,000 died as the buildings collapsed, were shown repeatedly.

We've said that premonitions are linked to synchronicity because they involve the coming together of inner and outer experiences that can't be explained by cause and effect and are meaningful to the observer. That's also true for dreams that provide glimpses of future events.

The Boundary Institute, a nonprofit scientific research organization dedicated to research of anomalous phenomena related to consciousness, collected dreams about the impending disaster to illustrate how the unconscious mind connects to such global events. The institute recognizes that the numerous dreams gathered were not scientific proof of anything, but were simply honest memories of dreams that occurred before 9/11.

Here are three of the numerous dreams they collected:

A few days before the attack I had the most vivid and terrifying nightmare I have ever had. I woke up in a sweat and told my husband about it. In the dream I was running down a city street. I could see the tall buildings around me, I was passing parked cars and I could hear people all around me screaming as they ran along with me. I looked back and could see the debris and dust cloud gaining on me and I thought that if I ditched under one of the parked cars that I could somehow avoid getting hit by the larger stuff that was being carried along in the cloud. I covered my face once under a car and remember feeling like I was choking. End of the dream.

The next few weeks as the 9-11 footage played on TV, I relived that dream over and over as I watched the big clouds of dust and debris move down the street. The closest thing to the dream I could describe to my husband up until 9-11 was that it was so much like that scene from the movie *Independence Day*. It was so strange to have seen this before it happened.

I saw in my dream a building with two towers smoking. The next morning I asked if the World Trade Center had two towers and confirmed it did... If the dream had confirmed the presence of aircraft I would certainly have e-mailed the White House. (received September 15, 2001)

My most scary psychic dream was of 9-11. It is so close to the facts that many people simply cannot believe it. I have a piece of paper where I wrote down two things upon waking: the date of the dream and around 200 days. I had my dream on March 2, 2001.

The first thing that happened was an intense shaking in a major city. It looked like New York but it was hard to tell. Suddenly a huge plume of smoke came out of nowhere and people were running down the street. People were shouting and very scared. I was watching out a window or on a TV screen. I was scared but was far removed from the actual situation.

A voice stated that in around 200 days this would happen. I have calculated many times and it was 192 days between March 2 and September 11. This to date is my most accurate dream or prediction. I do not go around talking about these things because they scare me. In my dream I did not see any planes because my view was at street level. By the way, at the end of the dream, three buildings had collapsed, which is how many buildings actually fell in the attacks.

In the aftermath of 9-11, certain numbers, especially 11, have been shown to appear repeatedly in connection to the event. Many people find these coincidental connections, which have circulated around the Internet for years, both disturbing and meaningful. Others, such as Snopes.com, have dismissed them as meaningless. Synchronicity, as we've said, is in the eye of the beholder. So it's up to you to decide.

1. New York City has 11 letters
2. Afghanistan has 11 letters.
3. George W Bush has 11 letters.
4. New York is the 11th state.
5. The Twin Towers formed the number 11.
6. The first plane crashing into the Twin Towers was flight number 11.
7. Flight 11 was carrying 92 passengers. 9 + 2 = 11
8. Flight 77, which also hit the Twin Towers, was carrying 65 passengers. 6+5=11
9. The tragedy was on September 11, or 9-11 as it is now known. 9+1+1=11
10. The date is equal to the US emergency services telephone number 911. 9+1+1=11.
11. The total number of victims inside all the hijacked planes was 254. 2+5+4=11.
12. September 11 is day number 254 of the calendar year. Again 2+5+4=11.
13. The Madrid bombing took place on 3/11/2004. 3+1+1+2+4 =11.
14. The tragedy of Madrid happened 911 days after the Twin Towers incident.
15. Meaningless? Or synchronicity?

GLOBAL CONSCIOUSNESS PROJECT

While mainstream scientists have dismissed the significance of such multiple appearances of the number 11, scientists associated with the Global Consciousness Project search for meaning in random numbers. The project, based at Princeton University and co-sponsored by the Institute of Noetic Sciences, measures what author and parapsychologist Dean Radin calls "the global mind."

During events of high global interest, the focused emotional attention by large numbers of people can be measured by random number generators spread throughout the world. Researchers detected meaningful shifts in the recorded numbers during and even slightly before mass events, including 9-11, the devastating Oklahoma tornados, and more recently the Boston Marathon bombing.

According to the GCP website, there are currently about 65 or 70 nodes worldwide in the network, and at each one random data trials are recorded continuously—one trial per second—day after day over the past thirteen years. The data are archived on a server in Princeton, and subjected to formal analysis testing to determine if there are departures from expected randomness corresponding to global events.

"Blips" or deviations in the random number generators are known as eggs, but the analysis looks for an increase in the correlation between pairs of eggs, separated by hundreds or thousands of miles. This means that the changes occur in synchrony and lead to detectable changes in the network as a whole. "By definition the eggs are independent and should not show any relationship at all," said project director Roger Nelson of Princeton. "But during moments of importance to humans, the devices show slight correlations with each other. The probability that the effect could be just a chance fluctuation is less than one in a billion, an impressive bottom line statistic that is composed of small effects accumulated in more than 350 tests."

Radin, one of the researchers involved in the project, noted that "If the Global Consciousness Project is detecting genuine, large-scale mind-matter interactions, then it raises the possibility that some coincidences may be more than just dumb luck."

That's particularly true related to numbers. On the evening of September 11, 2002, the first anniversary of the 9-11 attack, the New York Lottery drew the sequence 9-1-1. Radin said the chance probability of selecting any given three-number sequence is one in 1,000. In fact, in the previous 5,000 drawings, 9-1-1 had appeared five times. "However, is it a coincidence that this number appeared on this date, in this city, and not in any of the other state lotteries? Given the massive attention placed on the sequence 9-1-1 on that day and in that city, it does make one wonder."

MOVIES ⚡ 9-11

Just as some people experienced premonitions related to 9-11, scriptwriters and cinematographers inadvertently peppered movies with 9-11 references in the years preceding the terrorist attack. In both cases, those involved apparently tuned into a deeper level of awareness through their creative impulses and brought forth words or numbers that would be significant at a later time. Here are some of the synchronistic references:

In the 1999 film *The Matrix,* a scene shows Neo's passport with the expiration date of September 11, 2001.

In the 1996 film, *Independence Day,* Jeff Goldblum opens his laptop computer to watch a countdown as the president and his family are being evacuated from the White House. The camera cuts to a close-up of the clock, which shows 9:11:01.

The Peacemaker, a 1997 film starring George Clooney and Nicole Kidman, includes a scene at JFK Airport, where the stars are pursuing a Yugoslavian terrorist. As Clooney steps off an escalator, two desks are visible behind him, labeled 9 and 11.

In *Enemies of the State,* a 1998 movie, a computer search by Gene Hackman and Will Smith turns up personal data on a corrupt politician played by Jon Voight. His birth date is 9-11-40.

In the opening scenes of the 2000 film, *Traffic,* a drug van is pulled over. When the cargo is revealed, every carton is stamped 911.

This sort of synchro explodes through the status quo and makes it difficult to write it off to random chance.

MAKING SENSE OF IT

Synchronicity reveals an underlying pattern, a deeper reality hidden from the everyday world. But how do we interpret this larger framework? Suzanne Collins, author of *The Hunger Games,* a trilogy of dystopian novels about young people who hunt down and kill each other, resides in Sandy Hook, Connecticut. That doesn't mean that if she lived elsewhere, the tragedy wouldn't have happened. But the coincidence might remind us that violence in society is taking the lives of many children.

While skeptics find no meaning in coincidences, there are those on the other extreme who read too much into coincidences, seeing synchronicity as evidence of vast conspiracy theories. Perhaps they might see certain

9-11 synchronicities as hints that George W. Bush was behind the attack on the World Trade Center buildings.

There are also people who attribute synchronicity to the hand of God. However, bringing God into the equation tends to muddle the issue. If you believe that a universal creative force is inevitably involved in all that unfolds, then yes, synchronicity is the work of God. However, like the conspiracy theorists, some religious people use synchronicities to promote their own beliefs and ideas.

For example, if you Google Hurricane Katrina and coincidence, you'll find blog posts informing you that God caused Katrina to smote New Orleans because a few days earlier a gay rights parade was held in the city. That might make sense to some people who find homosexuality abhorrent on religious grounds. But if you look more closely, even that cultural bias doesn't work as a basis for synchronicity in the case of Katrina: the parade was held in the French Quarters, which sustained little damage.

The Sixth Ward, where many Afro-Americans live, was ripped apart and thousands of people were trapped for days with little food or water or means of escape. That doesn't fit well with the God against gays idea; polls have repeatedly shown that blacks tend to disapprove of homosexuality in larger numbers than other races.

It's not God who muddles the picture, of course. It's man.

We find that it's best to view meaningful coincidence as a window to a deeper part of reality, the source. However, take caution in using synchronicity as evidence to support any prejudices or advance any agendas.

Chapter 4
CRITTER COINCIDENCES

THE SWALLOWS & THE SKYDIVE

From bats to whales, from the smallest to the most immense, the planet is filled with a great diversity of wildlife. And any of them can be a vehicle of meaningful coincidence. But when you're on this stretch of the synchronicity highway, you may have to research the animal's lifecycle, habits, how it's portrayed in folklore, mythology, even in fairy tales, before you understand what the synchronicity means.

With critter coincidences, it's necessary to make associations, to take note of the details. What type of action does the animal take? Does the synchronicity involve more than one of the same type of animal? Is there a number connected with the synchronicity? These types of details often provide vital clues.

On August 19, 2009, we moved our daughter, Megan, back to college on Florida's west coast. On one stretch of the highway between Florida's two coasts there's nothing but sugar cane fields covering land that once was part of the Everglades. Along this stretch, hundreds of swallows sweep across the terrain and the two-lane road nabbing insects on the fly. They're especially thick around dusk and seem oblivious to cars.

On the way back to Florida's east coast, around dusk, we entered this stretch. The swallows swooped and dived (literally 'sky-dived'), often winging away from our car at the last second. Then two of them, one after another, hit our windshield. At some deep level, we sensed it might be an omen. But of what?

On August 30, eleven days after we moved her back to college, we met her halfway across the state for her second skydive, for her 20th birthday. Her appointment was for 12:30, but they didn't get airborne until around 2 p.m. She was jumping tandem with an instructor. Notice the emerging pattern—2nd dive, 20th birthday, two swallows, a *tandem* jump at 2 p.m.

The tandem jumpers left the plane last and there were just *two* of them—Megan and her instructor, and another instructor with his student. We were standing outside, watching the jumpers with four of Megan's friends. And suddenly, something happened to Megan's parachute. It seemed to just… well, fly away.

An instructor standing next to Trish exclaimed, "Wow, look at that."

"What just happened?" we asked.

"The first chute failed. Don't worry. They'll free fall for a few seconds, then the *second* chute will open."

And that's exactly what happened. They landed safely and afterward Megan said she didn't even realize they'd lost the first chute. Later, another skydiver said it's an unusual occurrence. It didn't happen to him until his 1,200th dive.

Just look at the sequence of *twos:* an event *eleven* days earlier that involved *two* swallows, was related to a *tandem* skydive that started at *2 p.m.* on our daughter's *20th* birthday, and it was the *second* chute that enabled them to land safely. Even though we knew the event with the swallows was symbolic of something, we didn't have any idea at the time what that something might be. But we were alert for patterns. This critter coincidence proved to be precognitive.

Another facet of this synchronicity lies in the type of birds that flew into our windshield: swallows. These birds are known as *aerialists* because of their acrobatic twists and turns as they swoop after flying insects; a skydiver is a kind of aerialist, particularly during the free fall part of the dive. The incubation period for swallow eggs is from *eleven to twenty* days, more twos; *eleven* days after the swallows flew into our windshield, Megan went skydiving. *Swallow* is also a verb; it's as if the birds drew our attention to something we were supposed to *swallow*, to accept or understand.

CROWS & BLACKBIRDS

Birds are frequently associated with synchronicities, perhaps because they are so numerous. Take crows, for instance. The phrase "a murder of crows" may have originated from a fallacious folk tale that crows form tribunals to judge and punish the bad behavior of a member of the flock. If the verdict goes against the defendant, that bird is killed—murdered—by the flock. The basis in fact is probably that crows sometimes will kill a dying crow, who doesn't belong in their territory, or feed on carcasses of dead crows.

Esoterically, crows are associated with battlefields, medieval hospitals, execution sites and cemeteries, so there is considerable superstition about crows as bad omens. But that isn't always the case, as Jenean Gilstrap discovered in July 2011.

One morning she went out to get a breakfast sandwich and on the way home, started thinking about a poem she wanted to write for her blog. She pulled into a parking area to jot down her ideas and eat her sandwich. She brought out her notebook and within minutes, one word ran into another, then one line ran into another until she had several pages. "It was like an exorcism of sorts, a very dark and heavy piece from something many moons ago that I'd not thought of in years."

The initial words took on a life of their own and four pages later, Jenean looked at what she'd written. She was shocked about where the piece had gone and was mentally debating as to whether she would ever post it. "It was a bit overwhelming that I still carried such vehemence over the incident from so many years ago. I just leaned back to soak up the sun and closed my eyes to it all."

It was a hot, still day, Jenean recalled, not a breath of air. Her car windows and the sunroof were open, the sun blazing down. Suddenly, a wisp of wind whipped through the car and literally pulled a sheet of paper from her hands. "I was so shocked to have a single sheet blown out of my hand by a sudden breeze that I was immobilized and just sat there, looking at the sheet of paper on the ground beside my car. I debated whether or not to pick it up. Maybe it was a sign to just 'let it go' in the most literal sense, blow it off, and allow the writing to be the act of exorcism."

But she didn't want anyone else to see what she'd written, so she figured she should retrieve the sheet. She opened the door to pick it up and just as she bent over to get it, heard a loud, noisy bird call. It was different than that of the seagulls who lived in the area. And where were the seagulls, anyway? she wondered. The area where she'd parked was behind a busy restaurant and was usually packed with seagulls looking for free meals.

"Just as I was realizing which kind of bird call this was, I looked over to see not one but *three* black crows land just a few feet away. I was trying to assimilate what it meant, then got back into my car to grab my phone and snap a photo. By the time I turned around again, two sea gulls had landed near the crows. The piece I was writing was called 'The Sins of Sinnin'.'"

The most obvious synchronicity is that just as Jenean was about to pick up the page that had blown away, while still clutching the other *three* pages in her hand, *three* crows landed. But also her poem expressed feelings she had buried for so long that in writing the poem, she *executed* those emotions, severed their power over her. Again, crows are related to burial sites and places of executions. It all fit for her.

Lauren Raines, an Arizona artist whose work is steeped in Celtic mythology, noted that the crow's association with battlefields is due to the ancient Celtic goddess of battle and of justice, the Morrigan. "Her token was actually the raven, and whenever a raven was seen before a battle, the warriors assumed that the goddess was with them, and if they should fall, she would bear them to the next world on her black wings. Many Celtic works of art show warriors accompanied by ravens. Three is also the sacred number of the Celts, 3 and 9—all the goddesses were a triad, signifying the cycles of life (Maiden, Mother, Crone). So from that perspective, Jenean's experience with the crows could be a blessing from the Morrigan!"

This was certainly the case for Nicholas of Portland, Oregon. In September 2010, he was waiting at the bus stop for the bus he rode to work every morning and noticed a pair of crows sitting on a telephone wire near the bus stop. "I just had a creepy feeling. I don't know why." Then, as he was about to enter the building in which he worked, a third crow flew across his path. "I usually don't think of birds as omens, but for some strange reason I just felt like something bad was going to happen."

A few days later, Nicholas lost his job, which he detested but hadn't quit because he didn't have any other prospects at the time. In retrospect, he said, losing his job was a blessing. For both Jenean and Nicholas, their experiences with the crows signaled a finality.

Crows and ravens are often depicted as tricksters, mischievous devils up to no good. Yet, because they are birds, they may also be symbols of transcendence. In *Man and His Symbols*, Joseph L Henderson, a contemporary of Jung's, has a fascinating section on birds as the "most fitting symbols of transcendence." These kinds of symbols "point to man's need for liberation from any state of being that is too immature, too fixed, or final."

For Jenean, that state of being involved longstanding resentment about something that had happened years earlier. For Nicholas, that state of being involved his staying in a job he hated.

Writer Sharlie West had a simple dream about a blackbird, the sort of dream many of us probably have frequently and promptly forget about—unless or until the event happens in our waking lives. In the dream, the blackbird was perched by her window, asking for help, and she picked it up and helped it fly away. The next afternoon, a black bird banged against her window and just lay there, stunned, unable to move. As in the dream, Sharlie picked up the bird and murmured assurances that it would be okay. After a while it flew away. The next night she dreamed she was flying with the bird.

Esoterically, blackbirds symbolize the unfolding of psychic awareness, of new directions in creativity. The Beatles wrote one of the most memorable and beautiful songs about the blackbird.

Blackbird singing in the dead of night
Take these broken wings and learn to fly
All your life
You were only waiting for this moment to arise.

Sharlie's dream proved to be precognitive, but it and the bird's appearance the very next day may also have been a signal that she would soon experience a burst of creativity that would take her writing in new directions.

"Synchronicities are moments of epiphany that slow us down and bring us to the present moment," wrote Veronica Goodchild in *Songlines of the Soul*. "This slowing down occurs not by *thinking* about the moment, but by directly experiencing another world in the ordinary one."

The last part of this statement describes shamanic states, vision quests, moments that Jung called "numinous," when we are spellbound by whatever we are experiencing or perceiving. It's the world that Carlos Castaneda described in his early books about his apprenticeship with the sorcerer, Don Juan. It happens when we are at one with our environment, with nature. In such a state of being, we intuitively grasp the importance of the signs and symbols that surround us—even if we don't immediately understand their meanings.

DOVES & OWLS

Mike Perry of the U.K. received a story from one of his blog readers that underscores the importance of this sort of awareness.

Dan came home from work one day and found a white dove perched on the steps that lead up the front door of his house. No birds of any kind had ever landed before on the steps.

This white dove wouldn't let him move by. He made noises, waved his hands, stared at the dove. But the bird refused to budge. Nothing. Dan finally went inside his house through the back door. When he looked out the window, this lone white dove was still on the front steps at 4 p.m., 5 p.m., and 6 p.m.

At 7 p.m. that night he received an urgent phone call informing him that his aunt had passed away suddenly that afternoon. He looked out the window again and the dove had flown away. It never returned.

White doves have long been associated with peace. To the early Greeks and Romans, doves symbolized love and devotion to family. In mythology, the dove is sacred to Aphrodite and Venus, the goddess of love. There are also biblical references to the dove as a creature of love and loyalty and of the dove as symbolic of the Holy Spirit.

When World War II ended, Pablo Picasso was asked to create an image for the Peace Conference and he chose the Dove of Peace. The image went viral—even without the Internet—and he continued to portray doves for many years.

Perhaps due to the dove's association with the Holy Spirit, of the embodiment of Christ after his crucifixion, the bird is sometimes symbolized as a messenger between the living and the dead. The message for Dan was that his aunt was now at peace.

The owl also has a long, rich presence in mythology, folklore, and indigenous beliefs that span cultures and centuries. Among Native American tribes, its symbolism varies widely. The Cree believed the whistle of a Boreal owl meant a soul was being summoned into the spirit world. The Kiowa believed that after death, a shaman became an owl. Among the Apache, a dream about an owl portended death. Owls as spiritual symbols can be found in Australia, China, Greenland, India, Indonesia, Japan, Peru, Siberia, and Sweden.

More recently, owls have been associated with UFO encounters. Blogger Mike Clelland, an abductee from Idaho, has a number of fascinating posts about his various encounters with three owls on camping trips. He's now writing a book about owls and UFO encounters. Whitley Strieber, author of *Communion* and numerous other books about encounters and abductions, also writes about the significance of owls during encounters.

Regardless of culture or belief, though, owls are usually seen as messengers of some sort—between man and the spirit world, humans and aliens, and between the living and the dead.

Some years ago, we lived on a neighborhood lake that was frequented by all kinds of birds. A family of burrowing owls had been attracted to the lake and nested in our back yard, under a hibiscus hedge. The species is endangered and in South Florida, when the owls often make ground nests near schools or other public places, the areas are protected to prevent people from disrupting the nests.

We had just returned from New York, where we had seen our agent and touched base with Richard Demian, a talented psychic we had known for a long time. We were in the kitchen, talking about the Fids—our nickname for Richard—when we suddenly heard the high-pitched screech of some burrowing owls. We hurried outside, puzzled by why they were flying around in mid-afternoon; dusk is usually the time they come out.

We knew about owl symbolism and were concerned about what their odd appearance at this time of day might portend. That evening, we received a call from Fids's sister. He had been found dead of a heart attack in his apartment.

GREY WOLF IN DELAWARE

Some animal synchronicities present us with options. They seem to be showing us possible alternatives in relationships, careers, family structures, life's path. A grey wolf served this function for Jenean Gilstrap.

One day she was out driving with her grandkids. They were on a four-lane highway that runs from north to south across the entire state of Delaware, in the most heavily populated area of town. They were about to make the turnoff onto the road that would take them home when a grey wolf crossed the highway.

Brakes shrieked as drivers abruptly stopped to avoid hitting the wolf. Cars nearly rear-ended each other. Other cars pulled to the shoulder of the road. "I was northbound and the wolf was in the middle of the southbound lanes of traffic—but everyone slowed down or actually stopped for this magnificent creature." She wanted to turn around and go back to where the wolf was, but couldn't have gotten through the backlog of traffic. She finally saw a patrol car pull out toward where the wolf was, then lost sight of him.

Stunned by the absolute uniqueness of seeing a grey wolf in "this podunk Delaware town, on a major highway," Jenean Googled *grey wolf*

Delaware as soon as she got home. She has a blog called Gypsy Woman, with many references to Gypsy's caravan and traveling, and for some time had been entertaining the idea of buying a small camper and hitting the open road. So imagine her shock when the second site that popped up was one selling a *grey wolf camper in the town where she lived*.

Jenean felt this synchronicity might be a confirmation about buying a camper. But in the end, she stayed in Delaware with her daughters and grandchildren.

Bernard Beitman, a professor of psychiatry at the University of Virginia, calls these types of synchros *instrumental coincidences*. "You are presented with an option or feel confirmed about a decision. But that still does not mean you should make the choice that seems to be suggested."

In essence, these kinds of synchronicities are like the Robert Frost poem, "The Road Not Taken," which tells of two roads that diverge and the narrator is sorry that he can only take one of them. For now, the camper wasn't viable for Jenean. But one day it might be.

THOSE MICE

Our neighbors have a pet snake. That means that once a week or so, they must feed the snake a mouse. A live mouse. These mice are small and white, specially bred as a food source for pet snakes. They are the equivalent of the clones in Michael Marshall Smith's novel *Spares* that provide spare parts—kidneys, livers, eyes, hearts—to wealthy donors.

The other day, our neighbor's son, Dawson, proudly showed us the pair of mice he'd bought, a male and female, who would breed like crazy to provide live mice for the snake. "Because the ones you buy in the pet store get expensive," Dawson said.

This show and tell about his white mice seemed to be a giant exclamation point at the end of a cluster of synchronicities for us that involved mice— the wild variety, the larger gray mice that can inhabit any space, anywhere, as long as there's a food source. Ours started in the fall of 2012, around the same time that we learned that a contract for one of our steadiest sources of income for the last ten years would not be renewed.

One morning as we ate breakfast, we heard scratching sounds coming from the pantry. We opened the door, but didn't see anything. The next day, the scratching noises seemed to originate in the kitchen walls, then in one of the bathroom walls. About a week into this scratching sound mystery, we found a dead mouse in the shower, with our male cat, Simba, crouched nearby. We figured the mouse had come out looking for food and Simba had pounced on it.

Mouse taken care of, end of story.

But the next week, we heard more scratching noises in the kitchen. A second mouse was apparently living in the walls. The cats and the dog kept sniffing around one of the lower cabinets, so Rob set a mouse trap with a bit of cheese and peanut butter on it into the cabinet. But the mouse nabbed the food and set off the trap without getting caught. A few nights later, we heard a scuffle in the kitchen and ran out there to find another dead mouse and one of the cats sitting nearby, gloating.

Again, we figured the cats had solved the problem. But when we started hearing the scratching sounds again, we set out more traps. We now wondered if one of the cats had caught a pregnant mouse and brought it into the house where it had gotten loose and given birth inside the walls. We recognized three—or more!—as a cluster and began researching the life cycle and habits of mice for some clue about what this mice invasion meant on a deeper level.

Mice are adaptable creatures, quick and fastidious. Their senses of smell and hearing are excellent and they use their whiskers to feel their way through the dark. They stash food for lean times. During this period, we were without book publishing contracts for the first time in nearly thirty years. We fretted and argued about it, saw our savings dwindling, and felt uncertain about which direction we should take. The mice seemed to be telling us to feel our way through the dark, to conserve our resources, but to remain alert to everything in our environment that might indicate an opportunity. In other words, follow the synchronicities if and when they unfolded.

By January 2013, the ninth mouse was history. *Nine.* The number obviously didn't refer to days and we hoped it didn't refer to years, so we settled on months. We interpreted nine as the number of months our lean times might last. Our first mouse made its presence known in October 2012 and our lean times lasted until July 2013, when a combination of work-for-hire projects, e-book sales, royalties, new opportunities, and other financial venues began to pay off.

Dawson showed us his new breeding mice in late May, more than seven months after that first mouse had scratched at our pantry walls. The two little mice were in a cage with food and water, running around like maniacs, almost as though they sensed their purpose in life, but they were *contained,* their lives controlled by their overseer, Dawson.

We took it as a sign that we were nearly at the end of the dark financial tunnel. Our previous overseer—contracts/publishers were nonexistent. But we had been bringing out our extensive out-of-print backlist as e-books, then published an original book as an e-book, and things were starting to sell. One of Rob's former agents had gotten involved in a new project—bookazines—and asked us to do several of them. It was work for hire, which meant no royalties, but the projects we did were fun, paid well, and were about topics that interested us—ghosts and spirits, UFOs, astrology.

This kind of reasoning is not the sort of thing you talk about in the company of people who believe that what they see is all there is. It's not what you talk about with people who dismiss coincidence as random, as some odd blip in the scheme of things. It's not the kind of thing you share with family and friends unless they're open to it because, really, how would you even explain it?

Listen, there were these nine mice living in our walls...we were at this weird juncture in our careers...Steve Jobs and Jeff Bezos changed everything about the ways we buy and read books, and these mice meant...

Talk like that will practically guarantee that the eyes of the person you're talking to will glaze over with boredom or the person will think you're a mush head, guilty of anthropomorphism—ascribing human traits to animals. They might say that humans are connected to our domesticated creatures like cats and dogs, but not to any of the rest of the animal world.

And that kind of thinking keeps us isolated, segregated from what Jung calls the *unus mundi,* the one world that Hindus refer to as Indra's Net, what quantum physicists call the holographic universe, where you and you and you are interconnected, threaded together in some way we don't yet understand or haven't discovered.

OSCAR, THE CAT

In 2005, Oscar was adopted from an animal shelter and became a permanent resident of the dementia unit at the Steere House Nursing and Rehabilitation Centre in Providence, Rhode Island. The staff adopted him because they feel that animals make the facility a home. The facility, after all, is usually the final stop before death, where patients with dementia no longer recognize loved ones, can't talk, and are lost in chopped-up memories of the past.

After Oscar had been at the facility for about a year, the staff noticed he would spend his days pacing from one room to another. He checked out the patients—sniffing, looking in on them, but didn't spend time with anyone—except when they only had a few hours to live. Then he would curl up next to them, purring.

Nurses once put Oscar on the bed of a gravely ill patient whom they believed didn't have long to live. But Oscar refused to stick around and the staff figured his predictive streak had been broken. The patient, however, rallied for another two days, proving the staff wrong. When the patient's time of death approached, Oscar was there.

In Oscar's first five years at the facility, he predicted fifty deaths correctly and astonished Dr. David Dosa, a geriatrician and professor at Brown University who works with dementia patients. In 2007, Dosa wrote about Oscar in the *New England Journal of Medicine* and in 2010, published a book about him, *Making Rounds with Oscar: the Extraordinary Gift of an Ordinary Cat.*

Dosa can't explain Oscar's talent and after the article was published in 2007, was concerned that people might consider the cat a furry grim reaper. Now he knows otherwise. "People actually were taking great comfort in this idea, that this animal was there and might be there when their loved ones eventually pass," Dosa said. "He was there when they couldn't be."

Oscar is apparently so accurate that the nursing home staff knows to call the family when the cat curls up beside a patient. If Oscar isn't allowed into the room, he'll scratch at the doors and walls, trying to get in.

In his book, Dosa doesn't provide a scientific explanation for Oscar's peculiar talent. He theorizes that the cat imitates the nurses who raised him or detects odors emitted by dying cells. But perhaps Oscar is simply a talented cat with a sixth sense about death. He's closely attuned to his environment, deep in the timeless, synchronistic flow.

LADYBUGS

Several years ago, Katrina, a photographer and writer who lived in northern California at the time, had house guests for a couple of days, a man and woman who took in the sights in the area. As they hiked a trail in the Muir Woods, they came upon hundreds of ladybugs swarming on a fallen log.

Spellbound by the sight, they took photos. Later, while walking on Stinson Beach, they saw a solitary ladybug crawling on a rock. Seeing hundreds of ladybugs on a log in Muir Woods was startling enough, but here was a lone ladybug in an unlikely place. Katrina is sure this is when they understood these sightings might have a particular significance for them.

When they returned from their sightseeing excursion, they eagerly showed Katrina their photos. At this point, she knew it was the perfect moment to interpret the experience as though it were a dream. So Katrina began by asking them what ladybugs meant to them. But nothing came to mind, so Katrina turned to Ted Andrews's book, *Animal-Wise* to find out if there were any hints in the life cycles and habits of ladybugs that might provide insight.

In many cultures, ladybugs are considered to be lucky and portend joy and transformation. As Katrina discovered, they can also signal a time when we're pushing too hard for a wish to come true and should sit back and patiently wait for it to arrive in its own time.

"As we talked, the number three began popping up. One of my friends mentioned her brother had a recurring dream three times that my friend was pregnant with triplets. I realized that the date was 3/9. My friends mentioned it was their nine-month anniversary." Then Katrina read that ladybugs live for nine months, realized her friends' plane had arrived at 3:30 p.m., and that they were in town for three days.

"The number three is about expansion, creativity, and luck. It's a spiritual number as well: there is the Holy Trinity as well as the Triple Goddess and the Three Graces." The synchronicity of it all was inescapable.

Katrina's friends flew home the next day and that night, broke off their relationship. They realized their relationship had run its course and they needed to let go of it so their lives could expand.

No doubt the relationship was already precarious before the synchronicities with the ladybugs. Possibly a third person was involved, adding to the meaning of the threes. But the interpretation nudged them to act, rather than to wait until the relationship deteriorated even further.

FLIES

During hot weather, the common housefly can be a pest, particularly if your home is inundated with them.

Biblical interpretations of flies tend to view them as evil, as satanic.

Easton's Bible Dictionary refers to the fly as a "pest" and notes that the Phoenicians "invoked against it the aid of their god Baal-zebub."

Smith's Bible Dictionary discusses *arob—swarms of flies—*"as the name of the insect or insects which God sent to punish Pharaoh. Since the *arob* are said to have filled the houses of the Egyptians, it seems likely that the dictionary is referring to the common fly (Muscidae). The *arob* may include various species of Culicidae (gnats), such as the mosquito, but even in present-day Egypt, the common fly is regarded as a "plague."

The *Animal Totems Dictionary*, though, is far kinder. "The Fly teaches the ability to greatly multiply prosperity, endeavors and ventures at enormous rates. He shows how to be quick to act and respond to achieve results. Fly aids in demonstrating the power of keen eyesight along with expanding awareness in many directions."

Even though flies are known to be carriers of disease, the *Totems Dictionary* noted that the lesson of fly lies in "the value of carrying your emotions, thoughts, and feelings in order to act quickly in sometimes unfavorable or uncomfortable conditions."

The life cycle of the common housefly starts with an egg, then develops through three distinct phases—larva, pupa, and adult fly. Under the most favorable conditions—a warm summer—the entire cycle takes from a week to ten days. An adult housefly has about three months to reproduce before it dies. So the life cycle provides a couple of time frames—a week to ten days and three months.

In the mid-1980s, Anne Norburn lived in a townhouse in Asheville, North Carolina. One summer was exceptionally dry for the area and their home was inundated with flies. "Every time someone opened the screen door to go in or out, big swarms of regular house flies would come in. There were so many flies, I even hung up fly strips to get rid of some of them. It seemed as if we all marched around armed with fly swatters."

The flood of flies lasted for a couple of weeks, then they were gone. Over the course of the next several months, everything in her life and in the lives of her kids improved. "After this fly invasion, I was not nearly as stressed...for some inexplicable reason things just got better. I truly don't know how to explain it. The kids got healthier. I didn't have to take anyone to the doctor for several years or so unless it was for a regular check up. Ditto dentist. I started making more money, which somehow seemed to go three times as far. It just turned out to be a real pleasant few years. It's as if the coming of all those flies brought along something much better."

So the next time your house is inundated with flies, look on the bright side. Your situation may be improving shortly!

THE SWAN AND THE CORMORANT

Several years ago, we posted a story about writer Nancy Pickard and her new book, *The Scent of Rain and Lightning*, which hit the *New York Times* bestseller list. As a result of that post, Robin Yaklin sent us a moving story about how a swan and a cormorant proved to be powerful synchronistic symbols in a diagnosis and subsequent healing.

"Something went *pop* in my head and then came pain like the devil slowly inserting a knife through my skull. Pressing my hands on either side of my head, I rested my forehead on my desk and prayed God would make it stop. And, then it did, suddenly, like it had come."

In front of her lay a notecard, with half a sentence composed. She kept looking at it, waiting for the pain to resume. Nothing happened so she went to work on the note again. But when she came to the word *and* she couldn't get the correct order of the letters. Then she started feeling dizzy. "Long story short, medical referrals were made until I ended up with a neurologist and a prescription for anti-depressants. I didn't like the medication. No, I hated it. I complained repeatedly. No one listened."

Robin tried acupuncture as a last resort. During the treatment, she had two visions. First, she saw "a round bubble shape, brilliantly red, with white outlining a swan's wings. The wings were stretched out as though the bird would take flight. Beautiful. I wanted it to last, but it faded and another image came—this time, the cross section of a brain. I knew it was my brain. It was divided crosswise so that it had four quadrants. The front two were blue as well as the back left. Only the right back section was red. The acupuncturist, an internist from China, was troubled and he suggested I follow up on this because in traditional Chinese medicine blue means stasis. 'Just a hunch,' he said."

Robin didn't know what to do. She wanted time to mull over these visions. Several weeks went by. One day she was driving home, in tears, from an appointment with her "unyielding" female neurologist—and decided to take matters into her own hands. She called a friend who had multiple sclerosis and she recommended that Robin see her neurologist.

The second-opinion neurologist was friends with the former neurologist and was irritated that Robin had questioned her diagnosis. He demanded that Robin reveal the diagnosis of the first neurologist, but she refused and requested that he begin his analysis with a fresh perspective. They glared at each other. He finally asked what tests the first neurologist had performed.

"None," Robin replied.

The second neurologist then said she needed blood work and other tests done to eliminate other possible illnesses. This made sense to Robin and she was willing to do it, but his tone bothered her. His announcement was issued like a challenge, as if his long to-do list was intended to discourage her from returning. Last on his list was an MRI of the brain.

When the results came in, Robin received a dire phone call from her neurologist. "Put everything down. Don't lift even a purse or grocery sack. I don't want to hear you went mall walking for four hours. You can walk from your hall to the bathroom and that's about it. You have aneurysms. Call these surgeons." She had five lethal bubbles in her brain.

Four surgeries were needed. In an attempt to make believe their lives were still normal, she and her husband went to the grocery store each night before the surgery to stock up for her homecoming. "By our house is a lake. The night before the first surgery, a beautiful swan settled on it. A few hours later, he was gone. He did this each night before the operations."

During the last surgery, Robin had a small stroke that affected her language skills, a devastating turn for a writer. The beautiful Persian carpet on their floor became a towel because that was the only word she knew to describe it. And there were other problems. "I was still dizzy. Typing floundered. Handwriting stopped. My right side was weaker. Healing has taken years." She's now almost fully recovered and as a reward to herself, signed up for BONI—Breakout Novel Intensive, a writers' retreat/workshop.

"My hotel room had a view of the river and some rocks on which a cormorant sat. One sunny windy day, he splashed around in the water, then hopped onto the rocks and spread his wings—glistening, beautiful, powerful wings that were exactly what I'd seen in my vision."

The sighting of this cormorant certainly bodes well for Robin's full recovery.

THINGS TO KEEP IN MIND

When you have a synchronistic experience with an animal—whether a dream or in your waking life, pay close attention to the details. What is going on in your life at the time of the experience? Are you about to get married or divorce? Have a child? Are you moving, changing jobs or careers? Are you in the midst of any other major life transition? Are your financial affairs shifting in some way?

Research the animal's life cycle and habits. If nothing resonates, research the animal's meaning in folklore, mythology, fairy tales.

If you experience a cluster, as we did with the mice, make note of the number. It could be a clue about timing.

If the experience happens in your waking life, try interpreting it like a dream. This process often yields clues that you might not notice otherwise.

Make note of the weather, the time of day, what you were talking or thinking about when you became aware of the animal. What was your mood, your frame of mind? How was your health? Sometimes, the synchronicity, the message, will be immediately obvious. But when it isn't, the clues may lie in these kinds of details. And as we mentioned earlier, research the animal's life cycle for hints about timing. Often, the life cycle will provide vital clues about which area of your life the message is addressing.

Chapter 5
NAMES & DATES

TOCAYOS

By definition, one of the criteria for synchronicity is that it's meaningful to the person who experiences it. This means you may be the only person in the crowd *who gets it*. It means that when you try to explain the scenario to others, they may find the story somewhat curious, even intriguing, but they don't grasp it the way you do.

Then there are other coincidences so startling that even the people who don't usually understand the significance of meaningful coincidence are just blown away.

Synchronicities involving names are one category of coincidence that can evoke such a reaction. These experiences involve more than just interesting parallels, more than just intriguing anomalies that seize our attention. These kinds of synchros often lead us to question the very nature of reality, the hidden universe we sense beneath the hum of our daily lives, and we invariably ask, *Who's in charge?*

Connie J. Cannon has lived in the city of St. Augustine, Florida, for more than thirty years. Shortly after she moved to this medium-sized city in the early 1980s, she opened a bank account and discovered there was another Connie Cannon with an account at the same bank. Over the years, she received phone calls and mail for the other Connie. On the surface, that's not so unusual, especially since both her first and last names are fairly common.

However, in 1988, the apparently random aspects of the name parallels changed. A story on the front page of the local newspaper described a bad car accident in which the other Connie Cannon was involved. She wasn't seriously injured but from that article Connie J. learned that she and her namesake were the same age, were both RNs who had worked at the same hospital but on different shifts. She also discovered that she and the other Connie drove the *same car—same make, model, year, and color.* Compounding the synchronicity was that a few weeks earlier, Connie J. had been involved in a fender-bender in her neighborhood that had smashed the front end of her vehicle.

In a sense, the parallels are like those of identical twins separated at birth. "I keep telling myself I'm going to make it a point to meet her. Who knows what else we would find out. But we haven't yet done it."

Name synchronicities can happen anywhere, at any time. In the mid to late 1980s, as mentioned earlier, we led adventure tours to Latin America for a South American airline. On one trip, to the Caribbean island of San Andres, Rob MacGregor invited a friend, another Rob (Lockhart). One day the two Robs took a taxi ride across the island. When they passed through a small village, the driver slowed and yelled, *"Tocayo!"* to a man seated on a porch, and the man yelled the same word back to him.

As they drove on, Rob M. asked the driver what it was that they'd said to each other. The man explained that he and the other man have the same name and *tocayo* was a greeting. In English, the word means *brethren.* Rob pointed to his friend and said, *"Tocayo!"* Since then, they have always referred to each other as *tocayo.*

Years later, Rob invited his *tocayo* and a third Rob to join him and Trish at a waterfront house in the lower Florida Keys. So the morning after the three Robs had arrived at the house, Rob M. was making toast and found a jar of jelly in the refrigerator. To his surprise, the brand name of the jelly, made in Homestead, Florida, was *Robert is Here.* An odd name for a brand, but a good synchronicity for the three Roberts. Later that day, Trish and two of the Roberts went to Key West for lunch. While eating at a courtyard table a man with a Golden Retriever walked by, and Trish asked the owner the dog's name. The man said, "This dog's name is Robert."

Of course, Robert is a common name. Three of them coming together isn't that unusual, but then the jelly in the fridge and a random encounter with a dog, both named Robert, made it an exceptional name synchro.

As synchronicities, those involving names fall into a category of their own. That's because in most cases they are mind-boggling to outside observers as well as the people involved. In some instances, though, when the synchronicity develops over a long period of time, the instigator—the one whose thoughts led to the coincidence—never even finds out about it. In such cases, as in the story that follows, the coincidence is meaningful to those of us who are inspired by the mind-expanding details.

THE TALE OF RICHARD PARKER

In the spring of 1974, Arthur Koestler, author of *The Roots of Coincidence,* sponsored a contest in coordination with the *London Times* to find the best coincidence. Twelve-year-old Nigel Parker submitted an incredible coincidence that not only won the prize but was called the *best coincidence ever* by Koestler.

Nigel's story was about a relative of his who survived a shipwreck only to become a victim of cannibalism. Seventeen-year-old Richard Parker boarded the *Mignonette* in Southampton, England, in July of 1884 and set off on his first voyage on the high seas. When the ship reached the South Atlantic, it was pummeled by a hurricane and sank. The four survivors, including Parker, had few provisions on their lifeboat, and after nineteen days adrift grew desperate.

The men discussed drawing lots to choose a victim who would be eaten by the others, but settled on Parker, who had become delirious from drinking seawater. The remaining crew survived on Parker's carcass for another thirty-seven days until they were rescued by the *SS Montezuma,* aptly named for the cannibal king of the Aztecs.

The peculiar story from young Nigel Parker's family history became incredibly stranger when Nigel learned about Edgar Allan Poe's unfinished sea-adventure novel, *The Narrative of Arthur Gordon Pym*, published in 1837.

In one scene, three men and a sixteen-year-old boy are adrift at sea in a lifeboat after being shipwrecked. Desperate, on the brink of starvation, they decide to draw lots to determine which of them will be killed and eaten. The cabin boy, Richard Parker, picks the dreaded short straw and is promptly killed and eaten. The novel was written forty-seven years before the true story of cannibalism occurred that involved another teenage cabin boy named Richard Parker. In essence, fiction transcended the imaginative realm and became a full-blown scene from real life, complete with details matching the fictive version.

Richard Parker, of course, also became the name of the shipwrecked tiger in Yann Martel's novel, *The Life of Pi,* that became a hit movie. Martel knew the story of Richard Parker, both Poe's fictional version and the real-life version. So his novel was a salute to the strange story, but not a synchronicity. In describing his book on Amazon.com, Martell not only notes Poe's literary connection to the Richard Parker tragedy, but also writes that another ship, the *Francis Speight*, became disabled at sea in 1846, and there were deaths and cannibalism aboard. One of the victims was a Richard Parker. That makes three Richard Parkers, all eaten after death by fellow sailors.

What would Poe make of these coincidental events if he knew about them? It seems that he gave us a hint in the following quotation from *The Viking Portable Poe*: "There are few persons, even among the calmest thinkers, who have not been occasionally startled into a vague yet thrilling half-credence in the supernatural, by coincidences of so seemingly marvelous a character that, as mere coincidences, the intellect has been unable to receive them."

In other words, *synchronicity!*

While Poe wasn't alive to appreciate the startling and meaningful coincidences that developed from his novel, the two girls in the following story, first published in the *Swinden Advertiser* in the U.K., recognized that they inadvertently played roles in surprising and unlikely events.

THE RED BALLOON

When ten-year-old Laura Buxton of Staffordshire, England, was at her grandparent's golden wedding anniversary, she was given a helium-filled balloon. Before letting it fly away, she wrote her address on a label with the message, *"Please return to Laura Buxton,"* then watched it sail away.

Ten days later, a farmer in Milton Lilbourne, pulled the balloon out of the hedge that separated his fields from his neighbor's house. Since a Laura Buxton was his neighbor's daughter, he gave her the balloon. But this was a different Laura Buxton, though she was also ten years old. She lived 140 miles away from the Laura Buxton who had released the balloon.

Laura Buxton from Milton Lilbourne got out her pen and wrote to Laura Buxton in Stoke-on-Trent, Staffordshire. Since even the girls' parents recognized the significance of this coincidence, the girls were allowed to meet—and then things got even more bizarre.

The girls, both tall for their age, were the same height and both decided to wear pink sweaters and jeans for their first meeting. Their hair was brown and they both wore it in the same style.

Amazingly, both girls had three-year-old black Labrador retriever dogs and pet rabbits, both gray. They also had guinea pigs, which were the same color and even had the same orange markings on their hindquarters.

It was almost like these girls were identical twins, two halves brought together by a balloon.

It all happened in June 2001, but the two young women are still friends and feel the circumstances that brought them together are too significant to be written off as meaningless. It seems they are linked karmically, if not genetically, and they were meant to meet each other. In other words, they feel a sense of destiny. Name synchros often feel that way.

MORE DOPPELGANGERS

A doppelganger is usually defined as a ghostly double of a living person. The idea is found in mythology, folklore, throughout various cultures, and has been used in popular culture in movies, novels, and TV shows. Many notable individuals have seen them. Among them are: the sixteenth century poet John Donne, the eighteenth century writer Johann Wolfgang von Goethe, and Percy Bysshe Shelley, another eighteenth century poet. Others include Abraham Lincoln, Queen Elizabeth I, and the French novelist and short story writer, Guy de Maupassant.

It's interesting that Donne, Goethe, and Shelley were all poets. It suggests that their imaginations were well-developed and that perhaps they were deeply attuned to other realms and dimensions. Donne was in Paris when he experienced a doppelganger encounter—but it was of his wife, who was pregnant, and she appeared holding a baby. At about this same time, she was giving birth to a stillborn daughter. Shelley's encounter happened in Italy, where his phantom self pointed at the Mediterranean Sea. Not long afterward, Shelley drowned in a sailing accident in the Mediterranean. He was just twenty-nine.

The encounters both Donne and Shelley experienced were certainly precognitive—the foretelling of a future event. For both of these men, that future event spelled tragedy. For Goethe, the experience was simply deeply puzzling. It happened while he was riding on the road to Drusenheim, a city in northeast France. Riding toward him was his exact double, who wore a gray suit trimmed in gold. Eight years later, Goethe was traveling on the same road, but in the opposite direction. He realized he was wearing the same gray suit trimmed in gold that he had seen on his double eight years earlier. So even Goethe's encounter was precognitive. Can a doppelganger, then, be some sort of holographic projection from the future self? Perhaps.

Neurophysiologist Karl Pribram and physicist David Bohm were two of the early pioneers of the theory that we live in a holographic universe. Most of us are familiar with holograms. They're used at Disney World, in the train ride through the haunted house where three-dimensional ghosts leap out at you. They were featured in the movie *Star Wars*, when a light shoots from the robot R2-D2 and projects a three-dimensional image of Princess Leia. In the TV series *Star Trek: The Next Generation*, the ship has a holodeck and even a holographic medical emergency doctor. In the 1990 film *Total Recall*, the protagonist wears a wristwatch that projects a holographic image.

But suppose, as Pribram and Bohm suggest, the reality we experience is actually a giant hologram? As Michael Talbot so aptly expressed it in his brilliant book *The Holographic Universe,* "...there is evidence to suggest that our world and everything in it—from snowflakes to maple trees to falling stars and spinning electrons—are also only ghostly images, projections from a level of reality so beyond our own it is literally beyond both space and time."

And if that's the case, if we're living in a holographic universe, then synchronicity may be one of our most direct experiences with this deeper reality. We can reach this place "beyond time and space" in dreams, during meditation, heightened creative periods, during NDEs, and through other kinds of altered states. But synchronicity may be the most easily accessible *conscious* experience we have of this deeper reality. If so, it behooves us to pay attention.

In an interview in 1979 in *Psychology Today,* Pribram noted: "...it isn't that there *aren't* objects out there, at one level of reality. It's that if you penetrate through and look at the universe with a holographic system, you arrive at a different view, a different reality. And that other reality can explain things that have hitherto remained inexplicable scientifically: paranormal phenomena, synchronicities, the apparently meaningful coincidence of events."

Doppelgangers—and synchronicities—may also be projections from probable realities. In the early 1960s, author and mystic Jane Roberts and her husband Robert Butts began experimenting with a Ouija board as part of Jane's research into ESP. It quickly became apparent that the material/information that came from the Ouija entity—Seth- was profound. Not long afterward, Jane began channeling Seth, they stopped using the Ouija board, and Rob started transcribing these sessions. At some point between then and when they began writing *The Seth Material*—Jane and Rob took a break one night to go dancing.

During that evening, Jane suddenly spotted a couple on the dance floor who looked so much like herself and Rob that she drew her husband's attention to the couple. They were heavier than either Jane or Rob, didn't look happy, and radiated a kind of grimness that disturbed her. She later came to believe that the man and woman were probable versions of herself and Rob, the version they might have become if they hadn't pursued the unknown path that led them to Seth.

What else lies in this deeper reality? We suspect there are undiscovered gems, undiscovered truths, undiscovered places we haven't even imagined. Not yet.

Abraham Lincoln probably thought the same thing when he encountered a doppelganger on the night he was elected president. In Carl Sandburg's biography about Lincoln, he wrote: "On the evening of his election he had thrown himself on one of the haircloth sofas at home, just after the first telegrams of November 6 had told him he was elected president, and looking into a bureau mirror across the room he saw himself full length, but with two faces.

"It bothered him; he got up; the illusion vanished; but when he lay down again there in the glass again were two faces, one paler than the other. He got up again, mixed in the election excitement, forgot about it; but it came back, and haunted him. He told his wife about it; she worried too.

"A few days later he tried it once more and the illusion of the two faces again registered to his eyes. But that was the last; the ghost since then wouldn't come back, he told his wife, who said it was a sign he would be elected to a second term and the death pallor of one face meant he wouldn't live through his second term."

Lincoln's encounter is also an excellent example of precognition.

It's one thing to read about other people's encounters with doppelgangers, but something else to be mistaken for someone who not only looks like you, but has the same name. Just ask Mike Perry, the synchronicity blogger from the U.K.

When he and his wife Karin were on vacation in Wales, they decided they deserved a meal in a good restaurant. He phoned the place they'd chosen to make a reservation, and Mike noted, "Whoever I spoke to was extremely polite, almost over the top, and I booked a table for 8.30 p.m."

They arrived at the restaurant around 8:15. When he told the host he was Mr. Perry and had a reservation, the host said, "Ah, Mr. Perry. Lovely to see you again. How was South Africa?"

Mike was unsure what to say, since he hadn't been to South Africa and had obviously been mistaken for someone else—another Mike Perry. Much to his wife's embarrassment, he just went along with it. "South Africa was fine, thanks."

The meal, Mike said, was superb and they had one of the best tables in the restaurant and the service was first class. "We almost felt like royalty."

The second time this happened, he and his wife were on vacation in the U.S. They were traveling through Phoenix and Mike had booked a hotel room in advance for two nights. "I walked over to reception and the person behind the desk said, *'Mr. Perry, how nice to see you again. We have given you the same room.'*" He had never been to Phoenix before or, for that matter, to the part of Wales where the restaurant was situated.

"So what does this mean?" Mike wrote. "To be honest I don't really know, but there have been quite a few similar instances. All I can say is that mostly when it happens it's to my advantage, as I am well looked after."

It would be fascinating to know the identity and background of this other world-traveler named Mike Perry.

MATCHING TALES

In 1979, the German magazine—*Das Besteran*—ran a writing competition. Readers were asked to submit unusual stories that were based on true incidents. Walter Kellner of Munich won the contest and his story was published.

He wrote about a time when he was flying a Cessna 421 between Sardinia and Sicily and encountered engine trouble when he was over the open sea. He was forced to land in the water and spent some time in an emergency dinghy until he was rescued.

An Austrian, also named Walter Kellner, spotted the story and complained that the German Kellner had plagiarized it. The Austrian Kellner said that *he* had flown a Cessna 421 over the same sea, experienced engine trouble and was forced to land in Sardinia. It was essentially the same story, with a slightly different ending. The magazine checked both stories, and both turned out to be true, even though they were nearly identical.

How is such a thing even possible?

Both Pribram and Bohm theorized that our deeper reality, the implicate or enfolded order, consists of an "energy domain," as Pribram calls it, that lies beyond our normal field of perception. Mystics, shamans, and psychics, can access this domain. Author and medical intuitive Caroline Myss talked at great length about this domain in her groundbreaking book *Anatomy of the Spirit.*

"Everything that is alive pulsates with energy and all of this energy contains information. The energy field around the human body—what mystics refer to as an aura—holds all the information about who and what we are, where in the body we're suffering ill health, and why. It's this field that intuitives access."

But, bottom line, we can all access this energy field when we want or need to. It speaks to us constantly through meaningful coincidence and when we're paying attention, we are in that same flow that intuitives and shamans access. We become the moving river in our own lives.

Our names also hold particular frequencies. Trish's aunt was born as Barbara Janeshutz. During midlife, she legally had her last name changed to Jaynes, because it was "more in line with who she was," she once explained to Trish, and then proceeded to scribble out a bunch of numbers that supposedly proved her point. Eventually, Trish realized her aunt was doing numerology to illustrate why her name—her identity—was better suited as a Jaynes rather than a Janeshutz.

When women get married and take their husband's last name, they are doing more than just promising to love and honor. They are changing their vibrational frequencies. When writers write under pseudonyms, they also are changing their vibrational frequencies.

PSEUDONYMS

In her professional life, Trish's first two novels were written by Trish Janeshutz, her maiden name. Her editor asked her to use a different name when she started the Quin/McCleary series because mysteries and suspense novels by men were outselling those by women. She became TJ MacGregor.

When she wrote *Tango Key*, the first in a new series, her editor asked her to choose a female name because by then mysteries by women were outselling those by men. So she became Alison Drake. All of these names hold particular frequencies, particular patterns of energy.

Stephen King, at one point in his illustrious career, wrote several novels as Richard Bachman because his publisher didn't want to saturate the market with King novels. *Thinner*, written as Richard Bachman, King's version of Richard Matheson's *The Incredible Shrinking Man* sold 28,000 copies. And according to Wikipedia, once readers realized that Bachman was King, *Thinner* went on to sell more than ten times that.

Bachman just doesn't do it quite like King does.

J.K. Rowling knows something about this. As the author of the Harry Potter series, she broke every writing record, everywhere. She became the first billionaire writer—and is still young enough to enjoy her fortune. Joanne Rowling was advised to write as a man because fantasy books by men were outselling fantasy books by women so she became J.K. Rowling. But in 2013, it was uncovered that Rowling had written *The Cuckoo's Calling,* an adult mystery, as Robert Galbraith, and the sales of Galbraith's novels quickly soared. Her official statement about the pseudonym:

"I hoped to keep this secret a little longer, because being Robert Galbraith has been such a liberating experience! It has been wonderful to publish without hype or expectation and pure pleasure to get feedback from publishers and readers under a different name. The upside of being rumbled is that I can publicly thank my editor David Shelley, who has been a true partner in crime, all those people at Little, Brown who have been working so hard on *The Cuckoo's Calling* without realizing that I wrote it, and the writers and reviewers, both in the newspapers and online, who have been so generous to the novel. And to those who have asked for a sequel, Robert fully intends to keep writing the series, although he will probably continue to turn down personal appearances."

HARRY WHO?

Backtracking to the origins of Harry Potter, in 1990, Joanne Rowling was working as a researcher and bilingual secretary for Amnesty International. While on a delayed train from Manchester to London, she conceived an idea for a series of novels. During the subsequent seven years, she was divorced from her husband, her mother died, and she lived on public assistance. When her first book was published in 1997, it included a line that proved to be precognitive: "Someday everyone will know the name Harry Potter."

The novels, of course, went on to become the bestselling novels of all time, with more than 400 million sold, and were also made into hugely successful movies. And yes, everyone knows the name Harry Potter. He even has his own spot at Disney World.

THE UNSINKABLE HUGH WILLIAMS

If you scour the Internet in search of unusual coincidences, you're likely to run across a story—or, make that stories—about Hugh Williams. These seafaring coincidences span nearly 200 years. Here is one version:

A vessel went down in the Menai Strait off the coast of Wales on December 5, 1664. All eighty-one passengers were lost—except for a man named Hugh Williams.

On December 5, 1785, 121 years later, another ship sank in the Menai Strait, and again all of the passengers drowned except one—Hugh Williams.

Move ahead to December 5, 1820, and yet another ship, a twenty-five-passenger vessel, sank in the Menai Strait. And once again there was a sole survivor. You guessed it, his name was Hugh Williams. We could call him the unsinkable Hugh Williams. And notice that not only is the only survivor the same in each case, but so are the month and day.

Where did this story originate and is there any truth to it? Or is it just a maritime tale that has been passed down over time?

The first reference to the lucky Hugh Williams is found on pages 281-282 of *North Wales, Including its Scenery, Antiquities and Customs*, 1804, by Rev. William Bingley. It describes a Hugh Williams who escaped from a shipwreck on December 5, 1785.

A version of the story appears as a footnote on page 155 of *Cliffe's Book of North Wales*, published in 1851. The story includes the sinkings on December 5, 1664 and 1785, with Hugh Williams as the only survivor. The date of the 1820 sinking, however, is listed as August. 5, not December 5. Hugh Williams is still listed as the sole survivor. The footnote goes on to mention that, *"Again on May 20th, 1842, a boat was crossing the Menai, near the spot where the above catastrophes happened, when she upset with 15 passengers, and all perished save one; but in this instance the name of the survivor was Richard Thomas."*

Another book, *Guide to North Wales* by Francis Coghlan, published in 1860, repeats the story of the three shipwrecks, and includes the August date for the third sinking.

Coghlan's account of the three shipwrecks ends with the comment:

"This extraordinary coincidence can only be explained by the circumstance that the name of Hugh Williams is very common in these parts."

Blogger Rick Spillman, who gathered some of these references, noted that in Wales Hugh Williams is a common name and that the Menai Strait "is a particularly nasty body of water with strong currents and rough seas."

Yet, in spite of those reservations, it remains a baffling coincidence that three Hugh Williams were the sole survivors of three shipwrecks in the same waters over 150 years. Is it meaningful or merely a curiosity? That depends on your perspective. But if it is a synchronicity, what possibly could be the deeper meaning?

IN THE NAME OF MURDER

The fascinating thing about synchronicity is that it appears throughout history but is often called by different names, addressed in different terms, herded under different parameters. But in the end, synchros are often startling reminders that we are unified and united in ways that defy expectations. It's as if some super glue gloms us together, and synchronicity springs forth from that deeper reality, whispering, *See? Do you see how it all fits together?*

Historical synchronicities involving murder and matching names are numerous. You don't have to dig too deeply on the Internet to find them. Some of these stories were also found in *Mysteries of the Unexplained,* published by *Reader's Digest*. Here are some of the best and most puzzling:

1) On July 28th 1900, the King of Italy, Umberto I, dined in a restaurant in the city of Monza. There he met the restaurant owner whose name was also Umberto, and he looked very much like the king. Surprisingly, they were both born in Turin on March 14, 1844. Not only that, but the restaurant owner's wife and the queen were both named Margherita. The restaurant owner told the king that he had opened on the same day the king was inaugurated.

The next day, King Umberto was shot dead and—in a separate incident—so was the restaurant owner.

2) In 1872, Claude Volbonne killed Baron Rodemire de Tarazone of France. Twenty-one years earlier, the Baron's father had been murdered by somebody else named Claude Volbonne.

3) On February 13, 1746, a Frenchman, Jean Marie Dubarry, was executed for the murder of his father. Precisely 100 years later, on February

13, 1846, another Frenchman, also named Jean Marie Dubarry, was executed for the murder of his father.

4) On the November 26, 1911, three men were hanged at Greenberry Hill in London after being convicted of the murder of Sir Edmund Berry. Their names were Green, Berry and Hill.

BIRTHDATES

In *The 7 Secrets of Synchronicity,* one of the stories we include involved writer and past-life researcher Carol Bowman.

Carol, while visiting her mother in a small town in New York's Hudson Valley, went to the grocery store for some basics. While waiting in line, she noticed the woman behind her had a toddler in her cart, a cute little girl. Carol asked the woman how old her daughter was.

Woman: "She'll be two next month. She's an Aries."
Carol: "My Aries daughter will be thirty next month. Aries kids are a handful, aren't they?"
Woman, laughing: "That's for sure. And I'm married to an Aries."
Carol's antenna twitched. "Me, too!"

So we can imagine these two women in line at this store, suddenly aware of some sort of connection, both with Aries daughters, both married to Aries men.

Woman: "I'm a Libra."
Carol understood that something odd and fascinating was happening. "I'm a Libra, too. What's your birthdate?"
Woman: "October 14."
"That's, uh, my birthdate, too."

Yes, it sounds like an episode out of the *Twilight Zone,* weird music and all. But the upshot was that Carol handed the woman her business card and said she would be conducting a past-life workshop in the area in June. The woman said she would definitely attend.

Now: fast-forward about four years. On July 3, 2013, Carol received a call from a Philadelphia woman whose therapist has recommended that she get a past-life regression. The woman looked for past-life therapists in the area and ran across Carol's name—and suddenly remembered reading about her in 7 Secrets because they share the same birthday—October 14. The same week she came for a regression, so did two other people who also shared Carol's birthday—so that was three clients in one week who were born on October 14.

In Carol's sixty-two years, the only other people she'd met born on her birthday were the woman from the grocery and Dwight Eisenhower, whom she met at West Point when she was ten years old. When she shook his hand, she told him they had the same birthday.

So Carol had called to thank us for the mention—which had brought her a new client.

This kind of connection is gratifying to writers. It means you're creating ripples in this huge pond of life that positively impact other people. This woman will now experience a past-life regression with one of the pioneers in reincarnational research because a friend gave her a book with a story in it that she remembered.

"But what do you think it means that I've gotten three clients this week who share my birthday?" she asked.

"It qualifies as a cluster," Trish replied, and looked to Jung for the possible significance.

Jung experienced numerical synchronicities throughout his life and believed that numbers symbolize "an archetype of order that has become conscious." Adding together the numbers in Carol's birthday, 10+14=24 and 2+4=6. Six is the number for service. As soon as Trish mentioned this, Carol said, "That fits. Past-life therapy is my work, but there's a strong service component to it. This therapy can heal."

Chapter 6
LOVE & SYNCHRONICITY

ANGIE'S STORY

Love is the single most powerful emotion we humans feel and experience. Whether it's romantic love, a parent's love for a child or vice-versa, the love between siblings or between friends, the love we feel for an animal companion, or the love we feel toward a particular place, it's like a force of nature. It sweeps through us, changing us forever. And, not surprisingly, love creates a fertile atmosphere for synchronicity.

"In all synchronicities what is important is not the 'objective facts' of the coincidence, but the emotional impact they had on the people involved," wrote Robert Hopcke in *There Are No Accidents.* Just ask Angie, a forty-eight-year-old hair stylist.

Angie has two grown children and a son headed to college next year. The kids are from her first marriage, which ended after twenty years. After the divorce, Angie met Patrick, who is Mexican-American, and in 2008, they got engaged. Several months into the engagement, Angie broke it off because Patrick's young children from his first marriage came to live with them and it didn't work out. After a separation, his kids returned to Texas to live with their mother and Patrick and Angie got back together and were married. Not long afterward, Patrick's teenage daughter moved in with them again and in late 2012, they got divorced.

When Angie broke off the first engagement, she had what turned out to be two pivotal dreams. In the first, she was in a market to buy bread. "The clerk told me not to buy bread from the front of the store because it was stale. She directed me to the back of the store for fresher bread. A bald-headed man who spoke with an accent told me I'd have to wait, that the bread had to be kneaded and baked. So I waited. In the dream, my mother told me that the kneading of bread means I had to be patient. Very patient."

On March 26, 2013, Angie met the bald-headed man who spoke with an accent. He pulled in behind her at the garage where she'd taken her car and they got to talking as their cars were worked on. Eduardo is Brazilian. His job? It turns out he owns a business that distributes *bread* around our county. Bald, accent, bread: Angie suddenly remembered her dream from five years earlier. She also realized that exactly five years earlier *to the day*, on March 26, 2008, she had received her first passport. At the time, she was still with Patrick and he was annoyed by it. "Why do you need a passport?" he'd asked her.

"I don't know," she'd replied. "Maybe we're going overseas."

In July, she and Eduardo traveled to Brazil and she met his family. They recently celebrated their six-month anniversary.

In the second dream she had that same night in 2008, she and Patrick were in a parking lot, about to drive somewhere and they were already late. Two young Mexican women came up to the car window and asked him for directions. He told Angie he was going to help them and when she pointed out that they were already late, he got out anyway to talk to the women. Angie drove off, leaving him behind. The dream turned out not only to be symbolic of a future split, but actually came to pass five years later, on the day their divorce became final.

When Angie and Patrick left the courtroom after their marriage had been dissolved, they walked downstairs so they could sign papers that would enable her to revert back to her maiden name. As they were leaving this area, the papers signed, two young Mexican women stopped Patrick and asked for help. "They were the same women from my dream, young, with long, dark hair. Patrick asked me to wait, said he would be right back. I kept on walking and left him behind, just like in my dream."

When our lives are in transition, synchronicities proliferate and our unconscious, it seems, is eager to help out. Even though Angie didn't have any idea what the two dreams meant when she had them, they were vivid enough so that she remembered them. When details from the dream began unfolding in her waking life five years later, she recognized the synchronicity and precognitive elements of the dreams and felt she was being guided.

TIMER

A timer is typically a kitchen device that you set for something you're cooking—a roast, a turkey, rolls, a pie. When it dings, you run over to the stove and remove the item and, in an ideal world, it's done to perfection. But *Timer* is also the name of a movie.

Here's the concept: as a result of a new invention, people have an opportunity to find their true love—that perfect person—by having a timer-strip injected into their wrist. The strip is visible, about two inches long, half an inch wide. On it is a digital timer ticking down to the moment when you'll meet your true love, who will show up with his or her own timer simultaneously ticking down to zero—the moment of truth and true love.

Although the story was intriguing in a humorous way and the characters surprisingly believable, the concept didn't seem very well thought out. For instance, the main character's timer was blank. No explanation was given and she didn't seem interested in a refund. Finally, when she wanted it removed, it wasn't because it didn't work, but that she didn't want to play the timer game any longer. The clinician who was going to remove it confessed he had never heard of anyone doing such a thing. So apparently no one had their timer removed after their true love was found. Why not?

We also wondered why so many people would want a timer to lead them to true love. Timers were wildly popular and you were a dork if you didn't have one. In spite of the plot flaws and obvious questions raised by a digital implant guiding, if not directing, your love life and future, we enjoyed the movie.

But as we watched it, we started thinking there was something somewhat familiar about the concept. Something from the past. At first, we thought it might've been a story we'd read or maybe one we'd written long ago. Then we remembered.

Back when we first met, Rob took a course in hypnosis and started guiding people—mainly friends and family—into past-life regressions. He had a knack for it. Trish was his favorite subject; she was susceptible and imaginative. One of those regressions involved a true-love timer. In that session, Trish moved into an alternate reality. She had just met Rob—an alternate Rob—and speeding ahead now in this alternate reality—we were making love for the first time when alarms attached to Rob's bed went off, ringing loudly, filling the room with sound. The alternate Rob bolted up, and shouted: "You're the one!"

Apparently, he had invented a gizmo that allowed him to monitor his compatibility with women that he bedded. The alarm had a variety of tones that allowed him to judge the level of compatibility. Apparently, nothing had ever happened even vaguely close to the alarming reaction set off by the alternate Trish's appearance in his bedroom. We hope they had a good life, filled with love.

Ironically, Jung had trouble defining love. In his autobiography, *Memories, Dreams, and Reflections,* he wrote that even though he had been confronted with the mystery of love in his medical practice and in his personal life, he had never been able to explain what it was. But he then went on to describe it in terms of extremes that lead, ultimately, to God.

"Here is the greatest and smallest, the remotest and the nearest, the highest and the lowest, and we cannot discuss one side of it without also discussing the other. No language is adequate to this paradox. Whatever one can say, no words express the whole." He saw it as a "unified and undivided whole" that was superior to the individual, and man was at its mercy. "He may assent to it, or rebel against it; but he is always caught up by it and enclosed within it… Man can try to name love, showering upon it all the names at his command, and still he will involve himself in endless self-deceptions."

If man, says Jung, has any insight at all, he will "name the unknown by the more unknown, *ignotum per ignotius—*that is, by the name of God. That is a confession of his subjection, his imperfection, and his dependence; but at the same time a testimony to his freedom to choose between truth and error."

Most of us probably don't think about love in the philosophical terms that Jung did. But we know when we feel it and sometimes, it does seem to have a divine source, as Renee Prince discovered through a hawk named Tennerin.

RENEE AND TENNERIN

Renee Prince used to be a marine biologist, a field she abandoned after she worked closely with captive dolphins. She now works as an artist on movies and TV series in Oregon. Every autumn for years, a hawk she called Tennerin would frequent the trees near her home and they developed a special friendship. She's writing a book about this friendship called *Hawk Diaries.*

But in the autumn of 2012, Tennerin failed to appear. Every day, Renie would walk out into the trees, looking for her beloved hawk, but he wasn't there. One afternoon, she set out around 3:15, calling Tennerin's name. Just as she reached the preserve, she saw a hawk swerving toward her over the river. Her heart soared with joy; was it Tennerin? She kept calling, but the hawk turned back toward the water and kept flying until it was out of sight. She hadn't seen any hawks for over a week and hoped she would see it again when she got to the big hill in the center of the nature preserve.

When she reached the top of the hill, she called and called for Tennerin, her voice echoing across the expanse of trees. No hawk appeared. Feeling dejected about it, she started back down the hill and listened to a podcast of the TED Talks radio show about the genesis of creativity. Elizabeth Gilbert—author of *Eat, Pray, Love*—was the guest. Renee had heard this particular talk some months earlier, and almost decided to stop the playback and choose the next show down on the podcast list. But since she was busy looking for hawks, she figured it wouldn't hurt to listen to Gilbert's talk again.

"As I reached the center of the grassy bowl in the middle of the woods and stood looking at the trees, Gilbert began talking about the people of the Sahara Desert who had danced for a thousand years to call down divinity. When a dancer connected with the divine, it could be seen in the beauty and power of the dancer, who became more than himself—he was infused with divinity."

When people watching the dancer saw this, Gilbert said, they called out "Allah! Allah!" Just as Gilbert said these words, a beautiful Red-tailed Hawk flew alongside me, so close that I thought he would land on the tree in front of me. But he continued past and into the shadows. As I stared at him, marveling at the beauty of his feathers, which glowed even in the darkness of the rainy afternoon, Gilbert was saying, …and this meant God is here!

"I suddenly woke up to the synchronicity of the hawk's appearance and heard Gilbert say again, God is here! And I saw in that moment that God is here, in this hawk flying in front of me, a copper and gray and brown dancer who shone with divinity and I was here to witness: God is here!"

The hawk disappeared into the woods and Renee called Tennerin's name again, hoping the hawk was coming back to land in his favorite tree and interact with her. She had some hawk food in her pocket—a couple of mice and some beef, and was primed to begin interaction, to make progress with a friendship with this hawk. But the hawk didn't return.

"And then I realized this was my hawk, my dancer, who showed me that God is here, and this was my gift. And that gift was enough. I understood this was all I could ask for—divinity in response to my heartfelt wish to see a hawk and feel my beautiful Tennerin's magic. And so it was that I encountered divinity on my walk today. Let me not forget that God is here. *Allah! Allah!* Whatever the name, without a name, even, Tennerin is here; the magic and the great synchronicity of love—it is right here."

SYNCHRONICITY & ALCHEMY

Synchronicity sometimes acts as a kind of alchemy that transforms us, or a decision we're making, in an essential way. The alchemy occurs because of what the synchronicity says to you, its impact on you. This was certainly the case for Jung during a visit in the 1950s with Henry Fierz, a chemistry professor with whom he had become friends over the years.

Friez had dropped by at five o'clock one afternoon to talk with Jung about a manuscript by a scientist who had recently died. Friez felt the manuscript should be published, but Jung, who had read the manuscript, thought otherwise. Their debate about the manuscript apparently became somewhat heated and at one point, Jung glanced at his watch, as if he were about to dismiss Friez. Then he seemed puzzled by the time and explained that his watch had just been returned from repairs, but it read five o'clock, the time that Friez had arrived. He asked Friez the time; it was 5:35. As Richard Tarnas recounted the incident in *Psyche and Cosmos,* Jung apparently said, "So you have the right time, and I have the wrong time. Let us discuss the thing again."

In the ensuing discussion, Friez convinced Jung the manuscript should be published. "Here, the synchronistic event is of interest not because of its intrinsic coincidental force," Tarnas wrote, "but because of the meaning Jung drew from it, essentially using it as a basis for challenging and redirecting his own conscious attitude."

Many of us might not draw a correlation between the stopped watch and the discussion. But synchronicity, by definition, is the coming together of inner and outer events in a way that is meaningful to the individual and can't be explained by cause and effect. This means that the outer world—and all of nature and our surroundings—can carry meaning just as the inner world does. Jung, accustomed to perceiving and thinking symbolically, recognized the synchronicity and changed his thinking accordingly.

When we train ourselves to read signs and symbols in our environments, especially those that may not be glaringly apparent, the deciphering of the synchronistic messages becomes easier. Our lives are enriched, our insights are deepened.

When alchemical synchros occur in relation to *big* events in our lives— like life and death—the meaning is often in-your-face obvious and can provide unexpected comfort and reassurance. This is what happened to Trish, when she took our seventeen-year-old cat, Tigerlily, to be put down.

For all these years, Tigerlily had been eager to eat anything—our daughter's coffee yogurt, cheese, tuna of any kind, broccoli cheese soup, fish, sweet potatoes. She was our feline vacuum cleaner. And when she wasn't eating, she did what cats do—chased lizards through the back yard, tried to catch dragonflies and birds, snoozed in patches of sunlight, explored. She always stuck pretty close to home, though, and was never much interested in other cats.

Tigerlily liked her humans well enough to sleep at the foot of their bed when she was younger and ruled the roost. But once we adopted two other cats, she was equally comfortable in another room, where she ruled whatever piece of furniture she had chosen. When Trish's dad lived with us for several years, Tigerlily used to follow him out to the pool every morning when he took a daily swim. She occasionally slept at the foot of his bed, as if keeping an eye on him, and when Parkinson's confined him to a wheelchair, she occasionally consented to a ride in his lap.

She eventually warmed up to our first Golden Retriever, Jessie, never bothered our Dusky Conure, Kali, and always, she ate and retained her usual slender form; sleek and fast, that was Tigerlily. In the last month of her life, she began to ail and Noah, our Golden Retriever, sensed it. When they slept on the couch together, he would lick her, nudge her, stay close to her. He was attentive, solicitous.

Eating became a challenge for her. We knew she was dying and hoped that nature would take its course. But nature didn't cooperate. It eventually got to the point where we no longer knew what to feed her because she had trouble eating everything. She tried, but she couldn't chew and then she would start choking.

One morning, Trish gave her some cheerios in milk, mixed in well-squashed sardines and she ate what she could. But when Trish went into the kitchen to check on her minutes later, she found Tigerlily foraging in the cabinet where the cat food was kept. She emitted a soft and pathetic meow. A bib of milk and food covered her snout and chest and she suddenly reminded Trish of her father in his final days, when the mere act of lifting a fork to his mouth was nearly impossible. Trish knew it was time.

She was visibly upset when she walked into the vet's office. One of the clerks, who had worked for the vet, Ira Grossman, for the many years we'd been seeing him, came over with a box of Kleenex. "Listen," she said quietly. "A friend of mine had a near-death experience several years ago. When she returned, she became psychic, she sees spirits—of humans and animals. They really do go to a better place. Tigerlily will be back."

Trish already believed that, but it was comforting to hear it. Then the woman told Trish that the other day, she'd found an injured kitten—part of one rear leg had been torn off, possibly by a hawk, and the other leg was broken. She had rushed it to the office and they were able to save it. "We lose one, we save another."

In the examining room, Ira's son, who's in his early twenties and is studying to be a vet, explained that Tigerlily would be sedated first, then put to sleep. "I took a double take when I saw her name," he said.

"Why?"

He told her the same story about the wounded kitten that the female clerk had just finished relating. "We fixed her one broken leg, but had to amputate the other to save her. She's doing fine now. I named her Tigerlily."

Stunned at the synchronicity, at the strange comfort it provided, Trish just looked at him, then managed to stammer, "That's an uplifting coincidence. Thank you for that."

"Hey," he said softly, passing her the box of Kleenex, "they come into life and they leave life. You're doing the right thing. Seventeen is a long life for a cat."

The message of this synchro was obvious. Even though Tigerlily was facing the ultimate transformation, from life to death, Trish found enormous comfort that the kitten with the amputated leg had been given the same name. Out of all the possible names in the universe, why that one? What are the odds? The kitten with the amputated leg could have been named Lia or Isabel or Anne. But she was named Tigerlily, the same as our cat. It was as if the universe was reassuring Trish that Tigerlily would be fine and would be back. And what is life, death and rebirth if not a kind of alchemy?

FULL CIRCLE

In 1993, psychic Debra Page gave birth to her second daughter, Laryssa. The infant was born with a rare, spontaneous genetic mutation and was given just twelve days to live. But she lived for almost two years. During Laryssa's brief life, Debra and Larry, her husband, met many helpful, caring individuals from the local hospice who came out to their home to help with Laryssa's care. She passed away on October 9, 1995.

Twelve years later, in 2007, Debra and Larry were searching for a physician in their area who could treat her autoimmune disorder. Through a neighbor who worked in the administration of the largest hospital system in San Diego, Debra learned about a new physician who was taking patients and was supposedly the best in the area for autoimmune disorders.

On the day of her appointment, the doctor, a woman, read through Debra's medical history and suddenly looked up at her and Larry and blinked away tears. "I worked with Laryssa as a hospice volunteer. I remember you both."

Debra suddenly remembered her, too, a caring young woman who had lost her mother to cancer. The three of them cried and hugged, and talked about Laryssa. Then the doctor said that she now had a daughter and Debra asked when she was born.

"October 9, 1995," the doctor replied.

"The very day that Laryssa passed away. All of us were amazed at the synchronicity."

It was as if Laryssa's life, brief as it was, had come full circle. Debra embraced the synchronicity as a "beautiful gift from the past." She felt as if her daughter had reached out to help her find the physician she needed, the very woman who had helped to care for Laryssa in the final weeks and days of her life. The fact that the doctor's own daughter had been born on the day that Laryssa died was the synchronistic exclamation point to the entire experience.

Six years after Debra's experience with the physician, she e-mailed Trish just as Trish was going over her notes from a couple of years earlier about Laryssa's story. Not only was it a synchronicity, but it seemed as if Laryssa was reaching out to Debra once again.

HOW SHE SAID GOOD-BYE

There are many different kinds of love, of course, and the bonds that develop among family members throughout years and decades can be immensely powerful. Sometimes we don't know just how powerful those bonds are until death. In times of major transitions—death being the most profound transition—synchronicities proliferate, almost as a kind of closure.

Jeri and Steve Young, like so many Boomers, not only have their own family—two sons and a daughter—but are dealing with aging parents as well. Jeri's father recently died of Parkinson's and Steve's mother recently died from complications of Alzheimer's. What is unusual about his mother's death is the way she said good-bye.

Steven's mother and Jeri and the kids always had a thing about the Goodyear Blimp. It is seen frequently in the South Florida skies, humming along the coast and sometimes headed inland, over the Everglades. Whenever they saw the blimp, it was a moment of great excitement. They exclaimed how cool it was, how they would love to ride on it, and the kids were particularly curious about how something so huge could be airborne! So the Goodyear Blimp was a family *connection*.

When Steve's mother was in the advanced stages of Alzheimer's, she lived in an assisted living facility

One Friday evening, Jeri and Steve left their house to eat at a Chinese restaurant. Their son, Kyle, was with them and so was their daughter, Nicki, who they were going to drop at a local barn to go horseback riding. At the time, Steve's mother was in the advance stages of Alzheimer's and was in an assisted living facility.

As they left their neighborhood, Jeri noticed the Goodyear blimp seemed to be following them. "The blimp followed us from our house to the stable. We were all fascinated that it was staying with us and for such a long time. A few blocks away from the restaurant we got a call that Steve's mother had just passed. We made a U-turn turn to drop Kyle at home so we could go to the facility to see her and the blimp also made a U-turn!"

All the way back to their neighborhood, the blimp continued to follow them. When they turned on to their block, the blimp also turned and showed a digital display that read www. Alzheimer's. com, the very disease Steve's other had. "And because the blimp was such a big deal for all of us, I knew, I just *knew*, it was Steve's mother saying good-bye."

Synchros like this one are so powerful they leave an indelible impression. You have to wonder at the orchestration of all it. Are there invisible gnomes who move pieces around on some cosmic chessboard?

Jeri says the blimp "followed them," but it was probably following the road they were on. Even so, why did it make that U-turn at the same time they did, just after they'd heard Steve's mother had passed on, enabling Jeri to see the message on the other side? *Alzheimer's*. It could just as easily have read *breast cancer* or *diabetes* or, for that matter, *Google*. Instead, it was an example of the inner world manifesting in a unique way with a personal message in the sky.

Chapter 7
SYNCHRONICITY & HEALING

THE LEGACY OF BRUGH JOY

In 1975, W. Brugh Joy had a flourishing medical practice in Los Angeles, life was good. Then shortly before his thirty-fifth birthday, he was diagnosed with chronic relapsing pancreatitis. There's no cure for this disease, which causes debilitating abdominal pain that may persist for several days, as it did for Joy. He knew the disease was unpredictable, that it might end abruptly on its own or that an attack could turn into fulminating pancreatitis, which had a mortality rate at that time of eighty percent. With each attack Joy probed his own psyche, struggling to understand why he was manifesting a disease that could severely restrict his activities or lead to his demise.

"I examined the stresses in my life, but they were inconsequential in comparison to the disease process and thus not powerful enough to lead to it. I talked to my body, trying to find some symbolic aspect that a malfunctioning pancreas might reflect, but nothing appeared. I simply could not see the dynamics of my problem."

One Saturday morning while working on some medical charts in his office, he felt a powerful urge to enter into meditation. Even though he meditated daily, this urge was exceptionally strong, so he finished up what he was doing and began meditating. "A vortex of energy, of a magnitude I had never before experienced, reverberated through my body and threw my awareness into a super heightened state. Then a loud voice said, in essence: *Your experience and training as an orthodox physician is completed. It's over. The time has come for you to embark on a rededication of your Beingness to a deeper commitment and action.*"

The voice proceeded to lay out the journeys Brugh would be taking—Findhorn, England, Egypt, India, Nepal, trips that would "reawaken old soul memories." The voice told him that his vision of being a physician was distorted and overemphasized "the body and external causes and ignored the journey of the soul." He was to start studying alternative healing techniques and practices so that he could develop a more integrated approach to healing.

The experience was so powerful that within six weeks, Joy had resigned from his medical practice and walked away from all that was familiar to him. "The wellspring that nourished my awareness was the knowing—the absolute *knowing*—that the course of action I was following was true to my soul."

When he arrived in Findhorn, his first destination, he realized he hadn't had a single attack of abdominal pain since that voice first spoke to him. His body had spoken and its message was clear: it was time to restore his soul. Joy went on to write several books—*Joy's Way: A Map for the Transformational Journey* is the best known—and for years conducted workshops on his healing techniques.

Michael Crichton, in his book *Travels*, has a chapter called *Cactus Teachings,* which is about the Brugh Joy retreat he attended in 1982. It's one of the best chapters in the book and provides a powerful glimpse of the techniques Joy used. The conference was held at a facility in the desert and early on, Joy had told the attendees to walk in the desert until they found a rock, tree, or plant for which they felt a particular kinship. Then they were supposed "to spend time with this teacher, and talk with the teacher and learn what the teacher has to teach us." So Crichton set out to find his teacher.

As other attendees excitedly reported finding a teacher, Crichton got annoyed because he hadn't. He finally found a cactus in an artificial rock garden in a meditation room. "I didn't like the cactus," he wrote. "It was common, a sort of phallic cactus shape with lots of thorns. It was rather battered, with scars on one side. It was not in any way an attractive cactus."

Days passed. Crichton kept talking to the cactus, visiting it, but the cactus refused to speak to him. Then finally one day on his way to the meditation room, he thought that if the cactus was really his teacher, it would speak to him. "And the cactus said, 'When are you going to stop running around and talk?' Irritably. Like a grouchy old man."

After this, Crichton kept firing questions at the cactus. It refused to speak to him. Every day, the same thing happened: no response. The conference continued, Crichton was exposed to new things—healing techniques, chakras, perceptual changes, the tarot, the *I Ching.* "On the final day of the conference, I visited the cactus to say good-bye. The cactus was just sitting there. It wouldn't speak to me." Crichton told the cactus that he appreciated what it had shown him and said he'd enjoyed spending time with it. "Which wasn't exactly true because I felt frustrated a lot of the time, but I thought it was more or less true." Still no response.

"Then I realized that from its position in the garden, the cactus could never see the sun set. The cactus had been years in that position and been deprived of seeing sunsets. I burst into tears. And then the cactus said, 'It's been good having you here with me.' Then I *really* cried."

Eight months after that conference, Crichton's life had completely turned around. He had changed his relationships, residence, work, diet, habits, interests, exercise, goals—in fact, anything in his life that could be changed, was changed. "These changes were so sweeping that I couldn't see what was happening while I was in the midst of them. And there was another change, too. I've become very fond of cacti, and I always have some around, wherever I live."

Neither Crichton nor Joy followed what could be called a conventional path. Generally, someone with pancreatitis consults a physician who then prescribes a course of treatment to alleviate symptoms. But Joy was already a physician who used a non-traditional approach to his health problem by engaging his body in conversation and searching for the root of the problem within himself. Illness as metaphor. When he couldn't find any answers or insight in this way, he then followed an overwhelming impulse to meditate and this enabled the powerful voice of his soul to speak. Joy still had a choice, of course, whether to dismiss the voice as nonsense or to take the advice. He listened, took the unconventional path and was healed.

For Crichton, the emotional release he experienced with the cactus at Joy's retreat apparently caused the tectonic shifts in his life during the subsequent eight months. Hardly a conventional path.

"The synchronistic field points toward a less certain and less predictable world, a world that is continually creating and being created, a world in which our affects, interests, institutions and irrationalities find a home," wrote Veronica Goodchild in *Songlines of the Soul*. "In fact, the irrational and the impossible become the transformative moment."

Perhaps the first step in healing yourself is to follow your impulses, as Joy and Crichton did. Impulses often lead directly into the synchronistic field.

MASS BELIEFS

Even though Joy was a medical doctor, he followed his own path concerning his treatment. But suppose you're not a physician and are given a dire diagnosis? What then? Do you follow the promptings of synchronicity and your own inner wisdom or do you seek traditional treatment and fully enter the mass beliefs—many of them negative—that permeate the medical profession? That depends as much on your personal beliefs as it does on your finances and whether or not you have health insurance.

When author and publisher Louise Hay was diagnosed with incurable cervical cancer, she didn't have health insurance. She believed she had contributed to the disease by holding on to resentment about childhood abuse and a rape she had suffered at the hands of a neighbor when she was just five. She set out on a course of forgiveness, exercise, and nutritional therapy and within six months, there was no trace of her cancer. Her journey is recounted in her bestselling book, *You Can Heal Your Life*. In 1984, she established Hay House, which today is one of the leading publishers about alternative thought and now publishes such luminaries as Esther Hicks, Deepak Chopra, and Wayne Dyer.

Some years ago, when Jenean Gilstrap was in her mid-thirties, she was diagnosed with a rapidly growing grapefruit-size tumor in her uterus. "I was starting a whole new part of my life and simply refused to allow something like this to happen." The night before the emergency surgery was performed to remove the tumor, the doctor came into Jenean's room and stayed until nearly midnight to console her. But Jenean was so certain the tumor was gone, *she* ended up consoling *him*.

When Jenean was opened up the next day, there wasn't any sign of a tumor. It had vanished in the twenty-four hours between her last radiology results and the emergency surgery. "The doctors were aghast. But I knew, I just knew. I refused to accept their diagnosis."

She experienced a similar incident when several cardiac tests indicated ischemia—a restriction in blood supply to tissues, which causes a shortage of oxygen and glucose needed for cellular metabolism. "The doctors were all upset, but I told them I was fine. Again, I refused to listen to their diagnosis." During stress testing, Jenean closed her eyes, and visualized her cells swimming through unclogged arteries. She recalls that the technician told her that her hands were making back and forth movements during the test. Jenean laughed because she had been mentally swimming but didn't realize there was a physical movement at the time. She wasn't surprised at the bottom line: a clean bill of health.

"Anyone can do this," Jenean says. "It's really simple, a matter of mind over matter, a belief or *deep knowing* that you can do it."

Natalie, a medium who lives in Australia, experienced something similar several years ago. She had a growth about the size of a dime near her right eye on her cheekbone. She was scheduled to have it surgically removed on a Tuesday morning. On Sunday night at church, she asked the angels to take the growth away because she was afraid of the doctor at the clinic. "I woke up on Tuesday to go to the clinic and it was gone! The surgeon couldn't believe it, as he had only booked me the previous Thursday."

These kinds of healings may be more common than we know. We make a significant connection, as Jung's patient did when the beetle fluttered at the window just as she was telling Jung about the scarab beetle in her dream. Something within us is galvanized, a belief changes instantly— or we refuse, as Joy, Jenean, and Louise Hay did, to buy into a mass belief system that pronounces a condition as incurable. Essentially, the outer event triggers an inner vibrational change that attracts the desired outcome—synchronicity.

HOMEOPATHY & MEDICAL INTUITIVES

This alternative medical system, which dates back to the late 1700s, is based on Samuel Hahnemann's principle called the Law of Similars. It says that a substance taken in large doses that causes the symptoms of a disease in a healthy person will cure similar symptoms in sick people when taken in small, heavily diluted doses.

If you drink too much coffee, you feel over-stimulated, irritated, hyped up, more alert, and probably have trouble sleeping. The homeopathic remedy for insomnia, though, is *Coffea Cruda,* a vastly diluted remedy made from coffee. The idea here is that insomnia has the same *vibrational qualities* as coffee so, essentially, you're treating like with like.

The late Edward Whitmont, a psychiatrist and student of Jung's who became a homeopathic physician, noted in his book, *Psyche and Substance,* that every illness and disease originates in both body and mind. This is why each patient manifests an inimitable configuration of mental, emotional, and physical symptoms. This pattern is an external representation of the patient's vibratory state. So when a remedy's vibratory state matches that of the patient, the result can be therapeutic. And the reason this happens? *Synchronicity.*

"These two levels of expression appear to be in a relation of what we may call associated coexistence or synchronicity, rather than of one-sided, fixed causation," Whitmont wrote.

Mainstream medicine, however, dismisses homeopathy as quackery. But many of the clinical studies on this subject have been performed by pharmaceutical companies that stand to lose billions in profits if homeopathy is shown to be effective. Pharmaceutical companies probably don't put much, if any, credence in synchronicity or energetic healing, in alternative medicine or intuitive diagnoses, either. But that doesn't invalidate their efficacy.

In *Awaking Intuition*, author and physician Mona Lisa Schultz, like Louise Hay and author Caroline Myss, takes readers through the world of a medical intuitive. She looks at illness and disease from an energetic level that is a mix of body, mind, and spirit. "If we ignore our emotions or our memories from the past, our bodies will express them all the more forcefully," wrote Schultz. "We're paralyzed until we deal with the emotions that are playing out in our bodies' symptoms, trying to get our attention. Every one of us can start to learn the intuitive language of our own body that tells us which aspect of our lives requires our attention."

Louise Hay knew that for her: incurable cervical cancer = childhood abuse and rape.

We live in a symbolic universe where everything is connected.

One scientific study that Schultz mentioned involved mammograms and breast cancer. Women who were about to have mammograms were asked a series of questions about events in their lives during the last five to eight years. "Researchers discovered that they were able to predict which women would be found to have cancer on the basis of the answers they gave to those questions." Women who had experienced a severe life event within that time frame "were consistently more likely to be diagnosed with cancer."

Yet, as Schultz pointed out, the determining factor in treating the disease was the person's emotional reactions and subsequent activism in dealing with the new condition. "We want to pay attention to body memories and figure out what emotions are related to the body symptoms we're experiencing." This is the same thing Louise Hay accomplished in *You Can*

Heal Your Life when she provided a chart of illnesses/disease, the probable emotional trigger, and the affirmation that could help reverse it.

Yes, it sounds facile. But it also works. At some point in the late 1980s, Trish noticed that whenever she finished a novel, her left eye would usually become inflamed and she would have to consult an ophthalmologist. The diagnosis was always the same: iritis, an inflammation of the iris. In Hay's scheme of things, detailed in *You Can Heal Your Life*, any disease ending with *itis* denotes anger. Eyes relate to how we perceive and explore the world. The left side of the body relates to the right side of the brain, that part that is creative, holistic.

Once Trish understood this, she realized the iritis she developed when she finished a novel was connected to the anger and frustration she felt about not knowing what to write next and a kind of postpartum depression that the novel that had consumed her for months was finished. After this realization, iritis no longer happened in relation to her writing. It occurred with other things that she was irritated about, but never again did it coincide with the completion of a novel. She got the message.

In spring of 2013, Angelina Jolie had a double mastectomy because she carries the breast cancer gene. Her mother died of the disease in her late fifties. So Angelina elected to have a double mastectomy at the age of thirty-seven so she could reduce the chance that she would contract the disease.

Some years back, Trish's agent, Al Zuckerman, asked if she would be interested in writing a book about four women in the Boca Raton, Florida, area who had elected to double mastectomies because they carried this gene. Even though she had profound reservations, she called one of the women and they had an interesting conversation. In the end, she told Al she couldn't be a part of this project because she didn't believe in bottom line: *if you carry the gene, you will get this disease.*

While it's likely that, in consensus reality, you are more prone to breast cancer if you have this particular gene, it isn't a foregone conclusion that you will contract breast cancer. Al counteracted with statistics—big statistics, overwhelming statistics—but she knew this project wasn't for her.

A few years later, we were having dinner with another couple when the woman suddenly announced she was going to have a double mastectomy. "I've had so much of my breasts removed in the past few years that I've decided to just get it over with."

Trish was so shocked that she didn't know what to say, and finally muttered a weak, "But why? "

"Because I feel like I'm waiting for breast cancer to hit me."

If that was her belief, Trish said, then she should have the surgery. And she did. Which leads to an interesting question. Trish's parents died from complications of neurological diseases—her mother from Alzheimer's and her dad from Parkinson's. When should she schedule her brain surgery so she won't contract either of these diseases?

And that's the bottom line with any therapy. How does it fit into *your* belief system?

"The unconscious helps by communicating things to us or making figurative allusions," wrote Jung in *Memories, Dreams, and Reflections*. "It has other ways, too, of informing us of things which by all logic we could not possibly know. Consider synchronistic phenomena, premonitions, and dreams that come true."

Jim Banholzer knows a little something about the "synchronistic phenomena" Jung mentions, and about healing, as the following story reveals. And really it's about recognizing that help is always available, if we're open and receptive to it.

SPIRIT HEALER

Some years ago, at the little Idaho hideaway where Jim lived, he pruned back a sugar maple branch so he could install a small suet feeder six feet off the ground. The maple was adjacent to some cottonwoods by a trickling creek, a lifeline for birds, especially magpies, kingfishers and an occasional owl. After attaching the birdfeeder, he discovered that he needed to refresh the suet twice a month.

He usually remembered to do this on time. However, toward the end of summer, he realized he'd forgotten to check the suet for awhile and when he did, discovered it was filled with a black goo. At first, he thought the suet had turned rancid, but while prying the object out, he realized black feathers were attached to the goo. "A poor blackbird had become stuck inside the feeder and was unable to extract itself, leading to its untimely death. I shuddered slightly and immediately looked at it as a bad omen. To me the bird augury was powerful enough that I decided to keep it a secret from my housemate, so as not to frighten her."

He didn't think much more about it until a few weeks later, when he was winterizing the grounds and placed a large tarp over a tent next to the maple. As he made a broad sweeping motion with the tarp, the same sharp branch he had pruned earlier speared through his ear and into the side of his head.

It was a Tuesday afternoon, nearly five p.m. After standing there stunned for a few seconds, trying to figure out what had hit him, Jim realized the gravity of the situation. He was alone and bleeding profusely from the left side of his head. He hastily rounded up the dog, grabbed a towel to press against the wound, and drove several miles to the local ER.

Although the hospital was small, it was well-staffed. As he arrived, something deep inside Jim switched his gears into survival mode, and helped him rally. He cracked a few jokes about his dilemma to the physician and his assistant, hoping this would put all three of them more at ease. It helped, but while the young doctor examined the complexity of damage, he expressed hesitation as to whether he could stitch Jim's ear back together properly, and suggested that he might need to transfer to a Boise hospital.

But that would be a long, expensive haul and Jim wasn't looking forward to seeing a specialist three hours away. "Right then, a visiting plastic surgeon *just happened by* our emergency room to see the problem. He encouraged the attending physician to try a specific stitching method and even made some animated motions of how to do this." After the physician made a few careful stitches with the newly suggested method, he gained more confidence. The visiting plastic surgeon saw that the doctor was getting it right, so he left them alone.

Jim was back at work the next afternoon. But a few weeks later, his housemate told him the bad news: the developer who had bought their tiny shack would soon be demolishing it and they would have to move. "Meanwhile, the trauma from the sweet sugar maple seeded something new in me. It forced me to reflect hard about the haphazard direction of my life and slowed me down enough to dedicate some quiet time to writing. I feel strongly that writing about items of a meaningful nature is something I should be dedicated to for several hours each week."

Not long afterward, Jim recounted his experience to a new friend, a professional hypnotherapist who had relocated to Idaho from South Africa. While getting to know her, she earned Jim's trust in her powers of intuition, so when she expressed a new viewpoint about what had happened that evening in ER, Jim sat up and listened.

"When I told her that I never caught the name of the plastic surgeon that walked by at that synchronistic moment, she suggested that I have not yet fathomed the extent of what actually occurred. She claims that even if I tried hard, I would not be able to discover the Good Samaritan's name, because he is not a human being. She believes he is a guardian angel, who sensed that my time here on earth was not yet finished, and that I still had some good work to give."

Richard Martini, in his marvelous book *Flipside: A Tourist's Guide on How to Navigate the Afterlife,* related similar stories about apparent helpers who appear and disappear mysteriously. "There are many familial stories of people on their death bed seeing other people in their room, departed loved ones, or strangers," he wrote. "Sometimes the departing ones return for a few moments of lucidity to say something profound to their loved ones about what's on the other side…"

For ten years, Martini was involved with Luana Anders, an actress and writer. Their relationship eventually evolved into a close friendship and he took care of her during the last couple of years of her life, when she was dying of breast cancer. Her death proved to be the impetus for Martini writing his book.

When a close friend of Luana's was battling cancer, she told Martini that a "handsome young man would come in every day and tell her stories and make her laugh. She called him the 'Jazz Man' because they talked about jazz and other things…" One day, some of her friends dropped by and she was eager to introduce them to Jazz Man. But at some point, she realized something was amiss. "You can't see him, can you?" she asked one of her friends.

The young man, wrote Martini, smiled at her and faded away.

When Trish's mother had Alzheimer's and was confined to a dementia unit, she used to talk about her mother—Trish's grandmother—stopping by periodically, sitting at the foot of the bed to trade gossip and news. Nana Rutledge had died decades earlier, on the day that Neil Armstrong walked on the moon, but when Trish's mother talked about her visits, Trish believed her.

Alzheimer's, after all, is a disease that robs you of memory. Eventually, it destroys who you are because if you have no memory, if you have no personal history, you are adrift, without identity. If your consciousness isn't focused *here,* then it's focused *elsewhere,* and in this place called *elsewhere,* it's perfectly plausible that you see the dead. Talk to them. Commune with them. There may be a spiritual component to this disease as well. Trish's mother was afraid of dying and Alzheimer's gave her a way to explore the other side before she crossed over.

Spirit helpers and healers are probably always around us, ready and prepared to aid us in whatever way they can.

CAROL & CHASE BOWMAN

In the 1980s, when Carol's son and daughter were very young, her son, Chase, suddenly developed a horrible fear of firecrackers. Carol realized the fear was symptomatic of something, but of what? She eventually took Chase to a hypnotherapist and Chase recounted a life as a Civil War soldier. He, a five-year-old boy, accurately described a bayonet, the "firecracker-like noises" around him on the Civil War battlefield, and said he had been wounded.

After Chase remembered his death on the battlefield, his fear of loud noises vanished. Carol suddenly knew that the recovery of that memory had healed him.

She began researching children's past lives and a friend was so impressed with what she was doing that she wrote Oprah about it. A year later, before Carol had even written her first book, *Children's Past Lives,* Oprah invited Carol onto her show. Carol went on to write a second book, *Return from Heaven,* about reincarnation within the same families. In the years since, Carol has established a practice as a past-life therapist. She has been on innumerable national and international TV and radio shows and was the first person to be contacted about the James Leininger case, which is probably the most solid case for reincarnation in the Western world. She discussed that case on ABC's *Primetime.*

Through her research, Carol isn't trying to prove whether these memories can be validated. Her focus is on healing through past-life regressions, an aspect her mentor—Ian Stevenson, and his protégé, Jim Tucker—summarily dismissed. Carol knows otherwise. And the universe seems to be cooperating. Recently, she was going through her cases for her next book, and ran across a regression she did in 1994, of a woman who had been plagued by the same nightmare for forty years.

In the nightmare, this woman saw herself as a young boy in tattered, dirty clothing. She/he was with a group of children and was urgently telling them to be quiet. The boy sensed a dark shadow following them. Then the woman would wake up in a panic.

In the regression, she saw herself as a fifteen-year-old boy, trying to usher a group of Italian children to safety during WWII. Everything goes wrong. The boy is found—and tortured—and he and the children are all killed. As he was dying, the boy felt terrible guilt about what happened, and blamed himself for not saving the children. He felt it was his responsibility, and he failed. He carried the guilt he felt into this life, which came up through the woman's dreams. Through the regression she saw that her past self really had died a noble death by sacrificing himself to try to save the children.

Nearly twenty years after that regression, Carol synchronistically heard from the woman, who gave her permission to use the story in her new book. Since her regression, she has never had the nightmares again. The regression provided closure when she saw herself as that boy who had done all that he could do to save the children in such a desperate situation. This insight, the shift in perspective, healed her.

That's what Carol's work is about. She's convinced that past-life therapy heals.

Richard Martini is convinced of the healing aspects of regression as well. When he underwent a regression, he saw himself as an American Indian whose wife and tribe had just been slaughtered and whose son had been taken. He found her body in a teepee. When the therapist took him to the final day of his life, he reported that he committed suicide by drowning himself while in a drunken stupor.

As the therapist took him between lives, Martini was reunited with his wife and son from that life and discovered that as an Indian, he was a healer, a man who healed through touch. He also learned that when he chose his life as Martini, he hoped to heal through the cinematic arts. "I saw myself describing it as an 'outside the box' way of viewing energy transfer between people, and how the healing energy of the Universe can be drawn down in a variety of fashions, including, surprisingly, film, music and art."

Knowledge of a larger picture about the nature of reality, particularly about the nature of our personal reality, our souls, our spirits, is both empowering and healing.

A SECONDHAND FURNITURE STORE

Sometimes, healing finds its way to us through strange, almost incomprehensible venues and synchronicity is usually involved.

One day Jane Clifford, a healer in Wales, and a friend were in a town near to where Jane lives. They ate lunch, then had twenty minutes to fill before her friend's dentist appointment. Jane mentioned a secondhand furniture place close by. It was a real shack, grubby and chaotic, but in the past, Jane had enjoyed poking around in the merchandise and had found some real treasures.

As they approached the place, Jane noticed a blackboard propped up near the door. On it was the following notice written in wobbly handwriting: *Prophecy and Healing*. It struck her as an odd combination for a secondhand furniture store, so she and her friend went inside.

Jane chatted with the clerk and asked about the prophecy and healing. "Where does it take place?"

"Here," the man replied.

He explained that a man named Richard did the healing, so Jane asked about the prophecy. The clerk replied: "If Richard gets a message from the Lord for you whilst he is doing the healing, he passes it on."

When Jane said she would like to try it, the clerk called Richard from the back of the shop. To her astonishment, the reading/healing was going to take place right where she was standing. She asked her friend if she would like to try it, but she shook her head and told her to go ahead. She sat nearby to wait for Jane.

Richard was a big, tall South African guy. He stood facing Jane and took both of her hands in his. "You are a healer," he said immediately. "And the Lord wants to use you as an instrument of his healing."

She confirmed she was a healer, and Richard continued: "You don't attend a church, but you have the Lord in your heart."

Jane agreed.

"What do you want healed?" he asked.

"My arthritis has been very painful."

"Do you know that bitterness, anger and the need to forgive are a component of arthritis?"

"Yes. We've also just had the coldest winter in sixty years and the cold is another component."

"Do you have any forgiveness issues?"

"I do. A family member has stolen hundreds of thousands from my elderly mother without her knowledge and I've been working on forgiveness for some time and reached compassion for this individual. But then the person stole more money, and I am back to zero again. So I understand I have more forgiving to do." Jane also told him she has several collapsed discs that cause severe back pain.

Richard then asked God to assist Jane in forgiveness and to realign her spine and ease her pain. "I wouldn't have been surprised to hear a few praise the Lords and all that happy-clappy stuff. But I could tell he was a genuine medium and clairvoyant."

He asked Jane if she minded if the clerk placed his hand on her lower back; she said that was fine. "As Richard was praying for my spine I definitely felt something going on there. Then it was done! He said the forgiveness issue would be worked on overnight."

By the next morning, her discomfort from the arthritis had eased considerably.

Her back felt more comfortable and she was in a much better place concerning her feelings toward the family member.

"Well, the Lord sure does work in mysterious ways! That secondhand furniture shack was the last place one would expect to find healing or prophecy, but there it was!"

A HEALING MEDITATION

It's well documented that meditation is beneficial. It lowers blood pressure and stress, helps with creativity, anxiety, depression, addiction, eating disorders. It also changes the actual structure of your brain.

The prefrontal cortex controls the "executive functions" of the brain and is often called its CEO. It helps us to organize our thoughts, solve problems, strategize, focus our attention, weigh the possible consequences of behavior, and to make predictions when we consider the future. In short, it's the prefrontal cortex that enables us to make good judgment and distinguish between right and wrong. As we age, it thins and this leads to the decline in cognitive function in later years. But studies have found that people who are long-time meditators don't experience this thinning.

In an interview with *Huffington Post*, Hedy Kober, a neuroscientist who studies the effects of mindfulness meditation at her lab at Yale and has practiced meditation for a decade, noted: "It did to my mind what going to the gym did to my body. It made it both stronger and more flexible."

And, as we know from Brugh Joy's story, meditation can also heal.

Rob periodically teaches a six-week meditation course at a yoga studio. Right before one of the classes, Trish had noticed that a lower tooth didn't feel right. She figured she would be spending part of the next day at the dentist and dreaded it.

This particular class involved a shamanic meditation with drumming, her personal favorite of the various types of meditations Rob teaches. At one point, she became aware of Rob's voice directing the class participants to heal themselves of some physical, emotional, or spiritual injury. So Trish focused on her tooth. She asked it to please be healed and felt confident that it could be healed, that such a healing was not only possible, but that it was going to happen, that it had happened already.

Suddenly, she was aware of a brilliant light on the right side of her head. It was so bright she thought that Rob had turned on a lamp and was holding it up to her face. The light went *into* her face.

Her eyes snapped open and the room was still dark. Rob was walking over to his iPod to turn off the drumming and she thought, *Wow, what was that about?* A while later, as she and Rob were walking back to the car, Trish realized the pressure in her tooth was gone.

There are innumerable anecdotes like this among meditators. When healing through meditation works, it's because you're focused, your desire for healing is profound and genuine, and you *allow* the healing to take place.

Part Two:
THE INNER WAY

"There are few persons, even among the calmest thinkers, who have not been occasionally startled into a vague yet thrilling half-credence in the supernatural, by coincidences of so seemingly marvelous a character that, as mere coincidences, the intellect has been unable to receive them."

—Edgar Allan Poe

"The whole history of science shows us that whenever the educated and scientific men of any age have denied the facts of other investigators on a prior grounds of absurdity or impossibility, the deniers have always been wrong."

—Alfred Russell Wallace

Chapter 8
SPIRITS SPEAK

HANK & JUDY

Imagine that everyone who dies receives a welcome package upon arriving on the other side. In this package, they would find an orientation schedule, a scrapbook featuring scenes from their life, and a book called, *A Field Guide to the Afterlife*. They might page through the book and pause when they find a chapter called, *How to Make Contact with the Living*.

What they learn is that communicating with the living is possible, but it's not likely that they will materialize as physical beings and hold a conversation with a loved one. Instead, they might learn techniques for contacting someone through the dream state or through meaningful coincidences. If the living person is reaching out to them, the process becomes easier since the person might be watching for clues that a loved one is in contact.

Such contact can manifest as a voice, a scent, a type of food, a song, a name heard over and over, through art, books, animals, or clusters of objects or numbers. It can come through a dream, meditation, vision, through a person with mediumistic abilities, or simply through events in your everyday life. It might occur when you least expect it or when you most need it. Unlike scary ghost encounters, the essence of spirit contact is overwhelmingly one of benevolence that provides comfort, confirmation, hope, and healing.

Contact comes most frequently with loved ones who have recently passed away. That was the case with Judy, a professional photographer in Manhattan and a woman Trish first met when they were both in college. For thirty-five years, she was involved with Hank, also a professional photographer. Their relationship went through various permutations over the years, but they always remained close.

After Hank died in 2009, Judy felt lost without him. But it wasn't long before she started getting hints that Hank was trying to reach her from the other side. Each time, the contact involved an object—a lamp, a button, a clock and a coin. The first incident took place a few nights after he died.

Many years ago, Judy's sister had given her a lamp filled with seashells, and it always reminded Judy of the summers that she and Hank had spent on Martha's Vineyard. Judy was certain that she'd turned off the lamp before she fell asleep. But sometime around midnight the light turned itself on and she woke up. If it was a coincidence, it was a meaningful one—a coincidence with a connection to the other side. "It had never happened before, and I knew it was Hank."

Another incident took place after Judy cleaned out Hank's place. She had decided to make a time capsule from a briefcase that her dad had made for Hank when they were a couple. It was one of her last days there and she was delighted because she had found letters, old photos, and some of his favorite shots, both professional and personal. Another photographer was there with her that day to help her finish cleaning out so she had a witness for what happened next.

Hank loved Hank's Soda and sent out cases of it to family and friends for Christmas one year. As a result of his large order, the company sent Hank a T-shirt and a button that said, "Hank's Soda." For the last four years of his life, that button had been hanging on a bulletin board, and Judy decided to include it in a time capsule she was creating. When she picked it up, she was surprised to discover that there was a little light on the button that had turned on.

"I called Mel to take a look and he said it was just because I touched it. But it blinked for two days until I sent the briefcase to the place where Hank's ashes were going to be buried. The day before his memorial, we opened the case again. The button wasn't blinking. You actually had to latch the little pin on the back to make it blink. It still gives me chills to think of that day. I am *sure* Hank turned it on."

Judy recalled another incident that involved a clock that Hank's upstairs neighbor made for him. "Peter was an engineer and loved to create gadgets. He made Hank this cool clock out of copper. It had tiny lights that blinked at the 12, 3, 6 and 9 o'clock hours. But it wasn't blinking while we cleaned out the studio."

She tried to give it to friends or sell it, but no one wanted it. So she took it to her apartment and hung it next to the door. The clock still kept perfect time, but she thought the blinking mechanism had worn out. "One of the first evenings after I handed over the keys to Hank's studio I had a really bad night, missing Hank, crying and hardly sleeping. You know how it is after you lose a close loved one. Anyway, as I was leaving for work the next day the clock started blinking. It seemed to blink when I was leaving or when I came home. Eventually it stopped and even though I've put in new batteries it won't blink now."

Probably the most mysterious of all the synchronicities that Judy experienced in the aftermath of Hank's death involved a commemorative coin that fell from a shelf in her closet. It was inscribed with the phrase, *Angel in my Pocket*. She'd never seen the coin before and had no idea how it had gotten into her closet. She couldn't help thinking of Hank, and put the coin on her key chain.

One night, a few weeks later, she woke up at 2 a.m. and couldn't get back to sleep. So she turned on the TV and the movie *Angel in My Pocket* was on. She realized it was Hank's birthday. "He would have been sixty-seven and absolutely loved presents, even small ones." On that birthday, it seems he gave Judy a present—a reminder of their time together and a nudge from the other side.

SEEKING CONTACT

Incidents such as the ones Judy described are examples of synchronicity related to contact with the dead that appear to be instigated from the other side. Such events, whatever the mechanism of contact, tend to surprise, comfort and even energize the recipient. But on the *synchronicity inner way,* interaction with spirits is a two-way street. You can initiate contact yourself and one method for doing it is through meditation. When you quiet your mind, you're more receptive.

Sometimes contact comes during meditation without even making any particular effort. That was the case for British blogger Mike Perry. While Mike says he usually meditates in the morning, one evening he felt a need to enter a meditative state. He remembers checking the clock and telling himself that twenty minutes would suffice. He followed his usual routine and after about fifteen minutes he heard a voice in his left ear. This had never happened previously. The voice simply said, *Your dad is listening to you.*

"It was absolutely clear—though I didn't recognize whose voice said those words. I was still relaxed in my meditation pose so I followed my instinct and spoke softly, telling my dad how I missed him and my mother, and thanked them for all they did for me over the years, especially while I was growing up. I also spoke about my son and how he was doing. I then opened my eyes and that was it."

Although his father hadn't spoken, Mike had sensed his presence and was grateful for the experience.

A MEDITATION TO INITIATE SPIRIT CONTACT

As mentioned earlier, Rob has taught a meditation course for several years. During the last half of the course, some of the meditations invoke contact with spirit guides or power animals, and students have also reported interactions with deceased loved ones or ancestors. One woman reported that her brother, who had died a year and a half ago, spoke to her during a meditation and told her he was fine and not to worry about him. Another woman said that as she reclined on her yoga mat, she felt hands pressing against her back and an image of a deceased uncle came to mind.

During a shamanic meditation, Trish "saw" her deceased mother in a corner of the room. She looked young, vibrant, without a trace of the Alzheimer's she had for the last five or six years of her life. Her mother turned and waved at someone and Trish then saw her deceased father striding toward her mother. He was young and vibrant, without a trace of the Parkinson's he'd had for the last ten years of his life. Then they both looked directly at Trish, and when they realized she saw them, they simply faded away.

Here's a method you can try. You might record the meditation, speaking slowly, or someone could read it to you. Begin by taking several long, slow, deep breaths. Keep your focus on your breath as you take a few more deep inhalations. Then slow your breath.

Turn your focus inward and scan your body. Concentrate on how your various body parts feel—starting with your feet, ankles, lower legs, knees, thighs, hips and belly, back, chest, shoulders, neck, and internal organs. Take your time. Feel your body relaxing. Remain focused and concentrate. Nothing else matters.

Now turn your concentration to your bodily functions. Maybe you become aware of the beat of your heart, the flow of blood from your heart, arteries, capillaries, and veins taking it back to your heart. Listen for the beat of your heart. If you can't hear or feel it, imagine that you can. You might even go deeper into the self…beyond the physical and into interior landscapes the invisible non-physical part of your being, which is really your true self. Stay with it. Gentle breathing. Concentrating. Relaxing.

Next, imagine that you're following a path through a verdant forest. You feel the crackle of leaves and brittle twigs under your feet, and smell the fertile scent of growing things. You feel the warmth of the day. Gradually, you reach flagstone steps and slowly climb a slope until you reach a heavy wooden door with a rounded top. It opens into a shadowy tunnel, and you can see a bright light in the distance. You step inside and follow the tunnel until you reach a crystal cavern.

You see bright, glittering crystal everywhere, on the walls, ceiling, and floor. You feel a high energy streaming through you as you sense that you've entered a sacred place. Know that this chamber magnifies your ability to make contact with the other side. You also are aware that you will be safe and protected, and whatever contact is made will be comforting and elevating.

Think of a deceased loved one, a family member, relative or friend that you want to contact. Or maybe you're seeking communion with a spirit guide. Now you see a mirror like no other among all the glimmering crystals. The surface shimmers and swirls and you move closer. Take your time as you stare intently into the mirror. Gradually, an image forms and it's the one you are seeking. You feel warmth and happiness emanating from this spirit being. You might hear a message and maybe you start a dialogue. If the connection is strong, the spirit being might step out of the mirror and appear as a physical being to you. Take your time; stay focused.

Finally, you thank your loved one or spirit guide and the being fades away into the mirror. Now feel yourself lifting up with the energy and leaving the crystal cavern right through the roof. Go with the flow. Feel yourself becoming aligned with the energy, moving with it. And you're back where you began.

ANCIENT ORIGINS

Among the ancient Greeks, mirror-gazing was a well-known means of reaching out to ancestors for guidance. This method frequently involved the use of a psychomanteum, a dimly lit isolated room with a mirror or reflective surface, such as a pool of water.

You've probably heard about the famed Oracle of Delphi, where ancient Greeks journeyed to hear prophecies from a priestess serving as the oracle. Lesser known is the Oracle of the Dead, a site in northwest Greece that pilgrims visited to contact the dead and learn of their future. Built in the third century BC, the Oracle of the Dead included a complex of underground passageways and isolation cells. It was the ancient Greek's premier psychomanteum, and was also known as The Necromanteion of Ephyra. Placed in the cells, pilgrims fasted and underwent sensory deprivation, exhaustion and disorientation—all designed to create an environment to induce visions. They also wandered through dark passageways and a stone labyrinth.

After several days or weeks, pilgrims were ready to meet the souls of the dead. They descended to the Sacred Hall in an underground cavern where they were given hallucinogenic leaves or seeds to chew. The pilgrims then gazed into a large copper cauldron filled with water, where they saw visions of the dead in the dark, reflective surface. In their heightened state, it was said that dead friends and relatives sometimes even emerged from the reflective cauldron and appeared as if they were physical beings.

Very little was known about the Greek psychomanteums until 1958 when archaeologist Sotirios Dakaris and his team uncovered a series of small underground rooms connected by a passageway that led to the main chamber where they found the remains of a large copper cauldron ringed with a banister. They had discovered the Oracle of the Dead, spoken of by Homer and Herodotus.

THE AZTEC MIRROR

In the sixteenth century, John Dee, a famed English mathematician, astronomer and astrologer, used an Aztec mirror to make contact with the dead. Dee studied alchemy and divination while straddling the worlds of science and magic, and made extensive use of his mirror while pursuing his occult interests. He was also the official scryer or crystal gazer for Queen Elizabeth I.

The black mirror, made of highly polished obsidian, was brought to Europe after the conquest of Mexico by Cortés between 1527 and 1530. Mirrors in Mexico were associated with Tezcatlipoca, the dark god of war and sorcery, whose name can be translated as "Smoking Mirror." Aztec priests used mirrors for divination and conjuring visions.

No doubt Dee was knowledgeable about the Greek's use of

psychomanteum, or mirror-gazing and that added to his fascination with the Aztec mirror. One psychomanteum was creating In the late twentieth century.

RAYMOND MOODY'S PSYCHOMANTEUM

Years after psychiatrist Raymond Moody wrote *Life After Life,* the classic book on near-death experiences, he wanted to find a way that anyone could connect with the afterlife without having to die briefly and be revived.

Moody, a scholar of ancient Greece, eventually found his answer when he read the Greek magical papyri—scrolls of magical recipes found in Egypt, but written in Greek. By following the instruction of the magical papyri in a facility designed for just this purpose, he created a modern psychomanteum in the style of the ancient Greeks.

He named his psychomanteum the John Dee Theater of the Mind, and began looking for people willing to step into his "apparition booth." His goal was to answer the question: Can apparitions of deceased loved ones make themselves known in a controlled environment to normal, healthy people?

In preparation, he would spend hours with a patient, discussing the loved one they wanted to encounter. Then he would escort the person into his mirror-gazing booth and turn on a light that was about as bright as a single candle. He would tell the patient to relax, gaze deeply into the mirror, and think only of the one he wanted to see. They would remain in the booth for as long as they liked and Moody would discuss the experience with the patient afterward.

He was surprised that five of his first ten subjects saw and communicated with an apparition, and all five believed that they had actually connected with a deceased loved one. He had expected only one or two would report contact and figured they would have doubts about the reality of the contact.

His first subject, a forty-four-year-old nurse whose husband had died two years earlier, made contact, but not in the way that she or Moody had expected. They had talked for hours about her late husband. But when she emerged from the booth, her expression was puzzled. She had made contact, but with her father, not her husband. She was stunned by the experience, because he had actually come out of the mirror to talk to her.

In all, Moody led 300 subjects into the psychomanteum for his mirror-gazing experiment that he wrote about in his book, *Reunions*. He viewed the room as a therapeutic tool to heal grief and bring insight into the continuity of life.

VOICES OF THE DEAD

After Jung parted ways with Freud, he experienced what he calls a "confrontation with the unconscious." This period lasted from 1913 to 1930 and resulted in *The Red Book*, a strange and hauntingly beautiful journey through Jung's psyche, the mythology of his own mind. During this period, he had numerous experiences with ghosts and spirits.

In 1916, Jung experienced a slew of parapsychological events in his house. "It began with a restlessness, but I did not know what it meant or what 'they' wanted from me," he wrote in *Memories, Dreams, and Reflections*. "There was an ominous atmosphere all around me. I had the strange feeling that the air was filled with ghostly entities. Then it was as if my house began to be haunted."

His oldest daughter saw a "white figure" moving through her room. Jung's second daughter claimed that twice during the night her blanket had been snatched away. That same night, Jung's nine-year-old son had "an anxiety dream." The next morning, a Saturday, he drew what he'd seen for Jung and called it *The Picture of the Fisherman*. It depicted archetypal figures—a fisherman, a devil, an angel.

Around five o'clock on Sunday afternoon, the high strangeness began with the doorbell ringing frantically. "Everyone immediately looked out to see who was there, but there was no one in sight. I was sitting near the doorbell, and not only heard it but saw it moving. We all simply stared at one another." Jung described the atmosphere as "thick" and wrote that he knew something would happen. "The whole house was filled as if there were a crowd present, crammed full of spirits. They were packed deep right up to the door, and the air was so thick it was scarcely possible to breathe. I was all a-quiver with the questions: 'For God's sake, what in the world is this?' Then they cried out in chorus, *We have come back from Jerusalem where we found not what we sought.*"

And this is the beginning of *Septem Sermones*, which poured out of Jung over the course of the next three evenings. "As soon as I picked up the pen, the whole ghostly assemblage evaporated. The room quieted and the atmosphere cleared. The haunting was over."

Shortly before this experience, Jung had written down a fantasy of his soul having flown away from him. He believed this event was significant because of the relationship of the unconscious—the anima—to the soul. "In a certain sense this is also a relationship to the collectivity of the dead; for the unconscious corresponds to the mythic land of the dead, the land of the ancestors."

From that time on, Jung wrote, the dead became more distinct for him as the voices of "the Unanswered, Unresolved, and Unredeemed..."

Throughout the winter of 1924, Jung spent long periods of time by himself in the Tower of his home on Lake Zurich in Bollingen, Switzerland. One night while sitting by the fire, listening to the night sounds outside, he heard footsteps going around the Tower, then distant music that sounded as though it were coming closer and closer, then voices laughing and talking. He went to the window, but no one was out there. He figured he had dozed off and dismissed it as a dream.

He went back to bed and fell asleep and the dream started up again. He heard the footsteps, talk, laughter, music. "...at the same time, I had a visual image of several hundred dark-clad figures, possibly peasant boys in their Sunday clothes, who had come down from the mountains and were pouring in around the Tower, on both sides, with a great deal of loud trampling, laughing, singing and playing of accordions."

At this point, he woke up. Only much later did Jung find a parallel to what he'd experienced in the Tower. He came across a seventeenth century chronicle by Rennward Cysat, who was director of the Lucerne Passion play from 1575 to 1614. In the chronicle, Cysat recounts that while climbing Mount Pilatus, a place known for ghosts, he was disturbed one night by a "procession of men who poured past his hut on both sides, playing music and singing." It was exactly what had happened to Jung that night in the Tower.

He also discovered an actual historical reference to this type of gathering. In the Middle Ages, there were assemblies like this of young men, mercenaries who marched from central Switzerland to Milan. "My vision, therefore, might have been one of those gatherings which took place regularly each spring when the young men, with singing and jollity, bade farewell to their native land."

When premonitions or visions have a correspondence in physical reality, Jung wrote, then it's a synchronistic phenomenon.

THE MEDIUM WAY

Mediums are known as conduits between worlds and those who are talented can provide convincing evidence of contact. In one memorable incident, Rob recalled a reading in the spiritualist village of Cassadaga, Florida, in which a medium told him she was picking up contact by a man whose name began with the letter J. She said he had died from something related to his brain. The medium, Hazel Burley, paused and frowned, then added that there seemed to be two men present whose names began with J. Both men had died of brain-related illnesses. In the previous year, Rob's cousin, John, and a friend, Jay, had both died of brain cancer.

But you don't have to be a medium to attempt to make contact. There are a variety of mechanisms, known as divination systems, that serve as a means of access to the other side. They range from tarot cards and rune stones to astrological charts and Ouija boards.

A simple form of divination, one with a complex name, is stichomancy. All that is required is a dictionary or possibly a Bible. You pose a question, then randomly open the book and, without looking, stab your finger at a word or phrase on the page. That was the method that Gibbs Williams, a psychiatrist and author of *Demystifying Meaningful Coincidences (Synchronicities),* used when he asked himself if miracles might be real. It seemed appropriate to use a Bible, and when he did so he randomly turned to the story of Lazarus being raised from the dead.

"I was struck by the story's implications, reasoning that if the Bible is the revelation of divinity communicated to mankind so that events like the rising of Lazarus might be literally true, then such phenomena as contacting 'dead' spirits and personal spiritual guides at a séance…might in fact be valid."

Williams called a friend and excitedly shared his experience. To his surprise, she exclaimed: "How uncanny!" Earlier in the day, she was on a walk with her somewhat unconventional psychiatrist when he told her that in a previous lifetime he had been present at the raising of Lazarus.

Upon hearing this amazing coincidental reference to the raising of Lazarus, Williams felt a sense of awe, as if he were in contact with mysterious forces. "That verified the possibility that so-called occult energies were apparently real and this meant that virtually anyone could access them at will," Williams said.

ESTHER HICKS AND THE BIRD

In the spring of 2013, Trish and our daughter, Megan, attended an Abraham/Hicks workshop that was held some months after the death of Esther Hick's husband, Jerry. They arrived an hour early so they could get good seats and ended up in the fourth row, with a good view of Esther and the "hot seat," where selected participants sit to converse one-on-one with Abraham.

Trish had wondered what it must be like for Esther, a medium, to still be able to communicate with Jerry, but without the tangible benefits of physical existence. She could no longer touch him, talk to him across a kitchen table, could no longer peer into his eyes. According to Ester, Jerry has joined the consortium of spirits known collectively as Abraham, but it has to be lonely at times for Esther.

The workshop started promptly at nine a.m. and the instant Esther strolled out in her stocking feet, the audience gave her a standing ovation and cheered. She greeted everyone hello, then shut her eyes, bowed her head, altered her breathing, and went into an altered state. When her eyes opened again, Abraham started talking.

It's impossible to tell whether Esther channels the entire time she is on stage, but her presence is flawless. She—or Abraham—is funny, charming, and insightful and the message is positive and usually powerful. At one point, Abraham said that when Esther was on her way to the hotel the day before, she felt Jerry around, felt him appreciating the beauty of the South Florida landscape—the palm trees, the vast blue sky, the perfect weather. Esther, he said, began to miss him terribly. Even though she is aware of his spirit's presence, she missed talking to him, exchanging ideas, interacting with him in the physical universe.

So Esther got checked in at the hotel and went to her room. As she was opening the door, she heard noise inside and wondered if the room was occupied. The door swung open and she saw that the room was empty. But out there on her balcony, perched on the back of a chair, was a large blackbird just chattering away. It remained there for fifteen or twenty minutes, staring in at her, and she stood there listening to it, watching it, and knew it was Jerry, talking to her.

Abraham explained this as a coincidence—the bird had picked up Jerry's impulse to speak to Esther, and was attracted to her desire to speak to him, and found the right chair, on the right balcony. And Esther,

Abraham said, was attuned to her need for communication with Jerry.

It's a perfect example of spirit communication through synchronicity. Whatever you call it, whatever label you give it, the end result is the same: Esther recognized what it was and embraced it. Yet, for someone else, perhaps for the person in the room next to Esther's, that singing blackbird might have been just part of the background noise.

In his autobiography, Jung pointed out that if the paranormal exists, then the rationalistic picture of the universe is invalid because it's incomplete. "Then the possibility of an other-valued reality behind the phenomenal world becomes an inescapable problem, and we must face the fact that our world, with its time, space and causality, relates to another order of things lying behind or beneath it…"

That sounds a lot like David Bohm's implicate order, doesn't it? And within that implicate order, it makes perfect sense that the singing blackbird was Jerry, talking to his wife.

A SPIRIT REQUEST

Natalie Thomas, a medium in Queensland, Australia, had a blogging friend, Vicki, who also lived in Australia, but in another part of the country. They had never met physically, but felt they were connected on a soul level.

In 2010, Vicki told Natalie about Tony Stockwell, a famous English medium, who was coming to her state for a week-long retreat. Vicki invited Natalie to join her. Natalie paid her deposit, but couldn't make it due to family dramas. "I was to meet her face to face for the first time, and was bitterly disappointed to miss both her and Tony."

At the same time, Vicki's cancer flared up again and she couldn't attend either. In late 2011, Natalie once again paid her deposit to attend the retreat, which was scheduled for March 2012. The two women anticipated finally meeting, but Vicki died in November 2011.

"I was devastated to lose her, the world seemed so dreary without her. I was in the shower one day soon after and felt her presence for the first time. I said to her, 'Sweetheart, is that really you?'

"I felt, *Yes.*"

Natalie told Vicki that if it really was her, she wanted to thank her for their beautiful friendship and also for telling her about Tony Stockwell.

Vicki replied: "You and I are from the same soul group, you are my Earth Angel, and I will now be working with you from here. Don't you worry, I will be at the retreat with you."

"At this point, I thought I was imagining it all," Natalie recalled.

Vicki then asked Natalie to contact her husband, Patrick, whom Natalie had never met.

"I can't contact Patrick! I've never even spoken to him," Natalie burst out. "What would I say?"

Vicki replied: "Hi, Patrick, I was speaking to your dead wife in the shower this morning, and she says, *Hi Darling*!"

"Nope, no can do. If you want me to speak to Patrick, then *you* get him to contact me."

That was the end of the conversation.

Three hours later, Patrick sent Natalie a private message on Facebook, introducing himself and thanking her for being Vicki's friend. He also said she was so looking forward to meeting her at Tony's retreat. Not to worry, he wrote, she'll be there with bells on!

Natalie was floored.

Fast forward to March. Natalie was packing for the retreat and wanted to take a keepsake of Vicki's with her. She couldn't find it anywhere and had to leave without it. So she said to Vicki: "You better make an appearance, Lovie, because I am missing you like crazy."

And she heard: "Trust. I will be there."

On the first day, in the first tutorial, Natalie received her first reading. A spirit came through and said she was Natalie's soul sister, she was on the retreat with her, and would be helping her from now on from the other side. Natalie was impressed that Vicki had used other people to prove to her that their conversation was indeed real.

"Now, I just talk to her like she is in the room, but I haven't asked her any BIG questions yet."

As Jung wrote in his autobiography: "There does seem to be an unlimited knowledge present in nature, it is true, but it can be comprehended by consciousness only when the time is ripe for it."

And so it was for Natalie. Despite endless conversations with her deceased friend, she wasn't really convinced of the veracity of the contact until two things happened. First, Vicki's husband wrote her on Facebook after Natalie had told Vicki to get *him* to contact *her*. Second, a psychic who had never met Natalie and knew nothing about her friendship with Vicki told her that her "soul sister" was present, the very term they used to describe their friendship.

STRAIGHT PINS IN CASTILLO DE SAN MARCOS

Spirits sometimes use the most unlikely objects to make contact. As with any synchronicity, though, the objects must have meaning for you or be significant in some way to the spirit. Even so, straight pins seem improbable—unless the deceased was a seamstress when she was alive.

During college, Trish and her roommate, Linda, lived for a time in a cramped, third-story apartment in Utica, New York. They shared the place with a gray tabby cat and several house plants, including a beautiful begonia that Linda's grandmother had given her.

One day they noticed that the begonia had died. Within a short period of time, Linda's grandmother passed away. She had lived in a rambling house on the Hudson River, where she pursued hobbies that she had loved—gardening and sewing.

Not long afterward, Linda's mother found a straight pin on Nana G's tombstone. A few days later, Trish and Linda began running across straight pins all over the apartment—and neither of them sewed. They found pins scattered on the living room rug, stuck in couch cushions, laying around on the kitchen table, in the windowsills. Linda finally mentioned it to her mother, who laughed and said that Linda's grandmother was visiting, that was all.

"I've been finding straight pins all over my house, too. Even straight pins underlining passages in the Bible," she said. "You know how Nana loved to sew."

One weekend Trish and Linda drove to Albany to visit Linda's parents and her mother showed them the Bible, the straight pins. During their visit, they found straight pins around the house—on the kitchen floor, on the stairs, on top of the TV.

The straight pin phenomenon persisted for several months, then stopped. Ten or fifteen years later, Trish was visiting St. Augustine with Linda and her mother. They were in Castillo de San Marcos, the oldest masonry fort in the continental U.S. It was built by the Spanish between 1672 and 1695, a fortress that covers more than twenty acres. Declared a national monument in 1924, the fort is a popular tourist destination.

Inside, the rooms are bare—no furniture, no art, just thick, solid stone walls, well-worn stone floors—and the whisper of the past. Footsteps echo in the empty hallways and rooms.

Trish, Linda, and her mother were remarking about how the cooler air inside was a welcome reprieve from the summer heat outside. Trish happened to look down and stopped, staring at a single straight pin. She picked it up and showed it to Linda's mother. "What're the odds of finding a straight pin in *this* place?"

Linda's mother looked happy, but not surprised. "I've been feeling Nana G around."

"I guess she wants to tour the castle with us," Linda said.

Someone else might have noticed the straight pin and perhaps wondered how it had gotten there. It's not something that women usually carry in their purses or that men carry in their wallets or pockets. A curiosity. But for the three of them, the straight pin was significant and meant that Linda's dead grandmother had dropped in to say hi.

chapter 9
TELEPATHY

IDENTICAL TWINS

Telepathy. Psychokinesis. Clairvoyance. Precognition. These phenomena comprise extrasensory perception—ESP—and Carl Jung maintained that synchronicity is the basis for all of them. He believed they are part of how the unconscious constantly speaks to us, whether we listen or not, whether we're aware of it or not. When certain unconscious forces are activated—particularly during times of crisis and transition—the more likely it is that we'll experience ESP and synchronicity.

Telepathy—mind to mind communication—is probably the most common of these phenomena. Most of us have experienced it at one time or another. No words are spoken aloud. You and the other person might be sitting in the same car or could be thousands of miles apart. You simply know what the other person is thinking, feeling, or experiencing and that knowing is pure, undiluted, unfiltered by your left-brain. Married couples experience it frequently. Parents and children experience it. Friends experience it. Anyone can experience it. But identical twins are in a class of their own.

"Some of the most compelling evidence for telepathy comes from the study of identical twins," wrote physician Diane Hennacy, author of *The ESP Enigma: The Scientific Case for Psychic Phenomena*.

Hennacy noted that telepathy occurs most frequently between twins during a crisis. Here are a couple examples of "crisis telepathy" from her book: One day in 1977, Martha Burke felt as if she "had been cut in two" when a searing pain crossed her chest and abdomen. Hours later she discovered that her twin sister had died in a plane crash halfway across the world. In July 1975, Nita Hurst's left leg became agonizingly painful as bruises spread spontaneously up the left side of her body. She later discovered that her twin, Nettie Porter, had been in a car crash at the very same time four hundred miles away.

This type of story among identical and even fraternal twins may be much more common that we realize. For the last eight years, we have lived next door to Annette, who is several minutes older than her identical twin, Janette. They have numerous stories about their telepathic connections. One of the most dramatic events occurred in the 1990s.

At the time, Janette lived in Memphis with her boyfriend and Annette lived in Florida with her husband. Janette worked for Chanel, so numerous bottles of perfume lined her bathroom shelves. One night, a loud crash in the bathroom snapped Janette and her boyfriend out of a sound sleep.

"Someone's broken into the house," Janette whispered. "They're in the bathroom."

Her boyfriend bolted out of bed, grabbed a baseball bat and moved quickly and silently toward the bathroom, Janette right behind him. No intruder. But every bottle had fallen from the shelves and shattered against the floor, almost as if someone had swept an arm across them, knocking them down.

"Right then," Janette said, "I knew something had happened to Annette. I just *knew* it."

Moments later, Janette's phone rang. It was Annette, sobbing hysterically. She had just been robbed at gunpoint while delivering a night deposit to the bank for her employer. "As it was happening," Annette recalled, "I was praying the guy wouldn't kill me. I was telling God that if I were killed, Janette wouldn't survive it. My husband would somehow get past it, but Janette wouldn't. I called her before I even called the police."

The shattering of the perfume bottles proved to be the pivotal event for Janette, the telepathic signal that told her that her twin was in danger. But what caused the perfume bottles to shatter?

Is it possible that telepathy may be a different form of psychokinesis? Physicist David Bohm believes it might be. Even though we discuss psychokinesis (sometimes referred to as telekinesis) in the next chapter, it's intriguing to speculate about how these phenomena might be interconnected. If we are, indeed, living in a holographic universe, then consciousness suffuses everything—matter and mind—and the meaning or significance we attach to events is particularly powerful.

"When harmony or resonance of 'meanings' is established, the action works both ways, so that the 'meanings' of the distant system could act on the viewer to produce a kind of inverse psychokinesis that would, in effect, transmit an image of that system to him," wrote Bohm in the *Journal of the American Society for Psychical Research.*

You can be sure that Janette, at the time this happened, didn't give a damn about how or why it worked; she simply knew that something had happened to her twin. Information was conveyed to her in an immediate, visceral way, and confirmation arrived just moments later with a call from Annette.

For people who experience telepathy frequently, it's just a part of their lives, their norm, one of their senses. They don't analyze it any more than the rest of us would analyze why milk tastes like milk or why we see the sky as blue.

But how does this apply to identical twins separated at birth?

The James twins of Ohio were separated at birth and were adopted by different families who weren't in contact with one another. Both boys were named James. They grew up not knowing each other, but both sought law-enforcement training, had abilities in mechanical drawing and carpentry, and married women named Linda.

They both had sons—one named *James Alan* and the other named *James Allan.* The twin brothers also divorced their wives and married other women named Betty.

They both owned dogs named Toy.

Mere coincidence? Not in this case.

Maybe categorizing such astonishing and meaningful coincidences is immaterial. What's important is physicist David Bohm's contention that "deep down, the consciousness of mankind is one."

But if the collective consciousness of mankind is connected in this profound way, then why are we so divided? Why is there war? Religious strife? Why does a seventh of the world's population go hungry? It would seem that the connection exists primarily within what Bohm called the implicate order, that primal soup that births everything in the universe. The challenge for humanity, at this particular juncture in history, lies in bringing this connection into external reality as a collective.

E-MAIL TELEPATHY

The Internet facilitates connections among people and often acts as a vehicle for psychic phenomena and synchronicity. In fact, if you use your computer a lot, you've probably experienced Facebook or e-mail telepathy as Adele Aldridge did.

Adele, an artist and author who writes about the *I Ching*, a Chinese divination system, was writing a letter to an author when she received an e-mail related to her art business. The correspondent had ordered an *I Ching* font Adele had created, and wondered why she hadn't received it yet.

Adele stared in disbelief at her monitor. The e-mail was from Katya Walter, the author of *The Tao of Chaos*, a book about the *I Ching* and the genetic code. Not only was that book on the corner of her desk, but Katya was the author to whom Adele was writing, to ask if she would write a foreword to her proposed book, *I Ching Meditations*. "I'd placed the book on the corner of my desk to remind me to write to Katya. I kept putting that task off, not only because I was immersed in writing the proposal, but because I felt shy about approaching such a knowledgeable author."

Adele immediately wrote to Katya and sent her the font. Katya was so pleased to hear from her directly that she called Adele and they've been friends ever since.

This kind of telepathic synchronicity is so simple and straightforward it's as if the universe was saluting Adele for being in the flow. So the next time you experience something like this, pause for a moment and appreciate just how many details had to come together for the synchro to occur.

TELEPATHY WITH PARTNERS

Regardless of how long you have been with your partner, there's usually a point where you begin to read each other's minds, complete each other's sentences, and simply know what the other is feeling and thinking. This is as true in romantic partnerships as it is in business partnerships.

Our telepathic moments often happen in the car. Maybe it's the lure of the open road that triggers it. Or the fact that we're both anticipating whatever it is we're going to do. Regardless, Trish is usually the inadvertent sender and Rob, the inadvertent receiver. It can encompass big issues, but usually doesn't. Usually, it's as mundane as this:

Trish (thinking): Tourist season is up and running, the polo crowd is in town, and Rob's next meditation class should be filled.

Rob (speaking aloud): Twelve people have signed up for my meditation class.

There's nothing uttered aloud that leads to his remark. We both acknowledge it as a telepathic moment, and move on.

But within this telepathic matrix, there's also a need for privacy, for a place within yourself where your partner hears only white noise, the hum of your mind, the whirring of its restlessness, but can't detect the contents, the specifics, the myriad details. After all, we can't be connected to each other day in and day out, 24/7, without losing an intrinsic part of ourselves. We need moments of inviolate solitude and isolation in order to grow and evolve as spiritual and creative beings.

But it's wonderful when one of us expresses what the other is feeling or thinking. It's a moment to savor and devour, to wonder and question, *What makes this connection possible?*

We also experience telepathic connections in bookstores or through books, which isn't surprising since we're both writers who, after thirty years of marriage, understand each other's tastes in reading material. Shortly after Dan Brown's fifth novel, *The Lost Symbol*, was published, we stopped by a Barnes and Noble to browse. While Trish was looking at the novel, Rob picked up a different novel under new releases, read the first couple pages, then picked up another and did the same.

In the first novel, *Shimmer*, by David Morrell, the story opens in a chopper with a police pilot who is chasing a pickup truck along a desert highway. In the second novel, *The Sign*, by Raymond Khoury, the story opens in a pickup truck racing across the desert, pursued by a chopper. What are the chances of that: desert-desert, chopper-chopper, pickup-pickup. Point of view above; point of view below. But if it was a synchronicity, how was it meaningful?

Rob figured that because he was reading and editing our first synchronicity book for the final time before submitting it, he attracted what he was focused on. Or, more esoterically, *As above so below*: the macrocosm is the same as the microcosm. He suspected that if he read *The Lost Symbol*, which Trish bought, he would find out more.

Not long afterward, we were on a trip and Rob was reading *The Lost Symbol.* In the first hundred pages or so of the novel, one of the repeated themes was *As above, so below,* the very concept he'd noticed during our bookstore trip. The odd synchro had come full circle, a good example of the kind of telepathy involved in close relationships.

When we posted this story on our blog, Navine—a poet—commented that she and her husband had experienced something similar at a Borders Bookstore about the same time that we were browsing Barnes and Noble. "I'd just finished with an appointment at my hair salon and was at Borders, really, to pick up my husband, who was waiting for me there. I didn't find him, and I figured he'd walked to his favorite cigar shop around the corner." So she browed the new titles, saw that *The Lost Symbol* was available, as was Ted Kennedy's *True Compass*. Navine remembered her husband talking about Kennedy's book, so she picked it up for him and bought *The Lost Symbol* for herself. Then she walked over to the cigar shop to find her husband. As she walked in the door, she spotted him with a cigar in hand, smiling. And he said, "Check out what I got at Borders. I got *The Lost Symbol* for you, and *True Compass* for me."

A skeptic might argue that married couples know their partner's taste in books, so of course those two books would be logical choices. Both Dan Brown and Ted Kennedy are household names, one known for fast-paced storytelling, the other known for his progressive politics and family legacy. Maybe…but maybe not. According to statistics issued by UNESCO in 2010, the U.S. published the most books of any country in the world: more than 328,000.

Random choices? Or telepathic choices?

TELEPATHIC FRIENDS & SIBLINGS

Jane Clifford, who lives in Wales, wrote us about an impressive series of telepathic communications with her friend, Liz Whittaker, a British novelist. Four times in a single week, she had picked up her phone to call Liz, and each time, before she could make the call, Liz called her.

The two women also kept crossing paths with text messages. One would literally answer before the other one sent her text. And, neither of them do much texting. Another time, her friend had just pressed *send* for an e-mail to her when the phone rang and it was Jane. That happened twice.

But the synchronicities or telepathic links reached a new level when, late one night, Jane sent Liz a picture of the medieval library in Hereford Cathedral. Liz's novels—*A Court in Splendour* and *The Bardic Monk* are set in Medieval times—and Jane thought she would love the picture, especially since the ancient world map—*mappa mundi*—was located in the cathedral. Meanwhile, Liz was wondering if Jane would like to see the *mappa mundi* in Hereford Cathedral. Then the e-mail arrived. "What magic will occur next?!" Jane exclaimed.

Sometimes telepathy manifests itself as a kind of empathy, where you physically feel what another person is feeling. This usually happens with someone to whom you're emotionally close. It doesn't matter whether you've recently seen this individual or even how physically distance the person is from you.

Several years ago, Connie J. Cannon, a retired nurse and one of the abductees we wrote about in *Aliens in the Backyard*, noticed that her left breast began to ache and then really hurt. It was unusual in that she had never experienced any sort of breast pain—not during pregnancy or her menstrual cycles.

But the pain persisted. "Several days later, my sister—who lives in Missouri—called from the hospital there to tell me she'd had a radical mastectomy of her left breast, and hadn't wanted to worry me, so waited until after the surgery to let me know!"

Once Connie knew the source of the pain, it disappeared. But a year later, her right breast began to ache with the same kind of pain. This time, Connie immediately called her sister, who confessed that yes, she had developed cancer in her right breast and was going to have a radical mastectomy in a few days.

Both times and on other occasions, Connie and her sister have shared other physical and emotion connections even though they're separated by more than a thousand miles. "I have Parkinson's," Connie says. "Six months ago, my sister was diagnosed with Parkinson's. These situations slide from telepathy into….what? We are all connected, and often husbands and wives, close friends, siblings, parents and children, have umbilical cords that never break. It's awesome and mind-boggling."

TELEPATHY WITH STRANGERS

Although not as common as other forms, telepathy can also occur with strangers. Nancy Atkinson recalls when her daughter, Jen, was in a graduate class that was being taught by a student teacher. Just as Jen was thinking that the woman wasn't very organized, the student teacher became quite flustered and asked Jen to leave the room while she was conducting the class. "My daughter said she had not said or done anything to signal her thoughts. She said it was almost as though the new teacher could *read* her thoughts. I told her that she probably could. It's my belief that the veil between us is falling and telepathy is just one part of it. I think we can look forward to seeing odd things, hearing odd things, and all sorts of other paranormal events."

Sometimes, telepathy with strangers flourishes in an environment where paranormal phenomena are accepted—a workshop on the paranormal, for instance, a New Age bookstore, a yoga studio.

One Sunday afternoon in May, we drove to a New Age center in a nearby town where Rob was going to have a healing session with a Peruvian shaman. The center offers yoga and meditation classes, sponsors spiritually-oriented events and workshops, and also has a small New Age bookstore and gift shop. While we waited for Rob's session to start, we browsed through the store.

Trish was poking through the extensive collection of stones, hoping to find a piece of moldavite, a stone that has been used as spiritual talisman for at least 25,000 years. The stone has a colorful history. Nearly 15 million years ago, a meteor crashed in what is now the Bohemian plateau of the Czech Republic. It's believed that moldavite is a result of that meteor's impact, but there are several theories about its origin. One theory is that it's an earthly rock melted by the heat of the meteor's crash. Another theory contends that its origin is extraterrestrial.

According to author Robert Simmons, when you work consciously with the stone, it causes chakras to open, your dream life becomes more vivid and meaningful, healings occur, it's easier to communicate with spirit guides, and synchronicities increase.

Another woman was also poking through the stones and she suddenly spoke to the clerk. "Do you have any moldavite?"

Maybe two seconds had passed between Trish's thoughts about moldavite and the woman's question. "I was just going to ask the same thing," Trish said, startled by the synchronicity.

The clerk came out from behind the counter with a single piece of polished moldavite fitted for a pendant. "We have one piece. Moldavite is hard to find."

The price was a bit steep and Trish and the other woman passed. But Trish and the woman recognized the connection.

TELEPATHY WITH PETS

Rupert Sheldrake spent five years researching the perceptiveness of pets and did so with the help of more than a thousand randomly chosen pet owners. His conclusions are similar to what many pet owners say: *My dog (cat, parrot, horse) and I communicate.* "The most convincing evidence for telepathy between people and animals comes from the study of dogs that know when their owners are coming home," Sheldrake wrote in *Dogs That Know When Their Owners Are Coming Home*. "This anticipatory behavior is common. Many dog owners simply take it for granted."

However, mainstream science isn't so quick to accept such results. "… Within institutional science there is a taboo against research on telepathy and other unexplained abilities, and organized skeptical groups see it as their mission to debunk any claims of the paranormal," wrote Sheldrake.

In spite of the scientific debate, personal experiences are what count for most people. When our daughter, Megan, was in third grade, her class invited parents to a Thanksgiving presentation about gratitude. Each student made something that expressed their gratitude for an aspect of their lives. Megan had sculpted a dog from clay and when it was her turn to speak, she got up and presented her little sculpture.

"I'm grateful for the Golden Retriever I'm going to get," she announced.

We looked at each: *Huh?* We had three cats and no intention of getting a Golden Retriever, or any dog. And her little sculpture certainly looked like a Golden Retriever—right down to the ears, the tail, the body stance.

"And this is the dog," she finished.

"We're getting a dog?" we asked her later.

"I think so," she replied.

A couple of weeks later, a friend of Megan's asked if we would like a dog. The friend's father, a police officer, trained dogs to sniff out drugs and one of the dogs, a Golden Retriever, had washed out of the program. No dog, no way, we said.

And then we saw her, a beautiful reddish gold retriever about two years old, who had been given up by her original family when the son developed asthma. Now she had washed out of the drug-sniffing program, and was going to end up at the pound unless someone adopted her.

"We'll try her for a few days and see how she and the cats get along," we said.

Well, Jessie came into the house, the three cats came over, sniffing, checking her out, and Jessie's tail wagged and wagged. Then she plopped down in front of Rob's desk and that was that. She stayed for eleven wonderful years.

We've often thought that Megan's sculpture rendition of the dog *we were going to get* was an instance of precognition. But telepathy seems just as likely. Perhaps Megan's deep desire for a dog—her intentions to have a dog as a pet—enabled her to connect telepathically to the dog her friend's family was fostering.

While Trish was writing this story about Jessie, she took a brief break to read some more of Sheldrake's book, and experienced a synchronicity. In one section Sheldrake discusses how some dogs don't anticipate their owner's arrival when they have just gone out for the day, but react when their owner has been absent for a longer period. Then Trish read this: "Take, for example, the Marchioness of Salisbury's dog, *Jessie…*"

The synchronicity made her feel as if Jessie was in the room with her.

Jeri Gerard, who lived several years in Japan and travels annually to Nepal for her import/export business, says there is a Shinto belief that we all have a circle of spirits (ancestors) like a halo behind our heads. These spirit guides often include animals we have loved and "they come into our physical world as needed."

While dogs are known for their obvious outward delight at seeing their human owners, cats often act like they couldn't care less. Despite the obvious differences, some cat owners are adamant about their telepathic connection with their felines.

Adele Aldridge considers herself the Cat Mom of the planet, and says she has pondered the mystery of cats frequently over the years. Her question, though, is fairly specific: "Do cats understand English?"

Sometimes they seem to, she says, and other times they act like they don't hear her at all, in any language. She shared one striking example when her cat convinced her that she understood every word Adele said—but only when she felt like it.

"When I was living in California I had two brother/sister black cats, Magic and Mystery. I had a deck over the water with a hammock where I could relax in between bouts of work. I could let Mystery out with me because she would jump on the hammock and sit at my head at the top of the hammock and she seemed to enjoy the gentle rocking. I could not let Magic out because he immediately jumped over the rail to wander and that made me worry."

Both cats loved to be brushed. They loved this more than eating. All Adele had to do was hold the brush in her hand and say, "Do you want to be brushed now?" and they would come running. But since they saw the brush, that wasn't what prompted her to wonder if they understood English. "One day as I was brushing Mystery I said out loud, talking to myself and to her: *Why can't you brush me? That would be so nice to have someone pet me and brush me."*

When it was time to sit in the hammock, Mystery followed and perched herself above Adele's head, as usual. The next thing she knew, she felt a claw slowly and gently running through her hair like a comb, not piercing her skin. "I lay very still, not wanting to disturb what felt like my hair being combed. She did this for several minutes. Of course I wondered if it was a coincidence. Wondered if she understood my words. Whatever it was, I was thrilled. But after that I made sure to say to her, *Are you going to brush my hair today if we can sit on the hammock?* And she did.

"You tell me. Do cats understand English? Was that synchronicity?"

When Natalie, a medium in Australia, was a kid, she had a cat that used to walk to the corner every day at three p.m. to pick her up from school and walk home with her. She instinctively knew when Natalie would be coming home. "When I was sad, she would sit with me and lick my tears away. She never left my side. We even ran away from home together. When I first got her, I was five. She actually came up to me and I knew she was the one we had to buy. She died when I was twenty-three, and I have never replaced her."

In discussing cats who anticipate their people's return after an absence, Sheldrake wrote, "As in the case of dogs, it seems to be telepathic and depends on strong bonds between cat and person. These bonds are the channels through which telepathic communication can occur, even over hundreds of miles."

TELEPATHY WITH A DOLPHIN

One of the most moving stories we've ever heard about human/animal telepathy came from Renee Prince, who earned a masters degree in experimental psychology so that she could work on interspecies communication with cetaceans. She spent years working with dolphins and orcas, always with the hope that it would lead to building some sort of mutual communication system between their species and ours.

"Unfortunately, after working with dolphins in captivity I came to realize that life in the tanks is ultimately an early death sentence for dolphins, and the brief life they do have is impoverished and intolerable. After two of my dolphins died, I left dolphin research, in part because I couldn't face the death of another one of my friends, and I had no power to change their situation. Captive dolphins and whales are, to the rest of the world, simply property, to be sold, used, and disposed of quickly when they no longer can serve human purposes. Since then I've lived with the guilt and pain of having left the dolphins behind."

But even after Renee changed careers to work in the film business, her love for dolphins persisted. She lived near the beach in order to be near them and often jogged along the beach, always looking past the waves for the telltale arcs of fins or noisy exhalations of breath that meant dolphins were visiting her section of the beach. She would see them once in a while and would rush out to meet them, hoping they could stay and play.

One afternoon, while she was jogging on the beach in the Los Angeles area, she noticed a dolphin in the waves. She could tell something was terribly wrong. "The surf was washing over him, tumbling him over and over. He was trying to get to shore. I knew immediately what was happening. The dolphin was in serious trouble, and had to reach land because he was too weak to keep himself afloat. He was in eminent danger of drowning."

Renee ran out into the water and pushed out toward him. When the dolphin saw her, his eyes widened in fear but just for a moment. Then he headed directly toward her. "At that second, I had the odd, yet utterly certain feeling that this dolphin had been waiting for me. When we reached each other and I put my arms around him, in the way I had always done with my own dolphin friends so many years ago, he relaxed against me and looked up at me with complete trust. I held him upright, keeping his blowhole above water, and he helped us head toward shore, moving his pectoral fins to steer us and slowly pumping his flukes."

Renee and the dolphin kept in constant eye contact and she talked to him, promising that she wouldn't leave his side. She told him she could call the marine mammal rescue center—a number she knew by heart—and that she would ride with him to wherever they could keep him, even if it had to be Sea World, the place she had fled long ago. "And I told him this time I wouldn't let Sea World keep him captive—I would make sure he was released back into the sea when he was well."

But as they reached shore, in water only a few inches deep, the dolphin wanted to turn around, to face back out to sea. She helped him turn, and he came to a stop. "He lay back in my arms, looked deeply and calmly into my eyes, and died. I saw the light go out of him. Somehow this dolphin, who never would have been near shore—he was a deep-water species, Delphinus delphis—had traveled untold miles away from his world and had, in an utterly alien world, met the only human on this beach who could have seen him, who knew what he wanted and could help him get to shore. He died in the arms of someone who, he must have known, loved him instantly and without conditions; someone who knew dolphins and for years had longed with all her heart for another chance at contact with his kind."

It took Renee a long time to process this event. She had thought she was there to save him. She made promises to him, made plans to give him back his life, to make him well. "When that didn't happen, I was horrified, angry at God, fate, the Tao—whatever. I was angry at myself. What if I had seen my dolphin earlier, before he was too weak to make it? Was there something I could have done differently or better so that he could have been saved? But I was left with no explanation, only the power and soul-wrenching synchronicity of our encounter. I've come to believe that my dolphin wanted to die in the embrace of love. I had given him that, I was sure."

The telepathic connection between Renee and the dolphin is also about a much larger picture—that of the earth as a living, organic being that interacts with us constantly. Gaia. Among its messengers are the creatures of the planet—with dolphins and whales as the ones with the highest level of intelligence and understanding.

Chapter 10
PSYCHOKINESIS

PAULI & JUNG

There are some people who enter a room and *stuff happens* to electronics, machines. Appliances go berserk, computers crash, cell phones act up. Theoretical physicist and Nobel laureate Wolfgang Pauli, one of the early supporters of Jung's theory on synchronicity, was one such person.

From early on in his career, colleagues noticed that whenever he entered a lab, equipment broke down spontaneously. It happened so frequently when Pauli was around, his co-workers called it "the Pauli effect." Over time, most of the scientists with whom Pauli worked knew about it. Physicists at the university in Hamburg where he worked were convinced that Pauli's presence anywhere near a lab led to a breakdown in equipment. Otto Stern, a fellow physicist, eventually forbade Pauli to enter the lab.

Imagine what a dilemma the Pauli effect must have been for fellow scientists, particularly for Stern, a Nobel laureate in physics. Psychokinesis, which hasn't been proven, at least not to the satisfaction of mainstream science, happened often when Pauli walked into a lab.

"*The Pauli effect,* as it became known, was obviously impossible; it had to be just a matter of coincidence," wrote Arthur I Miller in *Deciphering the Cosmic Number: The Strange Friendship of Wolfgang Pauli and Carl Jung.* "But nevertheless, it happened again and again."

Miller's statement is an oxymoron. If something "impossible" occurs repeatedly, then it isn't impossible. And apparently the Pauli effect could happen even when Pauli wasn't present.

In Miller's book, he wrote about an incident that happened in the 1920s. One afternoon at the University of Gottingen in Germany, a complicated apparatus for the study of atoms collapsed, without apparent cause. Pauli was in Switzerland at the time. "At last, said his colleagues, relieved, here was clear proof it couldn't be the Pauli effect."

The professor in charge of the laboratory wrote Pauli, telling him about the event. After a protracted delay, he received a letter from Pauli saying that he had been on his way to Copenhagen, but at the moment the equipment broke down, his train had stopped for a few minutes at the Gottingen station.

Miller also relates another story that happened in 1955. In celebration of the fiftieth anniversary of the discovery of Einstein's special theory of relativity, Pauli was to lecture at the Zurich Physical Society. Three of his friends and colleagues had dinner with him beforehand, then they all set out for the lecture. One Swiss physicist was on his scooter, saw he was low on gas, and stopped to fill up. His scooter caught fire, was totaled, and he had to walk. A second Swiss physicist discovered that his bike had two flat tires, so he had to walk, too. The third man took the tram, which he did frequently, but forgot to get off at the right stop. They all made it to the lecture, but one of the men involved noted that with the Pauli effect, Pauli himself never experienced any harm.

As one of Pauli's close friends said, "It is quite legitimate to understand the 'Pauli effect' as a synchronistic phenomenon as conceived by Jung."

Jung probably wouldn't argue with that. In 1909, he experienced a psychokinetic event during a meeting with Freud. Jung had asked Freud about his views on parapsychology and when Freud dismissed the entire field as nonsense, Jung understandably felt stung and betrayed. His own research, after all, was taking him more deeply into the world of parapsychology, mythology, religion, and symbolism. He held back an angry response, but suddenly experienced an intense inner heat, as if his diaphragm were burning up. Right then, a loud cracking sound erupted from a nearby bookcase, startling him and Freud.

Jung suggested it was an example of "catalytic exteriorization phenomena." When Freud dismissed that explanation as "sheer bosh," Jung predicted the loud cracking noise would happen again—and it did.

"It's as if…a burst of mental energy is propagated outward into the physical world," wrote author and physicist F. David Peat in *Synchronicity: The Bridge Between Mind and Matter* when he commented on this event.

Yes, it is. But it also sounds like something you would read in a Stephen King novel or see in a movie—*Firestarter, Carrie, The Fury, The X-Men, Mathilda*. What happened during that meeting between Jung and Freud or whenever Pauli walked into a lab is mind-matter interaction, the movement of or effect upon matter through nothing more than the power of mind. Psychokinesis.

Not surprisingly, Jung witnessed the Pauli effect during their association. When the Jung Institute in opened in Zurich, Pauli attended. At the time, the two men were working together to merge psychology and physics by proposing that the three cornerstones of physics—space, time, and causality—should include synchronicity. So as Jung drew attention to Pauli's work in bringing together the two fields, a vase overturned, spilling water everywhere.

One of the most comical anecdotes about the Pauli effect that Miller reported in his book occurred in the late 1920s, when Pauli met Erwin Panofsky, an art historian and expert on Johannes Kepler, a seventeenth-century German mathematician, astronomer and astrologer. They were introduced by a mutual friend at an outdoor restaurant in Hamburg. Miller noted that for Panofsky, the meeting was unforgettable for many reasons, but mostly because he personally experienced the Pauli effect. At the end of the long lunch, the three individuals stood up and Panofsky and the mutual friend discovered that they—but not Pauli—had been sitting in whipped cream for the entire lunch.

"If our minds can reach out and alter the movement of a cascade of marbles or the operation of a machine, what strange alchemy might account for such an ability?" asked Michael Talbott in *The Holographic Universe.*

Is psychokinesis the power behind psychic healing? Teleportation? Influencing the outcomes of sporting events? Is it a skill we can learn and develop? Ask Uri Geller.

URI GELLER

When he first became well known to investigators like Andrija Puharich, M.D., the Israeli spoon bender claimed his powers came from ETs. Maybe they did. Enhanced paranormal abilities are often reported in the wake of UFO encounters and abductions. But Geller's problem isn't ETs, it's skeptics. His credibility was seriously undermined by professional skeptics, specifically James Randi, who insisted Geller's alleged telekinetic feats were sleights of hand, just stage magic. Even noted scientists attacked him. Physicist Richard Feynman claimed Geller was fraudulent in his claims.

At some point during 1974, Trish happened to see Geller on TV one night, at the height of his popularity. He was bending spoons. She thought how she would like to see him do this in person, close up. About ten years later, she had an opportunity.

We had been married about a year by then and happened to be in a South Florida mall, where Geller was demonstrating his psycokinetic abilities. We wandered over to the small group that watched—maybe two dozen people—and were able to move in close to the platform that elevated him somewhat above the crowd. It was hardly Madison Square Garden!

First he demonstrated spoon-bending and talked about what was happening as he ran his fingers repeatedly over the spoon. We were close enough to Geller to reach out and touch him, so we had an excellent view of the spoon. As we watched, the upper part of the handle started to bend, so that it curved downward, like something out of a Dali painting. Then Geller asked for keys from the audience. People gladly turned over their keys—but we didn't. We had just seen what he'd done to the spoon and we didn't intend to get stuck at a mall ten to fifteen miles from home.

As sets of keys were handed over to Geller, he ran his fingers over them, and a tight hush settled over the small crowd. Within a couple of minutes, keys were bent at weird and impossible angles and handed back to their owners, who held them up for everyone to see.

Sleight of hand? Plants in the crowd? We aren't professional debunkers or magicians, but were close enough to see the metal bend, to see what the keys—and the spoon—looked like when the owners dangled them from their raised hands for minutes after Geller returned them. *The metal was curved, bent, abnormal.*

Even though Geller has been attacked by a host of skeptics, when he was tested at the Stanford Research Institute, the results were impressive. He demonstrated telepathy, extrasensory perception, and the power to deflect a compass needle by concentrating on it.

In a new documentary film about Geller that aired on the BBC2 on July 21, 2013, the filmmaker, Vikram Jayanti, used footage from the CIA-funded film record of the Uri Geller experiments at Stanford, and then tracked stories about Geller's involvement in a wide range of events, including the Israeli commando raid on Entebbe, the search for Osama bin Laden, and his dealings with the Mexican government.

The film also draws on knowledge from someone "in a position to know" that the U.S. military's psychic spy program (Stargate) wasn't shut down in 1995, but simply went "deeper black." So, Jayanti speculates, perhaps Geller is still at work as a psychic spy. Jayanti's speculations, though, may only be that. In our interview with Stargate remote viewer Joe McMoneagle in chapter 13, McMoneagle spells out the reasons he believes the government's remote viewing program hasn't continued in *any* form.

In Dean Radin's new book *Supernormal: Science, Yoga, and the Evidence of Extraordinary Psychic Abilities,* there are several chapters on psychokinesis and the various types of scientific experiments used to investigate the phenomenon. When testing psychokinesis with inanimate objects, two types of experiments are conducted—Micro-PK, where the targets are microscopic (photons, radioactive particles) and macro-PK, where the target is large enough to see with the naked eye. Spoon-bending is considered a macro-PK. "This phenomenon has been studied a few times under quasi-controlled circumstances, and in my opinion it seems that something interesting may be going on." However, Radin says, since there are many ways of bending metal with conjuring techniques, the scientific evidence is insufficient.

"That said, if I were forced to decide whether it was *possible* to bend metal for real, without using blunt force or conjuring methods, then I would say yes, it is possible." And he says this because not only has he seen it done by ordinary people, but he himself did it at a spoon-bending party.

He was holding a large, heavy soup spoon and was mimicking the hand movements of a woman nearby. While watching the woman, he heard someone shout, "Look what you've done!"

He glanced up to see what the commotion was about and it turned out that *he* was the source of the commotion. "I had somehow bent the bowl of the spoon I was holding about 90 degrees. I immediately checked my fingers to see if I had unconsciously used force, because it would have taken an enormous effort to create that bend and the effect would have left clear indentations on my fingers. There were no signs of force."

Someone shouted at him to bend it all the way, so he pinched it with a thumb and forefinger. "After the bowl folded over, it stiffened, and within a few seconds it became as hard as steel."

Radin hasn't been able to repeat what he did. "So I can't explain how this happened, nor do I present it as evidence for macro-PK. But it did happen."

Perhaps one of the reasons Radin was able to bend the spoon at the party was because everyone around him was trying to do so as well and believed it was possible. The energy of the collective can create a powerful momentum and environment in which the paranormal flourishes.

PEAR: PRINCETON ENGINEERING ANOMALIES RESEARCH

Robert G. Jahn is a professor of aerospace sciences and dean emeritus of the School of Engineering and Applied Science at Princeton. He's also the program director for PEAR, which he started in 1979 after a student asked him to oversee an experiment on psychokinesis that she was doing as an independent study project. At the time, Jahn didn't believe in the paranormal. But he agreed to oversee the student's project and was so intrigued by the results that he founded the Princeton Engineering Anomalies Research—PEAR.

For the last thirty-four years, PEAR has conducted thousands of experiments that involved millions of trials performed by several hundred operators. The focus of their research has been in two primary areas: human-machine anomalies and remote perception. According to their website, the most substantial part of their research has been on the first area.

"In these studies human operators attempted to bias the output of a variety of mechanical, electronic, optical, acoustical, and fluid devices to conform to pre-stated intentions, without recourse to any known physical influences. In unattended calibrations all of these sophisticated machines produced strictly random data, yet the experimental results display increases in information content that can only be attributed to the consciousness of their human operators."

In other words, these human operators attempted to influence machines—psychokinesis. One of their most intriguing findings was that pairs of operators with *shared intentions,* especially when the two individuals were bonded emotionally, "were found to induce further anomalies in the experimental outputs."

The key phrase here is *bonded emotionally,* which suggests that psychokinesis may have an emotional basis—like when Freud's rebuttal of the paranormal made Jung feel betrayed.

Also, even more remarkably, "these anomalies were demonstrated with the operators located thousands of miles from the laboratory, exerting their efforts many hours before or after the actual operation of the devices."

This particular finding correlates with what happened in a lab at the University of Gottingen just as Pauli's train had pulled into the Gottingen station miles away.

The ramifications of the discoveries at PEAR suggest that the current scientific belief about the nature of reality may be seriously flawed. From the PEAR website: "Beyond its revolutionary technological applications and scientific impact, the evidence of an active role of consciousness in the establishment of physical reality holds profound implications for our view of ourselves, our relationships to others, and to the cosmos in which we exist. Our ability to acquire, or to generate tangible, measurable information independent of distance or time challenges the foundation of any reductionist brain-based model of consciousness that may be invoked."

JUNG & RHINE

Psychokinetic incidents touched Carl Jung's life early on. After his father's death, when he was in his first semester of medical school, he and his mother and sister lived rent-free in a former mill, a dilapidated structure owned by a relative. He was studying in his room one summer afternoon when a cracking sound resounded nearby. He hurried into the dining room and discovered that a seventy-year-old walnut dining room table "had split from center to rim in a way that had nothing to do with its construction or the natural grain of the wood," wrote Deirdre Bair in *Jung: A Biography*. It's unlikely that weather was a factor. Where this sort of thing might happen on a cold, dry day in winter, the day was hot and humid.

A few weeks later, Jung got home one evening to find everyone in the household disturbed by something that had just happened. There had been another loud noise. This one had come from a sideboard, a piece of nineteenth-century Swiss furniture with multiple drawers and cabinets for storing dishes and utensils. Jung's mother and sister and the maid were too afraid to look for the cause of the noise, so Jung did.

In a side cupboard, where the bread was kept, Jung found a bread knife with its blade neatly severed in several places. "It could only have been broken in such a manner if the blade had been snapped deliberately several times, but there had been only one resounding noise, and no one had touched the knife since the previous meal," Bair wrote.

Jung, of course, wanted answers. He took the knife to a cutler, who informed him the metal couldn't have shattered naturally and attributed it to "an act of mischief."

But perpetrated by who or what? Jung kept the broken knife the rest of his life.

Jung corresponded briefly with J.B. Rhine, one of the early parapsychology researchers who went on to establish the Rhine Institute at Duke University, and told him about the exploding table and the shattered knife. Rhine agreed these incidents were probably the result of psychokinesis, but was stumped about how to test such a thing in a laboratory setting. Then, one day in 1934, a gambler walked into Rhine's office and inadvertently solved his dilemma about how to test psychokinesis in a lab.

The gambler told Rhine he could influence the fall of the dice, and Rhine, a skeptic, said, "Show me."

"So the two crouched on the floor—the traditional gambler's pose—and the visitor proceeded to demonstrate," wrote Colin Wilson in *Mysteries: An Investigation into the Occult, the Paranormal, & the Supernatural.*

As the man tossed the dice, Rhine realized the gambler was illustrating how mind over matter could be tested in a laboratory setting. They wouldn't need professional psychics and mediums for the tests, as they did at the time to investigate telepathy and survival after death. Rhine realized that most students were experts at tossing dice. The upshot was that Rhine tried using students to influence dice and, as Wilson noted, "his results revolutionized parapsychology. For they showed beyond all possible doubt that when someone first made a determined effort to influence the dice, the results were significantly above expectation."

Rhine's experiments also showed that when students immediately moved on to a second attempt to influence the dice, the results dropped. With a third attempt, the results dropped even more. "In other words," Wilson wrote, "students could exert PK powers when they were fresh and really put their minds to it. Then their attention began to waver and the results fell off."

So we know some of the components that play into psychokinesis: emotions/emotional bonds; being engaged and interested; being rested. But sometimes, psychokinesis occurs within group settings, as it did for Radin at the spoon-bending party, where the collective energy of the group is powerful enough to impact matter.

THE POWER OF THE COLLECTIVE MIND

When you meditate, you're more inclined to look inward for answers, are more aware of living in the moment, it's easier to find peace of mind, and it may very well increase the incidence of synchronicity in your life. When you meditate as a group, a kind of collective energy builds up and, as we discovered, it can trigger telekinetic events.

In a meditation course Rob taught, we were in the midst of the final moments of the final class, finishing the last repetition of a Hawaiian shamanic chant—*I'm sorry, please forgive me, I love you, thank you*—when the lights suddenly went out. The class sat there for a moment in a stunned silence, recognizing the oddity of the event, the synchronicity. Rob closed with a *Namaste—the light in me greets the light in you*. More appropriate than usual since we were in the dark. When the class was done, Trish hurried over to the far wall and flicked the light switch. The room illuminated. But who or what had turned off the light?

Rob later e-mailed the owner of the studio and asked if the lights were on a timer. They weren't. It wasn't an electrical blackout, either, because the soft lights in the front room of the yoga studio were still on. It was as if the collective energy of the students acknowledged the end of the six-week course at the same moment. That energy was powerful enough to provide a punctuation point—the extinguishing of the light, a great example of psychokinesis and synchronicity.

YOUR PAULI EFFECT

What about the rest of us? Do ordinary people have telekinetic experiences? It turns out that we do, but may dismiss our "Pauli effects" as quirks and intriguing anomalies.

Vicki DeLaurentis says she tends to have an effect on electrical things. "If I am having computer problems I know to walk away and let someone else fix it. Also cash registers. I've been at stores and if I get upset 'my' register will have problems so I always try to be aware of that. When I was a child I loved to change red lights to green! I am not as good at that anymore."

However, during a vacation in Ocean City, Maryland, every time she and her family were on the boardwalk and stepped under a light, it would go out. At first, her daughters got a kick out of it, but when other people started noticing, they wanted her to stop doing whatever she was doing. But she couldn't stop it. It wasn't something she could just turn off and on.

Jenean Gilstrap says that when she was a kid, she used to be able to change stoplights. "I always thought everyone could do it." As an adult, this ability manifested itself with computers. "In my last job situation, it became an office joke that if I was feeling a certain way, computers would crash. I could walk into the office and just know it was going to be one of those days."

Mike Perry, the synchronicity blogger from the U.K., wonders if there are different degrees of the Pauli effect, perhaps brought about by expectations—in other words, "what we expect, we get." Mike offers a simple example of a friend who, before he goes away on vacation, actually says, "Wonder what will go wrong this time!" And sure enough, he invariably has problems on vacations. "His car will break down, in one instance his wife broke a bone in her foot, he got the flu and so on and so on. Then he arrives back home with some sob story or another."

Jeri Gerard had one such experience that she has never forgotten. "I have known my husband for twenty-two years and we are best friends. In all of that time, I think we have argued three times. One night when we were staying in my aunt's house, we had an argument. It was horrible. I couldn't look at my husband and I would not lay down next to him. I put my blanket and pillow on the floor at the foot of the bed. Neither one of us can tell you what the argument was about. All I can say is that the anger lifted from me suddenly about ten minutes later. I lay down on the bed next to my husband and we both stared up at the motionless ceiling fan.

"It began to move. It started to spin slowly at first and then faster and faster until it seemed as if it would fly apart. And then… it stopped. No one else was in the house at the time and the switch on the wall was off the whole time. To this day I am grateful for the shared experience. I could have done without the arguing, but my husband has never had the supernatural experiences that I have had except for that one time. He's a psychologist, very scientific, and has a practical explanation for everything. Without that shared experience, I would worry that he might question the reliability of my perceptions."

The movement of the ceiling fan, like the cracking sound that ensued after Freud had dismissed the paranormal as absurd, seemed to have been caused by a release of intense emotion. Is intense emotion and focus also behind winning at the slot machines?

Several years ago, we flew across the state with Bruce Gernon, Rob's co-author of *The Fog,* and his wife, Lynn. Our destination was a casino on the Seminole Indian reservation near Imokalee, Florida. At the airport, as we waited inside the small terminal for a ride to the casino, Lynn pulled out a small velvet pouch. "Let's see what the pendulum has to say about our trip to the casino." She grinned. "Are we going to win anything?"

The answer was a resounding *yes*. While Lynn knows her way around casinos, we were basically clueless and allotted ourselves twenty bucks apiece for the slot machines. We hoped to win grocery money, so you might say our intentions and expectations were somewhat low.

The inside of the casino was like another world altogether—no windows, no clocks, just a strange twilight lit up by hundreds of machines, and absolutely no sense of the outer world. It was a kind of *bardo*, a Tibetan word that literally means an intermediate state, the place we go in between lives, where our expectations and beliefs dictate what we experience. In this "between" state, we felt as if we'd entered Rod Serling's *Twilight Zone,* a vast emptiness of probability.

At the check-in counter, we received scratch tickets, free draws, because we'd never been to a casino in Florida before. Trish's was for $25, Rob's was for $10. The clerk said we could use the scratch ticket on every machine except the "progressives." Once we had placed a bet, we could cash in the value of the ticket. So Lynn led us off to the one-armed bandits.

She explained how you place bets on the various machines—bets from one cent to a quarter. You slide your ID card into a slot, then insert your free ticket, place a bet... Trish won $66 on her first try and quit the machine after she cashed out.

Suddenly, at one of the "progressive machines," where bets progress upward on an incomprehensible scale, a woman shrieked with joy. She had just won $237. She was on a roll and she knew it. "As soon as she gets up, we'll try that machine," Lynn said. "You want to use the machines that win." And she proceeded to explain which machines she had used in past visits that had surrendered their riches.

At this point, we started to wonder if psychokinesis is involved in lucky streaks. Do players, through their intentions, needs, desires and beliefs, somehow merge with the consciousness of the machine to bring about a win? Do their desires impact the machines? Or is it all random luck? When we left the casino, we had won $130 and Lynn had won several hundred. Lynn's pendulum had been right. Our expectations had been met—grocery money. If we visit the casino again, we'll be sure to have higher expectations and more focused intentions!

"The few times I've gone to casinos, I must be in a certain frame of mind to win," says Jenean Gilstrap. "By that I mean I must *know* that I'm going to win. When I get to the casino, I shut my eyes and *feel* which machine is the *winning* one—and then go only to that one or others that *feel* right to me." Jenean noted that she can't manufacture the frame of mind that enables her to win. It seems this frame of mind either exists—or doesn't.

One time she and her daughter were at a casino and Jenean *felt* her way toward a winning machine and told her daughter to play it. "I saw a large token left in the return of the machine and asked several people if they'd left the token. No one claimed it, so I told Heather to play it because it was going to win. Heather dropped the token into the slot, pulled the lever, and suddenly sirens and whistles went off, waitresses with trays of drinks gathered around, and $600 came pouring out. Heather was in law school then, and the winning cash went to buy expensive legal textbooks.

Chapter 11
PRECOGNITION

FREE WILL OR PREDESTINATION?

The 2002 movie *Minority Report* takes place in a future society where murders are prevented by three *precogs* who can see crimes before they happen. Once they finger the would-be perpetrator and the location, the PreCrime unit sweeps in and makes arrests. When the chief of police—Tom Cruise in the movie version—intercepts a precognition that he's about to murder a man he has never met, alternate realities and paradoxes unfold. The movie is based on a 1956 short story by visionary science fiction writer Philip K. Dick and both it and the movie explore the issue of free will. Does it exist or is it just an illusion?

Let's take a deeper look.

On the evening of May 22, 2011, a powerful tornado struck Joplin, Missouri. The photos and video of that devastation are eerily similar to the photos and videos of the tornado that swept through parts of Alabama a month earlier. It's impossible to look at these photos and not feel a deep communion and profound sadness for these people. One moment, life is humming along as usual, the next moment, your world is turned inside out like a filthy sock and you're in the middle of nature's washing machine.

The images prompted us to wonder about why these tragedies happen to particular communities. Yes, Missouri and Alabama are prone to tornadoes in the same way that Florida and the Caribbean are prone to hurricanes or that the countries perched on the rim of fire are prone to earthquakes and tsunamis. But why Joplin and not Springfield, Missouri, just seventy-four miles away?

Why did Hurricane Andrew in 1992 flatten Homestead, Florida, and not nearby Miami?

Why did the Indonesian tsunami hit where it did and not some spot two hundred miles away?

Does the mass consciousness in a particular place attract such a disaster for some unknown reason? Do the individuals involved agree at some unconscious, collective level to be involved in something like this? Just how far does free will go? Do we have any free will at all?

In Thorton Wilder's *The Bridge of San Luis Rey,* published in 1927, five people in Lima Peru in 1714 end up on a rope suspension bridge that subsequently collapses, killing all of them. The story is told by a Franciscan monk who witnessed the tragedy and investigated the lives of the victims, seeking an answer to why these particular five people were in the wrong place at the wrong time. Was it destiny or free will?

On an individual scale, the same question can be asked. Shortly before actor Christopher Reeve was thrown from a horse and became a quadriplegic, he played a paralyzed police officer in the HBO special *Above Suspicion.* Was the role a kind of dry run—a synchronicity—for what later happened to him? Reeve ultimately became *the* spokesman for individuals with spinal cord injuries. Did he agree to that role before he was born? Was free will operating? Was it predestination? Or was this tragedy just a *random* event and he simply made the best of a terrible situation?

Few events can be more heartbreaking than the loss of a child. We've often wondered whether child and parents agree to the possibility of this event before the child's birth—or perhaps even farther back—or if it's just a random tragedy. Gayle, a hair stylist, lost her son some years ago to an OxyContin overdose. She feels it was God's will. She believes his death forced her to grow and evolve as a spiritual being.

Perhaps there are experiences we agree to explore in our present lives—our appointments with destiny, an oxymoron in the free will scheme of things. Then the event approaches and maybe we're allowed to back out, to choose something else, or to go ahead as planned. One of the Weather Channel anchors choked up while viewing the ruin of Joplin, Missouri, in the aftermath of a tornado in May 2011. Only ten minutes before the tornado struck, he and his crew had to pull off the road into Joplin because of the intense and violent hail. If they hadn't been held up, they would have been in the middle of the tornado. Or, as another anchor put it, *You and your crew might be dead.*

If we follow this in a quantum sense, was an alternate reality created when he and his crew got held up? The Many Worlds Theory of quantum physics says that for every decision we make—or don't make—an alternate path is created.

What if. Our lives, as lived from day to day, seem to be predicated on these two words. But perhaps the deeper reality that underlies our everyday world is also built on this same premise. What if.

A SHAMAN'S PREDICTIONS

When Arizona artist Lauren Raines was going through a divorce, she heard about a shamanic practitioner in Crownsville, Maryland, who had studied with Sandra Ingerman and was also an energy healer and herbalist. She was at a point in her life where she was "very open to anything," and went to him for a soul retrieval.

This shamanic practice helps to regain a soul that has become trapped, disconnected, or lost through some sort of trauma. Depending on the circumstances, a divorce can certainly qualify as a trauma.

"He was very businesslike, and without knowing anything about me, put on his drums tape and headset, had me lie down next to him, and we tranced together. At the end of the session he blew soul fragments back into my body, and we talked about what he saw. We talked about cutting the cords from my ex-husband, and my former community (I had moved away). He concluded the session by telling me: You'll know it's all over when you see a magenta flower that looks like a cosmos, and a terra cotta angel."

Eight months later, Lauren crossed the country with her cat and all her possessions loaded into her van. She was determined to move back to Berkeley, California, and start a new life. She had decided she would sleep in her van if necessary until she found somewhere to move. "I began my adventure as soon as I arrived with a visit to a coffee house that I last visited twenty years earlier. Almost immediately I was greeted by a long-ago friend, Joji Yokoi, who recognized me, bought me a cup of coffee, and offered me a place to stay. I didn't have to spend a single night in my van—and when I walked into his living room there was a huge photograph of a magenta cosmos flower hanging above his fireplace!"

A few months after that, Lauren answered an ad for a roommate. She walked into a house with an altar—and in the center was a terra cotta angel. The woman who had placed the advertisement was a colleague of Starhawk, Lauren's heroine and the woman whose writings were the foundation of her MFA thesis more than a decade earlier. "Needless to say, just like that, my new life began, and I ended up working with the very people I most wanted to work with, never having had to even try! The shaman was entirely right in his prediction."

The shaman gave Lauren two specific bits of information about markers that would signal her transitional period was finished—the magenta cosmos flower and the terra cotta angel. How was he able to see something so precise, for a woman he had just met?

"Shamans are inspired visionaries who are able to access information through their invisible allies for the benefit of themselves, their families, and their communities. This process is known as divination, and it is usually accomplished through ceremony and ritual," wrote Sandra Ingerman and Hank Wesselman in *Awakening to the Spirit World*. "Through their relationship with these transpersonal forces, shamans are able to retrieve lost power and restore it to its original owners…"

So through the trance-state that the shaman and Lauren entered together, he retrieved the power that Lauren had lost and was allowed to see the most probable path her future would take.

IMPULSES, PRECOGNITION AND PREMONITIONS

Most of us have experienced impulses. You might be driving down a particular road or highway and have a sudden impulse to get off at a particular exit or to take another route altogether. Or you might be signing up for college classes and feel the impulse to take a course that you've never thought of taking before. Perhaps because of that first impulse, you avoided a traffic jam or car accident. Maybe because of that second impulse, you met your soul mate.

An impulse is often a whisper from the future, the way our intuition interacts with our physical bodies to seize our attention. It can manifest itself as a premonition, a feeling of anxiety or anticipation, or as a precognition, foreknowledge about the future. Either way, it's a good idea to honor an impulse, particularly when it's strong. During our daughter's third year in college, Megan followed such an impulse and may have averted a tragedy.

At her college, January was the month when students were involved in independent study projects that took many of them off campus or overseas for the entire month. Two of Megan's dorm roommates were doing their projects elsewhere, so it was just Megan and a young man who had moved into her campus apartment about two months earlier.

There had been some issues with this guy—namely, that he often talked to himself in the bathroom or in his room, shouting and ranting about what an awful person he was and no wonder he was disliked. Megan and the roommates had overheard these rants and had discussed asking the young man to move out. They thought he needed professional help.

Late one night, Megan was in her room and heard the guy out in the kitchen, yelling to himself again. "I had this impulse to record what he was saying, so I turned on my phone recorder." And recorded him yelling about how much he hated this group or that group—conservatives, liberal hippies, everyone—but it didn't matter because he was going to BLOW THEM ALL UP. Megan, alone in the apartment, was totally freaked out, and locked herself in her room.

When she told us about it, we encouraged her to go to the resident director and tell him what had happened and that she wanted the young man *out* of her apartment. So the next morning, that's what she did—and played the recording. Her impulse to record the conversation caused the resident director to take it seriously—otherwise it might have been her word against the young man's.

So Megan's precognitive impulse, like the pre-cogs in *Minority Report*, perhaps prevented some terrible scenario. Since she turned him in, we wanted her out of there and away from him as quickly as possible. She moved temporarily into a friend's room and the young man moved to another part of the campus and received counseling.

THE KOI POND

If necessity is the mother of invention, then our intentions and desires may well birth precognitions and manifestations. That certainly seemed to be the case with a Koi pond that twelve-year-old Dawson really wanted. He had been bugging his mother, our neighbor, about buying a Koi pond that he could set up in the backyard. His mother, Annette, told him that when his grandfather came to visit, it was something the two of them could work on together. About an hour after they'd had this discussion, their garbage disposal died and they went to Lowe's to buy a new one.

As they entered Lowe's, Dawson spotted a Koi kit at the end of the counter, one of those do-it-yourself things. "Mom, it's a synchronicity. It means we should get the Koi pond."

Dawson knew about synchronicity because his mother read our book, *The 7 Secrets of Synchronicity,* and every time someone in the family experienced one, Annette would point out that a synchro had just occurred.

"Well, we're here to buy a garbage disposal, not a Koi kit," Annette told him.

After they got home, Dawson, his sister Maddie and their friend Zack left with a fishing net and headed over to the nearby canal to see what they could catch—fish, lizards, armadillos. About twenty minutes later, Annette walked outside and saw a Koi pond in their driveway.

She explained that the pond had been left in the driveway of a house in the neighborhood that was in foreclosure and abandoned. Dawson, Maddie, and

The kids hauled the Koi pond back to Annette's driveway, piece by piece, stone by stone, and then the three of them—covered with dirt –were ready to install the pond in their backyard.

"Pretty cool, isn't it, Ms. Trish?" Dawson called as he was hauling stones. "Our synchronicity."

There's something gratifying about a couple of young kids experiencing and recognizing synchronicity. It's also amusing that Dawson, who really wanted the Koi pond, not only recognized the synchro, but tried to use it to convince his mother that they absolutely had to buy the Koi kit at Lowe's.

PRECOGNITION IN DREAMS & ALTERED STATES

At one time, dreams were thought to be nothing more than the detritus the mind regurgitates at the end of the day, the accumulated *stuff* of our conscious lives—worries, concerns, details. We now know that dreams are more than that, and there is plenty of evidence that some dreams connect us to something much larger and vaster than ourselves. "Bohm's assertion that every human consciousness has it source in the implicate implies that we all possess the ability to access the future," wrote Michael Talbot in *The Holographic Universe*. And one of the best ways of accessing the future is through dreams.

A number of surveys and studies show that more than sixty percent of precognitions occur during dreaming. Rupert Sheldrake, writing in *Science Set Free: 10 Paths to New Discovery*, noted that in his database of 842 cases of premonitions, precognitions, or presentiments, seventy percent are about "dangers, disasters, or deaths; twenty-five percent are about neutral events; and only five percent are of happy events."

But there are also precognitive dreams that can't be pigeonholed into any of the above categories. These types of dreams illuminate our personal history in some way and provide insights into the continuity of consciousness from life to life.

ROMANIA?

In 2010, Jenean Gilstrap dreamed she was living in another time, long ago. She was dressed in several long skirts and tops and wore a fitted jacket that fell right below her waist. Her hair was loose, she wore some sort of headscarf. It wasn't quite winter yet, but it was cold enough for the layers of clothes and the jacket she wore. She carried a valise and sensed that all her belongings were inside of it.

She was on foot, traveling along a rutted dirt road that carts or wagons used, which made it more difficult to walk. Other people were walking, too, and the road wandered through groves of trees. Jenean spotted a side path to her right that intersected her road and as she approached it, looked up to see a man moving toward her. He carried a walking stick. Their eyes caught and as they neared each other, she sensed he was friendly and not to be feared.

When Jenean asked where he was going, he gave the name of a small village some distance from them. "I asked if we might walk together and he said of course. I tried to walk more quickly to catch up to him as he waited. I was having difficulty walking because of a hip injury and told him I was unable to walk very fast because of it. He stood there, waiting until I caught up to him, and said, 'Here, perhaps this would help you. Take this.' He handed me his walking stick and we began to walk together. Then I woke up with a searing pain in my right hip."

The following day, Jenean couldn't get this dream out of her mind. She felt it might have been a past-life memory and that it had taken place in the Ukraine, Hungary, or Romania. Of the three, Romania resonated the most strongly. A day later Jenean found a photograph on a blog that depicted the road she'd seen in her dream. Walking along the road was a boy carrying the identical walking stick that had been in her dream.

She wrote to Marius Morar, the blogger and the photographer, and discovered that Morar is Romanian. In an e-mail exchange, he said the boy with the stick was actually his seven-year-old son and the road was leading away from Romania, about ten miles from the border, south of Cluj-Napoca, in historic Transylvania.

Not only did the dream have possible past-life roots, but it turned out to be precognitive. The other intriguing aspect of this dream concerns the present. Jenean has a blog called Gypsy Woman; today, Gypsies comprise about two percent of Romania's population. So the dream was like a timeline from past to present to future.

ADELE & JOHN LILY

In the 1970s, artist Adele Aldridge found out that John Lilly, author, physician, neuroscientist and dolphin researcher, was going to be giving a talk at Wainwright House in Rye, New York, not far from where she lived. One of his books had just been published and he was on a lecture tour. Adele hadn't yet read his book, but was aware of his research, and wanted to hear his talk.

On the night before the lecture, Adele dreamed she attended and was surprised at the way Lilly was dressed. "He was wearing a jumpsuit instead of the usual suit or sports coat of the time. I thought that very odd. He was dressed like an auto mechanic, and I couldn't figure out the symbolism of the jumpsuit."

In her waking life, she didn't have any idea what Lilly looked like, but when she arrived at the lecture, he was the spitting image of the man she'd seen in her dream—and was wearing a jumpsuit. "I've never seen a man, before or since, who wore a jumpsuit as his clothing of choice."

This dream falls into that neutral category that Sheldrake talks about. Although it's precognitive, it's not earth-shattering and doesn't concern a disaster or death or bad news. But it made such an impression on Adele that she has remembered it for more than forty years.

But even "neutral" precognitive dreams connect us to what Jung called the *numinous,* the interconnectedness of all life, and in that sense that we are even connected to the divine, to something so vast and profound that our consciousness is forever changed. "Synchronicities…reconnect the time-bound participant with the timeless dimension of the transpersonal, archetypal realm, the *unus mundus*, and such moments open us to knowledge or hints of things to which we ordinarily have no access," wrote Veronica Goodchild in *Songlines of the Soul.*

In the timeless dimension of dreams, we can "remember" the future. And perhaps that's what is actually occurring with precognitive dreams.

THE DROWNING

During WWII, Jung was on a train returning home from Bollingen, Switzerland. He had a book with him, but couldn't read it. "...from the moment the train started to move, I was overpowered by the image of someone drowning." During the entire journey, Jung couldn't get rid of the feeling. "It struck me as uncanny, and I thought, 'What has happened? Can there have been an accident?'" The feeling was apparently exacerbated by a memory of an accident that had occurred while he was in the military service.

He got off the train at Erlenbach and walked home, still troubled. His second daughter's family was living with the Jungs then and as he walked into the garden, her kids were all there, upset. "They told me that Adrian, then the youngest of the boys, had fallen into the water at the boathouse. It is quite deep there, and since he could not really swim, he had almost drowned. This had taken place at exactly the time I had been assailed by that memory on the train."

As he wrote in his autobiography, *Memories, Dreams and Reflections*, "The unconscious helps by communicating things to us, or making figurative allusions. It has other ways, too, of informing us of things which by all logic we could not possibly know. Consider synchronistic phenomena, premonitions, and dreams that come true. The unconscious had given me a hint."

If it's possible for the unconscious to warn and inform us about future events in dreams, visions, and other altered states, then it must also be possible for it to locate lost objects. It seems that's what happened with a lost checkbook.

LOST CHECKBOOK

Jenean Gilstrap's daughter, Lisa, had lost her checkbook and had looked everywhere in the house for it but to no avail. That night, Jenean dreamed she was outdoors and was looking around in the dark for the checkbook. She went over to a utility pole and there it lay, on the ground at the base of the pole.

She picked it up and exclaimed, "I found it!"

Even though Jenean couldn't see Lisa in the dream, she knew she'd said this to her, that her daughter was there. After she picked up the checkbook, she turned to her left and moved back a few steps to hand Lisa the checkbook. Then she woke up.

"That morning, Lisa came straight into my room and asked if I'd seen the checkbook she'd lost the day before. I laughed and told her I'd found it in my dream, at the base of a utility pole. I just didn't know where the utility pole was."

The next day, Jenean asked Lisa about the checkbook. She still hadn't found it. That evening, as Jenean was on her way to bed, she asked Lisa again.

"Oh, yeah, I did find it, and it's really weird," Lisa said. "I found it in my purse, but I don't know how it got there because I know it wasn't there. I *know* I lost it."

Over the course of the days the checkbook had been missing, Lisa had removed every single item from her purse several times, set everything out on the table, and the checkbook hadn't been there. She was totally mystified as to how it had gotten back into her purse. But Jenean wasn't mystified at all. "I remembered I had handed it to her in my dream."

So, can items we lose in waking life and find in dreams somehow make it back into waking life? Well, why not? If a shaman can travel into another reality to retrieve someone's soul, then why shouldn't any of us be able to able to access that same dimension or reality to find lost objects?

THE DREAM POST-IT

In the spring and summer of 2000, our lives were in a kind of turmoil. Trish's father, who had Parkinson's, was living with us and had taken over our daughter's bedroom. Megan was now sleeping in the living room. Trish's mother was in Alzheimer's unit and going downhill quickly. Rob's office was located in an alcove that we had managed to section off with bookcases for a modicum of privacy. We had outgrown our house, had found a home in a community twenty miles north of us that was perfect, and were due to close on both houses on June 15 and make our move.

In other words, this was a time of major transitions for us and the synchronicities were shooting at us from every side.

In late May, as were preparing for our move and packing up our belongings, Trish fulfilled an earlier obligation and attended a writers conference in Kentucky. Upon her return, she dreamed she was still at the conference and someone interrupted her talk by passing her a note scribbled on a yellow Post-It. That note read: *Your mother has just passed on.*

The next morning, Trish hurried out to the breakfast table to tell Rob and her father about her dream. Her dad looked shocked; he, too, had dreamed that his wife of more than fifty years had passed away.

Several weeks later, on June 23, the dreams came true. Around five p.m., Trish was getting ready to drive over to the nursing home where they had moved her mother a couple of weeks earlier. She was going to be transferred into hospice and Trish wanted to be there to facilitate the process. But a few minutes before she left, Rob was sitting at his computer and laid his head against his arms to rest his eyes. In those few moments, he saw Trish's mom smiling and waving good-bye. Before he even had a chance to tell Trish what he'd seen, the phone rang. It was the nursing home; Trish's mother had just passed on.

Even among people who believe these kinds of things are possible, there's a shock element, a kind of WTF moment when your head and heart do this entangled, complicated tango and whisper, *We told you so...* It's at this point when you know you have glimpsed the inner workings of synchronicity, of this deep, underlying implicate order.

Chapter 12
CLAIRVOYANCE

One morning author Kurt Vonnegut felt compelled to call his brother-in-law, whom he never phoned. He was concerned about his sister, who was dying of cancer. As Vonnegut was making the call, news about a train accident in New Jersey came over the radio and an image formed in his mind. Even though his brother-in-law never took trains, Vonnegut knew instantly that he was aboard that train and was dead. Within an hour, he was headed for New Jersey. His sister died the next day, and Vonnegut and his wife immediately adopted the deceased couple's six children.

That dramatic story was told to writer Allan Vaughn in *Patterns of Prophecy* after he asked Vonnegut about how he had come up with the idea of people being linked through meaningful coincidences. Vonnegut had expressed that idea in his own way in *Cat's Cradle* when he described a *karass*, a group of people who unknowingly work together to achieve some common goal. You knew you were a member of a particular karass when meaningful coincidences happened between you and other members of that group.

Telepathy typically is an impression of what someone else is thinking and precognition is a sense of an event at a distance time. But clairvoyance is about "seeing" events at a distance in space, as Vonnegut did when he heard about the train accident on the radio.

It can occur anywhere, at any time, and through any means, even dreams. Shortly after the Boston Marathon bombings on April 15, 2013, author and futurist Marcus Anthony e-mailed us a stunning dream that had been sent to him by a South African woman. At first, we thought it was an example of precognition. But due to the time difference between South Africa and Boston, it's a clear example of clairvoyance.

Nirissa Pilay dreamed she was at an event near a stadium with crowds of people outside. A bomb exploded and people started running and screaming and then she heard a second bomb go off. "I found myself in a hotel asking the person at the reception if he knew what number my room was because I could not recall. Repeatedly, he said it was number 141. This morning I opened my inbox and my husband had forwarded me an e-mail about the Boston Marathon bombing: two bombs—one of which went off across from a hotel—141 casualties (or close), a sporting event and people running into hotels."

Nirissa pointed out that South Africa is six hours ahead of Boston, so that the bombings took place while she was asleep. The first bomb exploded at 2:49 p.m. Boston time—8:49 South Africa time. "I have always been skeptical of everything and suddenly the concept of universal intelligence has become a reality," she wrote Marcus. "I'm shaken. I felt I needed to reach out and ask someone with knowledge surrounding this for some guidance on this, please."

We asked her if she might've picked up the information subconsciously, possibly from a TV playing in the background. She replied: "We have not had our satellite fixed for over a month now. We chose not to fix it because it didn't bother us much to not be able to watch TV. So it's been mainly talking, books and board games for a while. So the answer to that question is, 'no'—there was no other physical source of information available to me while I was sleeping."

We also asked her if she had gone online before going to bed that night. She replied that she couldn't remember, then added: "I am one hundred percent certain I didn't have any knowledge about the actual event, until the e-mail from my husband."

Casualties in the 140s were being reported on the morning of April 16. A week later, however, the number of casualties had risen to over 200. But the similarities between her dream and the actual event are remarkable.

Adelita Chirino, who leads dream workshops, says that clairvoyance and precognition are common during dreaming. "It's just that people don't remember."

Makes the case for a dream journal, doesn't it?

Sometimes, such a dream is startling enough to wake you, so you don't need a dream journal. Some years ago, we were staying at a friend's house in the Florida Keys. We'd gone to bed around ten o'clock and about thirty minutes later Trish bolted upright and said, "Something has happened to my Aunt Pat." She had seen her aunt vividly in a dream, but as a kind of ghostly figure. She noted the time and called her mother the next day to find out if something had happened to Pat, her oldest sister.

Pat lived in Tulsa, Oklahoma, then, was elderly and living alone. Sure enough, she had sustained a bad fall and had ended up in ER. Given the time difference between Florida and Oklahoma, we figured her fall had occurred about the time Trish dreamed of her.

ESP TRAINER

Thanks to the acceleration of technology and the proliferation of iPhones, the app store is stocked with some cool tools to help you unlock your clairvoyant abilities. One of these is called the ESP Trainer, a free iPhone app developed by Russell Targ at Stanford Research Institute, under a NASA program. Targ, a physicist and a pioneer in the development of the laser, was also cofounder of the Stanford Research Institute's investigation into psychic abilities in the 1970s and 1980s.

Using your intuition/clairvoyance, you're supposed to tap the color that hides a photograph. A set consists of twenty-four attempts. If you succeed, you hear a chime, feel a vibration, and then the picture is revealed. If you miss, the correct color lights up. There's a score indicator along the top of the app that counts the number of your correct choices. As you achieve scoring levels of 6, 8, 10, 12 or 14 hits, words of encouragement appear.

On his website, Targ notes that people using the tool have improved their ESP as they get in touch with the part of themselves that is psychic. The website also notes that the purpose of the trainer is to allow you to become aware of what it feels like when you psychically choose the correct square. When you don't have that special feeling, you're encouraged to press the pass button. In a year-long NASA program with 145 people, many were able to significantly improve their scores. If you continually score 12 or higher, then Targ wants to hear from you!

Trish downloaded the app to her phone and we gave it a whirl. On her first try, she only hit 4 out of 24, a surprisingly low number, since by chance she should hit 6 out of 24. On Rob's first try, he got 7 out of 24, slightly better than chance. On subsequent attempts, Trish took more time. She discovered that when she held her fingers up close to the screen and shut her eyes briefly to get a "feel" for where the picture was, her score improved. When our daughter tried it, her score was 8 out of 24.

The free app is a simple and easy way to experiment with clairvoyance. Since you're by yourself, there's no self-consciousness involved. You're not competing with or trying to impress anyone. It's just you—and your clairvoyance.

REMOTE VIEWING

In 1970, Prentice Hall published *Psychic Discoveries Behind the Iron Curtain* by Sheila Ostrander and Lynn Schroeder. This book apparently created enough of a stir within intelligence circles so that certain steps were taken. According to remoteviewed.com, one of these steps occurred in 1973, when the Rand Corporation was hired "to determine if paranormal phenomena existed, how the Russians were investigating it and how this tallied with American efforts."

The 33-page report, available at the above website, is fascinating to read. It covers the nature of paranormal phenomena, possible military applications, the differences between Soviet and U.S. research, paranormal research centers in the Soviet Union and the U.S., and funding in both countries. The study concluded that "if paranormal phenomena do exist, the thrust of Soviet research appears more likely to lead to explanation, control, and application than is U.S. research."

From 1972 to 1995, more than $20 million was poured into the government's psychic spy program, Stargate. The Army and various intelligence agencies including the FBI, CIA, and DIA, were involved. On the remoteviewed.com you can read the PDFs of actual RV sessions with some of the notable remote viewers—Joe McMoneagle, Lynn Buchanan, David Morehouse, Angela Thompson Smith. There's even a session where Linda A. is in training and attempting to read a sealed envelope with Uri Geller's photo inside. Even if you don't know much about the history of psi research in this country, these documents are compelling.

Most of the targets dealt with defense and national security issues and involved psychically spying on enemies. However, sometimes the targets were literally out of this world. One of the most intriguing sessions involved Joe McMoneagle, who was referred to as Remote Viewer #001.

The session took place on May 22, 1984 and the transcript was released on August 8, 2000. The cover sheet of the transcript reads:

Method of site acquisition:
Sealed envelope coupled with geographic coordinates.
The sealed envelope was given to the subject immediately prior to the interview. The envelope was not opened until after the interview. In the envelope was a 3X5 card with the following information:
The planet Mars

Time of interest approximately 1 million years B.C.
Selected geographic coordinates, provided by the parties request-
ing the information were verbally given to the subject during the
interview.

As we read through the material, our immediate question was who in the government had made such an exotic request. We contacted McMoneagle and asked him about the session. He said the target and coordinates were provided by the Jet Propulsion Laboratory, a federally funded research and development center associated with NASA. McMoneagle's monitor for the session was author and consciousness researcher Robert Monroe.

Considering that McMoneagle was asked to remote view information from a card sealed in an envelope, his response is stunning. He described enormous dust storms, pyramid forms, aqueducts, and underground shelters. At one point, he reported "severe clouds, more like dust storms" that were the result of and the aftereffects of a major geological problem. He described mountains of dirt that appeared and disappeared, large flat surfaces, and megalithic structures.

Monroe then asked McMoneagle to move back to the time before the geographical upheaval and to report any activity that he saw. His perceptions were of people who were very tall and thin. "It's only a shadow. It's as if they were there and they're not anymore."

Monroe instructed McMoneagle to go back to a period of time when these tall, thin people were there. Initially, McMoneagle encountered interference, like "static on a line," where the connection broke up and became fragmented. Monroe advised him to report raw data, to not try to piece things together.

"I just keep seeing very large people. They appear thin and tall, but they're very large…wearing some kind of strange clothes."

At this point, Monroe told him to hold onto this time period and to move to another physical location. He then gave McMoneagle a new set of geographical coordinates, within this same time period—46.45 north and 353.22 east. These coordinates yielded new information.

McMoneagle found himself deep inside what he thought was a cavern, but said it was more like a canyon and he was looking up the sides of "a steep wall that seems to go on forever. And there's like…a structure with a…it's like the wall of the canyon itself has been carved. Again, I'm getting a very large structure, no…ah, no, intricacies, huge sections of smooth stone."

Monroe asked if the structures he saw had interiors and exteriors. McMoneagle said they did. He described the interior as huge, but like a rabbit warren. "Perception is that the ceiling is very high, walls very wide."

Monroe told McMoneagle to move to another location nearby, within this same time frame: 45.86 north and 354.1 east. At these coordinates, McMoneagle described the end of a large road and a "marker thing that's very large, keep getting Washington monument overlay, it's like an… obelisk."

Once again, Monroe provided a new set of coordinates—35.26 north and 213.24 east. McMoneagle described a high range of ragged mountains that formed a very large basin range where he was. Everything was huge, and the only thing he saw was a "right angle corner."

With the next coordinates, 34.6 north, 213.09 east, McMoneagle reported a cluster of squares up and down that were almost flush with the ground. "It's like they're connected…something very white or reflects light."

Monroe asked what his position of observation was as he looked at these objects that reflected light. McMoneagle replied that he was at an oblique left angle and that the sun was "weird."

The next set of coordinates were close to where McMoneagle was situated: 34.57 north and 212.22 east. We wondered how geographic coordinates on Mars are calculated and a Google search, of course, yielded the answer. According to sunlight and time.com, latitude and longitude on Mars are similar to the geographic system used here on Earth. Planetary scientists use two different Martian coordinate systems: planetographic and planetocentric. In both systems, latitude is measured in degrees north and south of the Martian equator. But with planetographic, which was probably used in 1984 when McMoneagle did this viewing, longitude is measured from 0 to 360 degrees to the west; in planetocentric coordinates, longitude is measured from 0 to 360 degrees to the east.

With the new set of coordinates, McMoneagle described a radiating pattern of some kind, intersecting roads that were dug into valleys, "real neat channels… they're very deep, it's like the road went down."

Monroe remarked that McMoneagle had "nulled out a bit" and encouraged him to recapture his focus. He replied that it was difficult, information was sporadic. These comments were similar to what he'd said earlier about the static in the connection.

When McMoneagle became focused again, Monroe gave him another set of coordinates: 15 degrees north, 198 degrees east. McMoneagle reported things like aqueducts, road beds that resembled carved channels. The horizon, he noted, looked "funny and weird…misty…. like it's really far away."

Once again, Monroe provided a new set of coordinates: 80 degrees south, 64 degrees east. Here, McMoneagle reported huge pyramids that were shelters from storms. He was instructed to enter one of the pyramids and report on any activity he saw.

"Different chambers," he said, "…but they're almost stripped of any kind of… furnishings or anything, it's like ah…strictly functional place for sleeping or that's not a good word, hibernations… I get real raw inputs, storms, savage storms, and sleeping through storms."

Monroe asked McMoneagle to tell him about the ones who slept through the storms.

"Very tall… very large…people, but they're thin, they look thin because of their height and they dress like in, oh hell, it's like a real light silk, but it's not flowing type of clothing, it's like cut to fit."

Monroe then instructed McMoneagle to move closer to these entities and ask one of them to tell him something about themselves. And this is where things got very interesting.

"They're ancient people. They're ah…they're dying, it's past their time or age. They're very philosophic about it. They're looking for ah…a way to survive and they just can't…they're hanging on while they look or wait for something to return or something coming with the answer."

When Monroe asked what these people were waiting for, McMoneagle said there was a group or a party of them that left to find a new place to live. "It's like I'm getting all kinds of overwhelming input of the corruption of their environment. It's failing very rapidly and this group went somewhere, like a long way to find another place to live."

Monroe asked what caused the environmental disturbance and it's apparent from the transcript that McMoneagle was picking up a lot of raw data that was difficult to decipher.

"I get a globe…ah…it's like a globe that goes through a comet's tail or…it's through a river of something but it's all very cosmic. It's like space pictures."

When Monroe asked how the search party left, McMoneagle replied that he got the impression of a "large boat" with "rounded walls and shiny metal." Sounds like the interior of a spacecraft, doesn't it?

Monroe suggested that McMoneagle should accompany the search party to wherever they were going, so he did. His description is eerie. "...a really crazy place with volcanoes and gas pockets and strange plants." Joe described it as a volatile place, "like going from the frying pan into the fire." But he pointed out there was more vegetation here than in the other place, which had none. We wondered if their destination could have been Earth in its earliest, formative years.

This viewing took place nearly three decades ago and our knowledge about the red planet has expanded since then. When the rover Curiosity landed on Mars a year ago, it began transmitting data back to Earth. "As Mars became a planet and its magma solidified, catastrophic outgassing occurred while volatiles were delivered by the impact of comets and other small bodies," said Dr. Chris Webster at NASA's Jet Propulsion Laboratory in Pasadena, lead author on one of the studies of the rover's data. Webster and his team believe a major event destroyed the atmosphere around four billion years ago.

Even though the time frames don't match, is it possible that McMoneagle was viewing the collapse of the Martian atmosphere after the planet had gone through some sort of catastrophic encounter with a comet or some other space object? Is it possible these tall, thin individuals he saw had put themselves into some sort of hibernation in the hopes that they would survive until the search party returned? It sounds like science fiction…but suppose it's true?

In March 2013, newscientist.com reported that NASA's Curiosity rover had discovered definitive evidence that Mars was once suited for life. This evidence came in the scoop of grey powder that was drilled from Martian rock near an ancient streambed called Yellowknife Bay.

"This is probably the only definitively habitable environment that we've described and recorded," said David Blake, the principal investigator for the rover's Chemistry and Mineralogy instrument, known as CheMin.

According to New Scientist, the team was seeking three things that, when combined, spell habitability: a non-acidic environment; enough water for microbes to thrive in; and minerals that could act like batteries, allowing electrons to flow and bring energy to any potential organisms. They found all three.

The sample of grey dust indicated the presence of a clay mineral that forms in the presence of water. The CheMin also detected minerals that suggested the water was pH neutral and carried substances capable of supplying microbes with energy.

"We have found a habitable environment that is so benign and supportive of life that probably if this water had been around and you had been on the planet, you would have been able to drink it," says rover project scientist John Grotzinger.

Was McMoneagle actually seeing ancient inhabitants of Mars? Our interview with him in chapter 13 provides fascinating insights into all these questions.

THE MISSING MAN IN TOKYO

Since his retirement from the Army, McMoneagle has continued to remote view for private clients. In 2003, he was asked by a Japanese television station to locate a man who had been missing for thirty years. On May 10, a camera crew from Tokyo arrived at his home in rural Virginia. He was handed a sealed envelope containing the name of a missing man. The target was identified with a number on the envelope.

With that, he focused and, backed by years of experience, made a series of drawings and typed out a description of where to look for the man. Keep in mind that McMoneagle doesn't speak Japanese and didn't know his way around Tokyo or any other Japanese city—any more than he knew his way around Mars!

The first clue he provided was a large Ferris wheel with changing colored lights. He said he felt that it was in Tokyo near water and from the top of the Ferris wheel you could see four ball fields separated by walkways, which formed a cross. One of the walkways ended at a group of sculptures.

Near the complex of ball fields, he saw a river and across the river a "special train track." On the other side of the track was a raised highway that would lead to a multi-story hospital that he sketched in front of the camera crew.

Then the description took a bizarre turn, reminiscent of a psychic treasure hunt. He wrote that once they discovered the hospital, they were to give the name of the missing man to the first nurse they encountered. McMoneagle went on to describe the missing person as a man about seventy-seven years old.

When the crew returned to Japan, they started following the clues. They soon discovered there were thirteen Ferris wheels in Tokyo, but only four of them were covered with lights that changed colors. That immediately narrowed the focus to four locations. Surprisingly, you could see ballparks with intersecting walkways from all four. In all, at least sixteen ballparks were visible from the top of the four Ferris wheels.

Next, the crew began looking for sculptures at the end of those walkways, but they couldn't find any. They were ready to give up when they found a topiary garden—sculptured shrubbery—at the end of a path at the last location. That walkway ended near a river, which McMoneagle had drawn.

Across the river they spotted a train track—of a monorail, which was considered special, as McMoneagle had described. They also found an elevated highway near the track. After following it for twenty-eight miles they came to a hospital. As the crew left their vehicle, they encountered a nurse crossing the parking lot and, following what McMoneagle had said, asked if she knew the man they were seeking.

To their astonishment, she told them matter-of-factly that she knew him because he'd been a patient a few weeks ago. When they asked how they could find out where he lived, she surprised the crew again by directing them to the missing man's home three blocks away.

When they arrived, an elderly woman answered the door. They asked for the man by name and she said she would go get him. He was indeed the man they were looking for. A short time later, the seventy-eight-year-old man was reunited with his son, who had instigated the search, after a separation of thirty-four years.

By the end of 2004, McMoneagle had made ten trips to Tokyo for the television production company and found seven missing persons.

Rob e-mailed his cousin, Russell Walstedt, a nuclear physicist who lived in Japan, and asked him to watch the program. Since Russell was skeptical about psychic abilities and Rob had known McMoneagle for a few years, he was eager to hear Russell's assessment.

After watching the psychic detective program broadcast from Tokyo, Russell wrote back. "The remote viewing guy is indeed amazing, if actually genuine." He went on to say that the crew was still looking for two of the three people they asked McMoneagle to locate. However, Russell was baffled by how he had located even one of them.

"Remote viewing," McMoneagle wrote in *Remote Viewing Secrets* "is not simply using psychic ability to obtain information. It is using scientific protocol to *develop* and *extend* that ability, so that ordinary people can learn to do what psychics do."

RENIE WILEY, ADAM WALSH, AND CHRISTIE LUNA

Renie was a South Florida artist and psychic who often volunteered her services with the Cooper City police. Her work on two well-known cases beautifully illustrates two facets of clairvoyance—psychometry and empathy.

Renie was a tall, large-boned woman, a redhead with a kick-your-ass attitude who dominated any room she entered, any gathering she joined. She was opinionated, funny, stubborn, smart and sassy. She was an ace astrologer who mentored Trish and a psychic with such raw talent that one Cooper City cop began to use her in his investigations.

In 1982, Renie and the cop were driving near a mall in Hollywood, Florida, where Adam Walsh was last seen in Sears on July 27, 1981, shopping with his mother. The cop hoped that Renie might be able to pick up something psychically about the missing boy—where he was, what had happened to him, if he'd been abducted.

At this point, the police believed he'd been abducted, but didn't have any leads. Renie didn't have an object that had belonged to Adam, but posters of the boy were found everywhere around South Florida and they wrenched at your heart. His huge, innocent eyes whispered, *I am your son, your brother, your cousin, your neighbor.* His face had been burned into the collective consciousness and that seemed to be all that Renie needed.

When she and the cop were within a few miles of the mall, Renie's hands suddenly flew to her throat. She started choking, gasping for air. The cop had worked with her often enough to realize she was picking up something related to Adam and quickly sped away. Several miles later, he swerved to the side of the road.

"What is it, Renie?"

She sobbed. "Adam was decapitated."

Not long afterward, the head of the six-year-old boy was discovered in a canal in Vero Beach, Florida, more than a hundred miles north of the Hollywood mall. In 2008, Ottis Toole, a serial killer serving five life sentences for murder, confessed on his deathbed that he had killed Adam. Toole died of liver cancer at the age of forty-nine.

We observed Renie in action two years later, on a dismal, rainy night in late 1984. We drove with her to the police department in Greenacres, Florida to see what she could pick up on a missing girl. Eight-year-old Christie Luna had vanished near her home in Greenacres on May 24, 1984.

Around three p.m., she had walked to a store to buy cat food and never returned. Police suspected foul play.

Renie had requested toys that Christie played with, her way of connecting with the girl. She sat on the floor of the police station clutching an old teddy bear, running her hands over it. Her eyes were shut as she rocked back and forth, humming softly. Everything about Renie at that moment suggested a small, childlike person. She started to whimper, then cry, then sob, her body hunched over the teddy bear.

"The mother's boyfriend used to beat up on her," Renie murmured. "She's deaf in one ear because of it." The deafness was later confirmed by Christie's mother.

We left the station with the officer and drove around Greenacres, through the wet darkness. Christie's teddy bear was on Renie's lap as we passed the house where the girl had lived and the store where she was headed when she vanished. Renie directed us through one street after another until we came to a wooded area surrounded by a high wire-mesh fence. Renie disliked what she was feeling and turned to the officer. "You should search in there."

Renie felt the girl had been killed by the mother's boyfriend, but Christie Luna's body was never found and the case, as of 2013, remains open and unsolved.

Renie passed away in the mid 1990s. But in 2008, twenty-four years after she had clutched Christie Luna's teddy bear, both she and the case entered our lives again, through a strange and startling synchronicity.

Dennie Gooding, a psychic in L.A., called to say she was going to be in South Florida, and hoped we could get together. Nancy McMoneagle, Joe McMoneagle's wife, also called and said she was going to be in South Florida the same weekend. As it turned out, they had both been invited by the wife of a detective, who was investigating a cold case. They would be staying with her in Greenacres, less than ten miles from our home. Their visit synchronistically coincided with that of author and past-life researcher Carol Bowman, and screenwriter Julie Scully. So we decided to throw a party on the weekend when everyone would be in town.

The morning of the party, we found an uncashed check for $50 from Renie, dated 1987, the repayment of a loan. We wondered where the check had been all these years. We had moved twice since the check had been written and why had it suddenly turned up now? We didn't think any more about it until later that evening, when the party was in full swing, and we were catching up on things with Dennie.

"So what kind of case are you working on with the cop?" Trish asked.

She then proceeded to describe the unsolved mystery of a girl from Greenacres who'd gone missing in 1984 and was presumed dead. "But her body has never been found."

Goosebumps crawled up Trish's arms. "The Christie Luna case?"

Dennie looked shocked. "How'd you know that?"

Trish told her about Renie and that night twenty-four years earlier, then went over to a drawer and brought out the check from Renie.

"Synchronicity!" Dennie exclaimed.

Dennie wasn't able to locate Christie's body. But interestingly, when she and the cop in charge of the cold case were driving around, she pinpointed the same area that Renie had—several acres of undeveloped, government-owned land, enclosed by a metal fence. "I feel she's buried in there."

The synchronicities in this confluence of events are startling. Not only did Dennie pinpoint the same area that Renie had, but on the day we learned of Dennie's involvement in the case, we found the check Renie had written us decades ago. It was as if both Renie and Christie Luna were nudging us all and awaiting justice.

Chapter 13
REMOTE VIEWS: CONNECTING
WITH JOE MCMONEAGLE

Joe McMoneagle was born January 10, 1946, in Miami, Florida. He was Remote Viewer #001 in the U.S. Army's previously classified Stargate program, and was awarded the Legion of Merit for his contribution to various intelligence operations. He and his work have been featured in *Newsweek, Time, Reader's Digest*, and on ABC's *Nightline* and CBS's *48 Hours*, and on prime-time British and Japanese television. He currently teaches remote viewing at the Monroe Institute in Virginia.

He's the author of *Mind Trek: Exploring Consciousness, Time, and Space Through Remote Viewing; The Ultimate Time Machine: A Remote Viewer's Perception of Time; Predictions for the New Millennium; Remote Viewing Secrets: A Handbook*; and *The Stargate Chronicles: Memoirs of a Psychic Spy*. He and his wife, Nancy, and their many "fur children" live near Charlottesville, Virginia.

He graciously agreed to an interview.

Before you read this interview, be sure to read chapter 12 so you have a better idea of the process involved when Joe remote views and, specifically, about the remote viewing session concerning Mars.

1) In your book, *Mind Trek*, you talk about a near death experience (NDE) you had in 1970 as the event that charted your life's path. Can you tell us about that?

A very good friend brought my first wife to a Gästehaus, an inn, in Braunau, Austria where we would all spend a fun evening together. My memory is that it was sometime in July of 1970. It was early evening when we all arrived, so we decided to have a drink before our meal. After taking a few sips from my drink I began to feel very nauseous, so not wanting to be sick in front of many diners, I excused myself from the table and tried to exit the restaurant. I remember getting just to the door and as I pushed on it, there was a "pop" and I found myself standing over cobblestones in the street and watching rain passing through my upturned palms.

As I looked up, I could see a body laying half in and half out of a swinging glass door. While I slowly drifted over, I watched my friend exit the door and drop to the pavement, dragging the body up into his lap, where he began striking the body in the center of the chest with his fist while yelling at it. That's when I noticed the body was actually me.

They didn't wait for an ambulance, but instead loaded me into an automobile and drove me directly to a hospital located in Passau, on the German side of the border. As they drove away, I followed, literally flying along beside the car. I watched as they unloaded my body at the emergency room door. I watched the whole process as they cut off my clothing and inserted tubes in my nose and connected IV lines, and got progressively more bored with the whole thing. I was sure I was dead and wanted to just move on.

I felt heat on the back of my neck, so I thought I had floated up against the ceiling and the bright lights inside the emergency room. I turned to see what it was, and found myself falling downward through a tunnel, where I then reviewed the actions of my entire life up until that point. At the end of this life review, I fell out of the tunnel into an enveloping white light, which was soft, warm, but very intense. At that point I felt suddenly as though I was completely whole again, that I knew all the answers to any questions I might have. I was home again. I was complete and totally comfortable there, just being within the light.

But a voice deep inside me said; "You can't stay, you have to go back and finish what you've started." I tried to argue with the voice, but to no avail. There was a second "pop" and I found myself sitting up naked under a white sheet, staring down at another patient lying next to me. I told him in broken German and English, "You can't die, God is a white light, and you should fear nothing."

He quickly left the room and fetched the doctor who then sedated me. As a result, of this whole experience, I was transferred to a wing of a rest home somewhere in Munich, where they spent quite a bit of time trying to figure out how much brain damage I suffered.

What I didn't know was that during that evening before, I had gone into convulsions while lying on the ground outside the restaurant. I swallowed my tongue, which is why they couldn't wait for the ambulance. It took almost thirty minutes to get me to the hospital. Once you swallow your tongue, it's only minutes until you stop breathing, and then your heart stops and then you are dead. So, when they got me to the emergency room I was already DOA. I had been dead for fifteen to eighteen minutes. They have no idea how I survived, but were sure that I had suffered severe brain damage since I had been dead for that period of time.

Subsequent testing showed that aside from earlier damage as a result of my service in Southeast Asia, I had suffered no additional brain injuries. But the changes to my belief systems and how I understood things to work, were significant—like being hit by a Mack Truck. This was very disturbing to the United States Army.

2) In 1978, you began working with Hal Puthoff and Russell Targ at Stanford Research Institute International. How did those experiences help you understand the after-effects of your NDE?

My work with Hal Puthoff and Russell Targ at SRI International was only testing to determine if I was qualified to participate in the new US Army Special Project using psychics to target the Soviet Union. I later worked with Hal for a short period before he left SRI International for another lab in Austin, Texas.

The person I worked with the most at SRI International was Dr. Edwin May. He is the one who actually raised more than three quarters of the research money and did approximately seventy percent of what the program science requirements consisted of. He and I have worked together more than thirty-three years.

As to the second portion of the question, I'm not sure I'll ever completely understand the after effects of an NDE. I feel very strongly that I made some rather gross assumptions about what different things might have meant during the NDE, so my belief has changed rather radically since the experience. I no longer believe, for example, that the white light is God. It feels more like that's what we probably are when we are no longer physical. As energy beings, it makes sense, since we are created in the image of our Maker. It's the reason we feel so complete, whole, and feel as though we know all the answers to the cosmos. We truly are spiritual beings.

3) In 1979, you experienced a type of synchronicity that is often referred to as the "library angel." In this kind of synchronicity, you're browsing

a bookstore or library and a certain book "falls" at your feet or is on a table where you sit down. And this book happens to address a concern you have. It's the right information at the right time. In your experience, a book was lying on the floor in an aisle—*Journeys Out of Body* by Robert Monroe. Tell us why this synchronicity was so powerful for you.

It opened the original door I had tried to shut after my experience in Austria back in 1970. I had been having repetitive out-of-body experiences (OBEs) ever since my NDE in Austria. I couldn't stop them from happening, and I couldn't account for them. I didn't know what was causing them, and either wanted to understand why they were happening, or wanted them to stop.

When I read Bob Monroe's book, I understood that it was okay, the OBEs weren't something that should make me nervous, or something that I should fear. I made a point to visit with Bob Monroe very soon afterwards and as a result was able to open even more doors in my quest to understand. I visited him often, attended seminars at The Monroe Institute, and began working with Bob in his lab in Central Virginia. He expanded my awareness and abilities in a big way.

4) We ran across a transcript of an RV session you did in 1984 that was fascinating. You were handed a sealed envelope with a 3X5 index card inside with three sentences on it—the target you were supposed to view. You didn't look at the card and the envelope wasn't opened until the RV session was finished. Written on the card was: the planet Mars, time of interest approximately 1 million years B.C. Your monitor then gave you a set of geographical coordinates. Can you tell us about that viewing? Do you recall how you felt at the time about what you were seeing? How did your monitor choose those coordinates? And why were there so many of them?

At the time, I was working with Bob Monroe in his lab over extended weekends. This had been set up by the Army in the hopes that it would shorten my cooldown periods and extend my abilities to remote view. I was becoming very stressed by the demands within the Stargate Project. From approximately mid-1982 until September 1 of 1984 I was the only remote viewer left within the unit, so I was carrying the full load. This was beginning to wear thin. Bob was working with me in his lab to try and reduce the stress and increase my ability to respond. During this period of working with Bob, they would occasionally bring down a test target to see how I was doing. It could be a target of importance or simply one utilized to test my abilities.

On this one occasion, I was taking a nap during lunch hour inside the controlled isolation chamber in the lab, when Bob woke me up by announcing that he had a target for me. Lieutenant Skip Atwater had brought him a card with seven sets of coordinates on it, and an envelope that was sealed. Bob told me he had the target envelope in his shirt pocket and that he would read off the coordinates to me one at a time, and I was to describe what I saw at each set. I agreed.

What I remember is that the first coordinate was a huge pyramid, like none I'd ever seen before. I asked him if this was a new discovery, because it seemed this was larger than the one at Giza, Egypt. He said he didn't know, all he had was the sealed envelope and the coordinates. So, I described it to him. He gave me another coordinate and this one appeared to be some kind of a ruin. And on it went.

I remember at one point looking up at the location and getting a very strange impression of the sun. I told Bob, "The sun, it looks very weird."

He said: "I'm not interested in the sun, I'm interested in what's at the coordinate."

Onward we went. At the end of the session neither he nor I could figure out what this target was—it was mostly ruins, a few pyramid shapes, and feelings like the whole thing had to do with the preservation of life, the need to pass along a great deal of information. I began seeing a race of people who were very much like us, but much larger—like, *huge* larger—over ten feet in height. And these people were fighting to stay alive, were building hibernation chambers inside pyramids, and trying to put aside information for those who might come later, informing them of what had gone wrong.

In any event, when we finished the remote viewing effort, Skip Atwater asked Bob to open the envelope and tell us what was inside. The card within the envelope said: "MARS ONE MILLION BC." It really surprised both of us.

The coordinates were for specific locations on a certain area of Mars, which included what appeared to be ruins, lots of pyramids of different shapes and designs. I asked Skip where the coordinates had come from. He said they originated with the Jet Propulsion Laboratory (NASA).

When I was doing the viewing, I kept getting a really sad feeling—these people were losing their home, and a handful had volunteered to stay behind to try and set up messages for those who might come after them. I got the distinct feeling that the pyramids were being set up to be used as hibernation chambers, and some point at some time in the near future they had an expectation that someone would eventually find them and understand what they did to save their people. It was very moving. I don't think I expected such a powerful response to the remote viewing.

5) How does remote viewing differ from clairvoyance?

Remote viewing is being psychic under very strict controls, specifically a protocol that ensures the remote viewer or psychic does not know anything at all about the target they are viewing. Clairvoyance is being psychic, but within which there are no controls at all.

The other differences are that a remote viewer will also get more than just information about the target; they will get pertinent noises, tastes, smells, feelings, and sometimes actually hear things that are pertinent. Clairvoyance is almost always spontaneous; remote viewing is deliberately targeting something identified within a sealed envelope.

6) Do you think RV was used in the hunt for Bin Laden? If not, would his location have been determined much earlier with remote viewing?

I have no idea if remote viewing was used to hunt for Bin Laden. I have been used to hunt for numerous individuals but was never informed as to their identity. Sometimes I got feedback that my information proved to be of extreme value, and sometimes they never told me what my information was used for, or if it was used at all.

What one must understand about someone as important as Bin Laden is that they probably actually knew where to find him for some time. When it comes to intelligence information, everything has to be looked at within the context in which it exists.

For instance, they've been collecting information of all kinds on Bin Laden for many years. They probably knew more about him than he knew about himself. Over time, they developed an understanding for how he thought, what he was planning, who he communicated with and how he even communicated the information. It's probably the reason Al Qaida has been so ineffectual for so long.

So, once you've been able to eradicate a person's effectiveness, to otherwise neutralize them and/or eliminate them from the game, then even if you knew exactly where that person is, why would you want to pick them up and then have them replaced by someone you now know nothing about at all? That would be the last thing you'd want to do.

In Bin Laden's case, he outlived his ability to lead. His own people realized he had been marginalized, so they decided to sidestep him as their all-powerful leader and go to a new leader instead. Once they decided to go around him, his value as a leader dropped. Now his only value would be political. That's when someone within the administration decided it was time to take him out altogether.

7) In your book, *Remote Viewing Secrets* you have a chapter on the ethics of RV. What constitutes ethical behavior in RV and improper behavior?

Ethics and morality aren't something that someone should have to tell us about. It is something we should already be doing, simply because we feel an obligation. Our obligation is always to others.

A person who calls himself a remote viewer, by necessity, has to follow certain rules of the road, so to speak. The first question you should consider when asked to remote view a target is: "Should I be doing this?" If you feel the least bit nervous about remote viewing something, then you shouldn't be doing it.

It goes without saying that you should never use remote viewing for illicit reasons, in a way that violates someone else's rights or freedoms, nor should you use it to find something or someone that will violate the privacy of an individual. This means there are many cases where one shouldn't be using remote viewing because the target triggers one of these questionable issues.

As an example, industrial espionage is something remote viewing should never be used for. It shouldn't be used to promote profiteering or support increases in one's possessions in an unethical way. It should not be used to expand on acts of racism, to terrorize someone, to take something from someone that rightfully belongs to them, or be used against someone in a way that exceeds justice within the law. There are even times when the context within which it will be used might cast a negative view on its use, so it should not be used.

It is especially difficult keeping to its ethical use when making an appearance on television. For instance, when a person has been pulled from the crowd [the audience] and you are asked to do something with that person to prove remote viewing's efficacy—"Tell us what this woman's home looks like!"—it could be unethical under certain circumstances since it might upset the person dragged from the audience. A description of the outside of the house might be ethical, but the inside isn't. In such a case, the remote viewer may have to deliberately fail in the viewing or refuse to do it. Not something anyone wants to have to decide while appearing before millions on national television. But, it has happened.

Ethics and morality cannot be delegated to another individual. We are all responsible for our own actions and as to how moral or ethical they may be. This holds true, whether or not you are talking about remote viewing or anything else.

8) In precognitive remote viewing, do you see several possible paths or just one path? Or does that depend on what you're trying to view?

I never see possible paths of outcome. While there may be millions of other possibilities when it comes to outcome in the future, there's only one that will happen, that's the one that will occur. So, if someone says they can't see what will happen because there are just too many possibilities, they do not understand remote viewing. There is only one and will only be one outcome at the time the outcome must occur—so while there are a multitude of possible outcomes, there will only be one that is reported on using remote viewing.

Some will say: "Then that is called predestination or predetermination."

No, it isn't. Since free will decides the actions and the outcomes that will eventually occur, remote viewing only reports on what those will be. A remote viewer isn't determining outcome, he/she is simply reporting on what it will be—what free choice and action have already determined that it will be. So, no matter what a remote viewer or psychic says about the future, it is nothing more than a good guess as to outcome. If they are right, then that is it, they are simply right. If it is wrong, then they've missed. They should then accept full responsibility for failure and not try and blame it on anything else.

9) Other than the tall, thin entities you remote viewed on Mars, have you ever seen any other alien entities? Or the inside of a craft?

Yes, I have. I've been working on two or three UFO incidents that I believe are truly alien craft and not some mistaken crash site that includes our own aircraft. When I first started viewing these targets, I kept getting the same thing over and over again. It looked like the old hippie peace sign, a large "Y" inside a circle. Only the circle was missing. So, it looked like an equilateral "Y" with angles all the same, and lengths of each line all the same. I couldn't get past this image for many months until I finally had an epiphany.

The "Y" *is the inside or outside corner of an empty box.* I suddenly realized they, whoever they are, had given me a target so simple that it almost defied description or at least understanding. As soon as I discovered this, the target then constantly morphed into entire boxes. They have been able to block me on nearly a consistent basis. But, *nearly consistent,* isn't all the time. Once in a while I've been able to catch a peek behind the boxes, and to see things I'm sure they do not expect me to see.

Over more than three years, I've been able to see only once in a while. In those instances I've seen control systems that are part biological and part physical, so I would have to say their ships are hybrid systems made up of grown materials within material frameworks. They communicate with their ships much as we would consider mind-to-mind communications to be.

I've also seen what I call their "Skin Suits" which are the environmental suits they must wear if they are exposed to our atmosphere. They are highly vulnerable to our biological systems. They are deeply afraid of the many viruses and biological agents we carry within our bodies and that are swimming in our air and waters or found within our animals and plants, and the very dirt at our feet. They have little immunity to them. So, they wear hazard suits, or what I call skin suits, to protect themselves.

Whenever they re-board their ships, they must immerse themselves in order to eradicate all these elements. These skin suits hide their features completely, and make them all look the same. The large eyes people report are the protective lenses that cover their eyes.

Likewise, these skin suits protect them from us as well. Our instinctive reactions would kick in if one of them appeared in its natural state to us. Our reactions would be instant and violent. They understand that we are a violent and reactive species and that is one of the reasons they do not make contact with us openly, but only do so when the circumstances are right and they are in full control.

We think we are their equals, but this is simply arrogance. They are half a million years ahead of us, in capability. They jump star-to-star without effort, and operate on ancient rules that far and away transcend our understanding for how things work. Our belief in their abilities as alien creatures is pitifully underreaching, and we are quite primitive in our understanding for their limits and abilities. And while we might consider them butt ugly, they consider us to be half a step behind a chimp in our development.

I continue to try and remote view the interior of their craft and see what they obviously do not want me to see. Sometimes I get the sense that they let me see what they feel I can handle, and bit by bit I'm developing a slightly better view of what they are and what their intent might be. My feeling is that it would be seriously in error to believe that we have any kind of intelligent equality to their actuality.

But, one thing is clearly apparent to me—they do have a belief in a higher form or overall creator, but it is nothing like ours might be. Their God is not the god of our fathers, nor is it a God that aspires to know us better, or that we aspire to understand. It is a God of rules that are very clearly stated and understood. These rules as they understand them, dictate that if you understand, then you live—if you do not understand, you die.

10) Have you ever remote viewed the alleged crash in Roswell in 1947? If so, what did you find?

Yes, I have remote viewed the alleged crash at Roswell. I do not believe it ever happened. It is my belief that the real crash was a two-part crash that took place in Socorro, New Mexico, approximately 170 miles west-north-west of Roswell. It is actually almost due west, just south of Albuquerque, and just north of Truth and Consequences. A crash occurred there that is almost never referred to. If someone brings up the crash at Socorro, however, almost without exception, Roswell becomes the front-page news. They use Roswell as a distraction to draw people away from the crash site at Socorro, which I believe is the more important crash site.

There is still a great deal of material that can be found at and around the Socorro crash site, while there is none to be found near Roswell. Roswell is a cover. The materials found surrounding the Socorro site are well established as being from a very high intensity, very hot impact. The heat created at Socorro probably exceeded 1800 degrees in places immediately following the vehicle crash.

It is also my belief that there were at least two crashes at the Socorro site, which occurred exactly twenty years apart almost to the minute. There are reasons for this as well. The Socorro site represents an ingress/egress point into and out of our time/space locale—a specific requirement attached to their modality of travel star-to-star.

11) What is the most distant point in the past that you have remote viewed? What's the most distant point in the future you have remote viewed?

The most distant time into the past that I've remote viewed is the beginnings of life on planet Earth. This represents hundreds of millions of years and goes back to a time when the planets had different orbits and different positions within the solar system. Mars was inside Earth's orbit, and both of their orbits were outside those of Saturn and Venus.

Since then a lot has changed, to include the loss of a planet that now no longer exists, but has become the asteroid belt. Saturn has many moons, but now has a much larger orbit outside our own, and its rings are the remnants of three moons that used to circle the planet. We switched places with Mars approximately two million years ago, and this resulted in Mars's demise as a life-bearing world. There have been many changes.

The most distant time in the future would have to be the end of our star and the death of our world as a result. This takes place over a period of tens of thousands of years. It occurs in a number of steps that first freezes then heats up our planet Earth to the point it basically dissolves to dust and is sucked back into the core of our Sun. We will have chosen another place to live long before this should occur.

By the time this happens, we will have terra-formed Mars back into another Earth-type planet. We will have transformed a number of asteroids into a number of deep-space exploration ships, and we will have made contact with other beings from at least three other star systems. Our rule books will have changed by then to include those providing us with a deeper understanding of our origins than would have ever been possible with a belief in a Creator. Humanistic understanding will have reformed to an understanding of the importance of life itself, why we exist, and what our responsibilities are within at least our own universe if not back to the beginning of time, and other things which are just not explicable within our current context.

12) Do you think RV is still being used by the government, but outsourced?

No, I don't. The reason I don't is because I was intimately involved from the beginning to the end of the original Stargate Program.

It was my experience that the politics and general angst that developed between the people involved scientifically, politically, militarily, and in all ways was just too aggressively destructive and caustic to allow its existence at all. The damage caused by those who supported it was far more damaging and extensive than the damage caused by those who despised it. And those who despised it did sufficient damage to ruin what little was known and accepted as ground truth for decades to come.

It is inherently threatening to the very system it was designed to support. There is absolutely no known defense against it, except the fact that it fails sufficiently on its own. Everyone was afraid of it for obvious reasons, and no one was willing to trust it, since they couldn't come to agreement as to whether or not it was the work of the devil or a God-given gift. Remote viewers within the unit were sometimes egotistically out of control, believed things about it that couldn't possibly be true. Those who thought it was a ridiculous exercise in fraudulent behavior went out of their way to destroy whatever validity might have existed.

And in the end, those who might have liked to bury it within the system and to keep using it, lacked whatever courage might have been necessary to get the job done.

That doesn't even address the mechanics of its use—how to insert its product within a system that absolutely has to understand the origin and validity of its own information. This system must have full knowledge and understanding in order to choose participants with a stable and unbreakable mental stability, a lack of ego, a drive to succeed that transcended their own day-to-day needs, and who clearly had a desire to consistently and routinely do the right thing no matter the outcome. But this proved to be completely beyond the capacity of any governmental body or agency currently working in Washington, D.C.

And for those reasons, no, it's simply not possible. And I've not even gotten into the monetary, protection, application, or exploitation complications such a unit would be faced with in a day-to-day routine. I wish I could believe differently, but I don't.

13) What are your current projects? Any new books in the works?

I'm looking at ways that we may save our own planet from our destructive ways, and trying to come to grips with what the rules might be for making contact with another species from another star. Obviously this requires an understanding for a different set of rules than those within which we currently operate, and a completely different understanding for what is important.

I'm attempting to write a book on the ethics and morality for the field of the paranormal. Whether or not I'm able to finish this before I quit being human is another matter entirely. I'm also writing more within the non-fiction area regarding remote viewing and some of the deeper logic that supports it. Much of this is counter-intuitive and beyond the reach of many who aspire to be better remote viewers. So, I'd like to share this before I give up remote viewing completely.

I'm getting more and more into sculpture and art, specifically oils and drawings in ink. Whether or not I'm successful is probably going to be an outcome I can't hang around for. I've almost finished re-building a 1986 4x4 Chevy truck, to include a 400 HP engine. I needed it for dump runs. My next goal will probably be a much older car or some kind just to see if I can do it. The engineering challenges are wonderful mental exercises. I'm also trying to squeeze a jet-ski engine and propulsion system into a small fishing kayak about fourteen feet long and thirty inches wide.

I continue to provide remote viewing support to my Japanese friends whenever they approach me with a new inquiry about their history's mysteries. I provide support to the development of new medications as well as new methods for medication development. I ponder how and where we come from, why we have so many diversities within our species called human, and how to improve the human dilemma.

Sometimes I get the sense that there are more important things in life, and when I discover what those are, I will share them with others. Until then, I'll continue to use RV to support businesses and people in any way I can. I will use it ethically and in ways that are beneficial to as many as possible.

–Joseph McMoneagle, CW2, USA, Retired, CStS.

Part Three:
THE SKYWAY

"Because politics is the art of the possible, it appeals only to second-rate minds. The first raters… (are) only interested in the impossible."

–Arthur C. Clarke, *The Fountain of Paradise*

Chapter 14
THE ABDUCTION SCENARIO

ENCOUNTER IN GERMANY

In May of 2013, we received an e-mail from Katy Walker, a documentary film producer who had heard us on a radio show/podcast called *Mysterious Universe,* talking about UFO encounters and synchronicity. Coincidentally, her company was making a documentary film on synchronicity and she wanted to talk to us. We made tentative arrangements for an interview in Miami later in the year.

Katy told us that her life was not only filled with meaningful coincidences, but that she'd had an alien encounter herself years ago in a remote forested area of eastern Germany. So we turned the tables and interviewed her.

The incident occurred in 1998, and began after she and a friend, Oliver, arrived in a tiny remote village where his parents owned a cottage. They went to a restaurant not far from the cottage and while sitting outside, kept hearing a strange sound, like the bleating of a calf. "We thought it was an animal at first but then as it continued, it became really disturbing."

After eating, they went back to the cottage and Katy off-handedly said that it would be cool to talk to an alien. It was a peculiar thing for her to say. "It was not my thought. At age nineteen, I had never even thought about the possibility that there might be intelligent life other than humans."

Oliver looked at her oddly, then went outside to see if he could find what was making the noise. That was the last she would see of him for three hours.

As she puzzled over why she'd made such an odd comment, a blinding light beamed through the front window. After a few moments, she saw extremely long fingers touching the glass and the silhouette of skinny beings looking in at her. She knew instinctively that they were implanting thoughts in her mind so she would cooperate. But she wanted nothing to do with them. She scrambled away, raced up to the attic, and hid in the corner.

For three hours, Katy fought them off mentally, struggling to push them out of her mind, her consciousness, refusing to go with them. "It's not a good feeling to have something put into your mind when you don't really believe it. I'm extremely headstrong, and they finally gave up. I suspect they figured it wasn't worth it. Otherwise, they probably would've come up to the attic."

She's convinced that Oliver was taken and concedes that might be the reason they left her alone. "Maybe I wasn't really of interest to them." She noted that she's never had any other alien contact experiences and pointed out that most abductees are taken repeatedly over decades.

She also wonders if her and Oliver's memories were erased, because they never spoke about the incident. "I don't remember what happened when he came back. I just know it was a very long time and I was angry that he didn't have an explanation for why he was gone so long."

In late July, we heard from Katy again. The filming of the synchro project was underway in San Francisco and the entire crew was encountering synchronicities. Primarily, they were about owls, but also about butterflies. After several days of seeing these images on book covers, T-shirts, earrings, and elsewhere, something peculiar happened the day they filmed in the Mission District of San Francisco, near an area famous for its wall-to-wall graffiti murals.

Everyone seemed more emotional that day, and Katy wondered why she was feeling the same way. The owls and butterflies were everywhere. "There must have been six or seven murals with references to owls, some of them had hypnotic eyes, some looked sinister, and some looked half-asleep. To me, they seemed to represent mind control, anger, and complacency," she said.

Owls have been a red flag for her ever since her alien encounter. More than any other creature, they remind her of the aliens. In fact, in UFO lore, aliens have the ability to shape shift into owls and apparently do so at times in order to create screen memories for abductees.

Besides the owls, there were many Day-of-the-Dead Mexican folk art pieces and several Aztec murals. One mural in particular attracted Katy's attention. It featured a tiny owl in a tree and next to it was a Hopi Indian medicine man with light energy emanating from his hands. The light was directed at a hybrid human/alien. On the other side was a Gray. "Spaceships surrounded the scene, blending into the tail of a giant blue whale, which symbolized the merger of dimensions or realities. Even though these ideas were already familiar to me, I got a crazy feeling from the visionary mural."

After viewing it, she headed back over to where the rest of the crew was filming a sinister looking Aztec face with gigantic teeth. It was around this time when a rectangular UFO barely higher than the trees cruised by. Even though it was daylight, no one saw it. But it appeared on the monitor later when they reviewed the day's filming. It's visible for just a few seconds, but the image is clear and the UFO moves slowly before disappearing behind tall trees.

"My explanation for the UFO clip is that my higher self/spirit guides recorded this projection to prove the existence of aliens not only to me but to others who are on the fence," Katy said. "These various synchronicities have also opened my mind to the realization that not only do we have entities helping us, but we have many working against us."

ON THE FENCE

Let's say you have some doubts about the reality of UFOs and alien abductions. You're on the fence, not sure what you think. You've never seen a UFO or had any kind of encounter. But you've heard the stories and wondered why anyone would make up such crazy tales. And why there apparently are so many people telling similar stories.

Possibly, someone whose judgment you trust has said something like this: *There are no spacecrafts from elsewhere visiting this planet and therefore no one is being abducted by aliens.* Even if you tend to agree with that opinion, and many people do at this time, there's something disturbingly bizarre going on. Hundreds of thousands of people, possibly millions in the United States alone, believe they have been taken aboard alien spacecraft and subjected to experiments and medical procedures. So what's that all about?

But wait, you say. If that were true, why isn't the FBI looking into these cases? And where are the witnesses? Aren't these so-called abductions simply vivid dreams or instances of dream paralysis? Or perhaps they're due to overactive imaginations during hypnotic regression or outright hoaxes or evidence of mental illness.

Actually, studies have shown that abductees are no more prone to mental illness than the rest of the population. Many abductees recall their experiences, or parts of them, without hypnosis, and many were awake and not in bed when they were abducted, making the dream scenario irrelevant. Since most abductees avoid publicity and don't want their names used, it seems unlikely they would perpetrate hoaxes. Regarding witnesses, abductions are typically discreet and any witnesses tend to become abductees themselves. Such witnesses might have their memories of the incident erased or screen memories implanted.

It's a complicated matter, and it's best to let the experiencers tell their stories so we can better understand what might be happening.

MONTREAL ABDUCTEE

Shortly after *Aliens in the Backyard* was published in February 2013, we were guests on *Coast to Coast* with George Noory. In the aftermath, we received e-mails from listeners, some of whom had never told anyone about their life-long abduction experiences. A couple of abductees mentioned that they just happened to turn on the radio as we were talking about synchronicity and abductions. They had never heard anyone link the two, though it's exactly what they have experienced.

Maurice, a forty-three-year-old French Canadian, says that his experiences have been so strange he has had a difficult time believing them himself. They began in 1975, at the age of five. His mother had gone into labor, so his parents sent him and his older sister to their grandparents' home, where the first incident occurred.

"I know it was late because it was dark. I clearly recall playing in the basement with my tricycle. I looked at the window and saw six grey metallic boots and tight metallic pants covering very skinny legs. I was suddenly covered by a milky white light and I don't remember anything else. To this day, I can't go down that basement myself. I shift into a panic mode just at the thought of going down there. This is but one of the numerous unpleasant memories that haunt me."

On January 26, 2013, Maurice was in bed next to his wife, fast asleep, when shortly after midnight his lower body lifted off the bed. As he woke up, his upper body also lifted up so that he found himself completely suspended in the air over his bed, with his wife sound asleep. "I couldn't move. I was thinking, *You son of a bitch, leave me alone, I'm not in the mood for this crap tonight.*" Then he was flung like a whip to the door of the room.

"My head was pointed at the floor where a small, pale-skin humanoid with large eyes and a large head was standing. There was maybe an inch between my nose and his face A voice in my head said, *I own you.* That was all he remembered. When he realized he was back in bed, he glanced at the clock. It was 2:20 a.m. More than two hours had passed. "I have memories of such activities throughout my entire life."

The next day, his wife commented that she had never had such a good night's sleep. She suffers from sleep apnea and never sleeps more than two or three hours without waking up. On that night, she'd slept eight hours. Maurice has never spoken about his experiences to anyone except his wife, who thinks he simply has a fertile imagination. She always has discouraged him from talking to others about these experiences and reminds him that her uncle was ridiculed and ostracized by her family for talking about his UFO sighting.

But when Maurice heard us on *Coast to Coast* describing a UFO encounter experienced by another man from Quebec, it was a meaningful coincidence for him, and he decided to speak up for the first time. "It made me realize that I'm not the only person in this part of the world who has gone through some crazy stuff that can't be mentioned publicly. I work in the engineering field, and we are generally very analytical and pragmatic. If I speak of this using my real name, my job could be at stake."

However, as long as we used a pseudonym, he was willing to tell us about his experiences. When he was eight or nine years old, he woke up one night at about 2 a.m. and felt an urge to go the dining room. Once there, he looked out through a large bay window and saw a red dot in the sky. The dot grew larger until it was a big sphere. A beam of light shot from this object and lifted him up. "I recall seeing the window getting closer and closer. I was bracing for the impact and, just like that, floated through the window towards this red sphere. The next thing I remember, I'm in the basement. So I walked back to my room and the clock said 3:30 a.m. My mom woke up and asked me why I was awake. I just looked at her and didn't say a word. I had and still have today this feeling of helplessness."

About a year later, another incident occurred while he was on the playground at school during afternoon recess. The bell rang, telling the students to return to class. As he walked from the far end of the yard, he saw a metallic object moving at a slow speed directly overhead, at an altitude of 250 or 300 feet. "It was forty feet across and resembled two attached wok dish covers. The underbelly of the craft looked burnt, like someone had taken a giant blowtorch to it. I saw it for about ten seconds then it shot straight up without a sound. When I got inside, I started asking other kids if they had seen the strange object in the sky. Three of my classmates said that they had."

Sometimes after he has been abducted, Maurice finds what look like paper cuts on his arms and hands. He also thinks he might have an implant in his sinus cavity. A little over two years ago, he was hospitalized with severe stomach pains, and the nurse had to insert a tube down his nose to collect some gastric acid from my stomach. However, something in his left nasal passage prevented the tube from moving in to his throat. The nurse moved to the right nostril and the tube was inserted without any problem.

In 1994, when Maurice was twenty-four he moved to Austria to learn German and downhill ski racing. He wanted to race in the FIS World Cup, the top international circuit of alpine skiing, and he needed to improve his world ranking. He lived in a small town called Zell am See in central Austria, not far from the city of Salzburg.

One night in January, he woke up at 2 a.m. feeling terrified and overwhelmed by a sense of impending doom. His blinds were closed, but suddenly the room was inundated with white light. The next thing he remembered, he was pinned to a vertical table in what looked like an underground cavern with a rocky ceilings and rocky walls. Other people were also strapped to tables in the room, and they all appeared to be unconscious.

"Men in lab coats and small, milky, beige-colored beings were moving about. Two men with weapons were standing not far from me, and one of the little bastards was in front of me. A voice in my head said, *You are not to speak of this to anyone.* I felt my head being pushed down, my chin was driven into my chest and I felt the back of my neck being stretched to its limit. *I won't. I promise,* I answered. The next thing I remembered, I was back in his bed and it was 3:30 a.m."

In April, Rob contacted Maurice again and asked if he had any more contact with the beings. His answer was terse. "Please do not contact me again. After I told you my story, I started receiving telephone calls over and over again from distant places where I don't know anyone. When I answered, they would hang up. Maybe it was a warning. I don't know, but I am saying nothing more."

His terror is palpable—and all too typical. It's bad enough that people experience the inexplicable, but the aftermath is often worse. Abductees are traumatized by what has happened to them—*Did I imagine it? Am I losing my mind? And if it really happened, who's going to believe me? I'll lose my job. My wife/husband will think I'm nuts*—and it paralyzes them. All too many abductees exist in a cocoon of utter dread of discovery, a self-imposed isolation that can be as debilitating as the abduction itself.

What's astonishing is that we're more than half a century past the abduction of Betty and Barney Hill in September 1961, more than a quarter of century beyond the publication of Whitley Strieber's groundbreaking *Communion,* and not much has changed. We've been offered the insights of luminaries like John Mack, the Harvard psychiatrist who regressed hundreds of abductees and wrote books about his findings, and not much has changed in the scientific outlook on the subject. It essentially remains off-limits if you want to advance in your field. Meanwhile, popular culture has tackled the abduction phenomenon in so many ways—through novels, movies, TV shows—that you don't have to be a conspiracy theorist to wonder if we're being prepared for contact. Let's take a deeper look.

PRIMED FOR CONTACT

Hollywood is our visual cue, the pulse of the collective heartbeat where aliens and abductions are concerned. Since the late 70s, the number of movies about aliens is staggering, and we're only listing those that are best known:

Alien—1979 and its subsequent franchises
Alien Nation—1988
The Astronaut's Wife—1999
Avatar—2009
Battlestar Galactica—1978
Blob remake—1988
Close Encounters of the Third Kind—1977
Cocoon—1985
Communion—1989
Contact—1997
(The) Day the Earth Stood Still—remake, 2008
District 9—2009
Dreamcatcher—2003
E.T.—1982
(The) Fifth Element—1997
Fire in the Sky—1993

(Many) Flash Gordons—1940-1989
I Am Number Four—2011
Independence Day—1996
Indiana Jones and the Kingdom of the Crystal Skull—2008

Okay, we're only nine letters through the alphabet and a picture has emerged, right? And we haven't even talked about television series and novels in which aliens are central to the plots. If you want complete lists—Google it! The point here is that not only are aliens/ abductions /other worlds great fodder for stories, but an accretion of these types of stories help to mold our collective beliefs about what's happening now, what's possible, and what may be happening in the near future. But the bottom line is that your take on all this may be totally different than ours. That could mean that each of us has different parts of the puzzle.

DARREN'S STORY

Darren Rogers, an experiencer from Nebraska, is convinced that the beings he has encountered are both physical and non-physical and inter-dimensional rather than from another planet in our universe. He also contends that a person's beliefs play a major role in how we perceive these beings.

Rogers's encounters are seemingly frequent and exotic. In early August of 2013, he awoke on his couch to find fog or mist obscuring the hallway near the front door and his kitchen. As he studied the fog and made sure it wasn't smoke from a fire, he touched his upper right arm and wiped away blood from a small puncture.

Suddenly, something unseen silently approached and abruptly lifted him up by his feet until he was dangling upside down in midair. At that point, his recollection of the experience ended. He woke up sometime later on the couch and realized the fog was gone. It was still night and he went back to sleep. In the morning, he looked at his arm, expecting to find dried blood or a small scab. But there was no sign of a puncture mark.

Synchronistically, Rogers related the story via e-mail the day after Rob had written Maurice's story (which appears earlier in this chapter) in which he had dangled upside down in midair during an encounter.

Rogers speculated that he had encountered an artificial intelligence, an energy probe sent by an intelligent cosmic group to explore and study other species. "This encounter showed me some civilizations in the cosmos use energy that is programmed to perform certain tasks for them like we humans use drones and robots to perform jobs for us. What excites me about this possibility is that it might explain how some crop circles could be created. If a species can use programmable energy as devices or tools to accomplish and perform certain tasks, why couldn't the crop circles be created by such programmed energies?"

Rogers said that he has had numerous encounters with living beings from elsewhere. While many abductees can recall encounters when they were as young as two years old, Rogers contended that his first encounter took place *before* he was born. He said that while he was in spirit, in between lives, he agreed to work with the beings, that he *contracted* to work with them. "They said I would have a horrible accident, because it was fated, but I was being given an unusual option to recover from it by their superb medical assistance if I would agree to help them."

That accident occurred twenty years ago when he was thirty-three. "So I agreed and these beings entered my life at the fated accident's time and I miraculously recovered. These beings allowed me to remember all this at the necessary time when I began experiencing strange happenings in my house."

At first, though, he thought he was damned and that demonic forces were after him. But when he consciously recalled the agreement he made in spirit with these beings, he began to understand what was going on. "I think they put an energetic probe in my mind to be activated at the proper time."

In spite of his agreement—or possibly because of it—alien beings have abducted him. "Sometimes I'm physically taken, but more often it's an out-of-body experience. These beings only let me remember parts of some experiences because they say it would muddy the waters of what they're trying to learn from me if I saw too much of them."

Rogers said he is supposed to help them understand how emotions are affected under difficult circumstances. "Emotions apparently really puzzle them because they bled emotions out of their DNA and society a long time ago. But they say this was a huge mistake; without these emotions a race loses such a piece of itself that it begins to decay and die."

Other abductees have noted the same thing. Lifelong abductee Diane Fine, whom we wrote about in *Aliens in the Backyard,* contends that the Grays "desperately want to 'grok' us. They are obsessed with why we are attracted to other beings: mates, pets, children, even rock stars. Our nature to feel desire seems to interest them."

According to Rogers, these entities intend to reintroduce emotions into their genetic make-up. "They found out the hard way that the mind isn't enough to survive. One also needs feelings and passions that work as drivers to inspire others. Without emotions this isn't possible and eventually this leads to a pathetic emptiness and lifelessness."

He added that the symbiotic relationship he has with the entities is mutually beneficial. "I must say I'm glad I know them."

Rogers believes that other abductees also have made agreements at the soul level with the aliens. "These beings are interacting with people for a particular reason. I don't believe these beings enter other people's lives randomly or to be a demonic or evil influence on anybody."

A LIFELONG ABDUCTEE

Jenny Adams isn't as confident as Darren Rogers regarding the intentions of her abductors. She's a thirty-six-year-old therapist and mother of three who lives in Florida. Like many people who experience encounters, she doesn't want to jeopardize her family or her professional reputation, so we're not using her real name. Jenny contacted us after our appearance on *Coast to Coast*.

"I have never contacted anyone regarding the strange history of my family and myself until hearing your responses to callers on *Coast to Coast*. Two of them described experiences that sounded familiar to me. It was reassuring because who can you really talk to about these experiences without sounding nuts? I have a graduate degree and a professional reputation to uphold."

When Jenny was two years old, she and her mother saw a red glow at all the windows. Her mother looked out and saw a massive craft the size of a football field hovering above the house. Jenny doesn't remember the incident, but her mother described her absolute terror and panic as she realized that two hours had passed, the lights were gone and she had no idea what had happened to them during the missing time.

"According to my mother she saw these lights or crafts only when she was with me. She has told me she often felt they followed her home at night when I was in the car with her. I know it sounds like mental instability, but if you met my mother you would know that's not the case. She refers to them now as 'those damn things' when she talks about it with me as an adult."

The next incident occurred when she was seven or eight. Her mother was away at a church retreat and her two older brothers and their girlfriends were babysitting Jenny. She doesn't remember much about the evening except that she went to bed late. "The next thing I know, I woke up in the backseat of my brother's girlfriend's car. It was parked in the driveway. It was around three a.m., I didn't have a shirt on and wasn't wearing shoes, a coat, or gloves. It was freezing cold, the middle of winter, probably fifteen to twenty degrees outside in the middle of the night in upstate New York."

She was terrified, confused, and crying. She knew that she'd gone to sleep in her own bed. She ran back into the house, but everyone was asleep, the air was quiet. "I always thought I got to the car by sleepwalking, even though I'm not a sleepwalker. Then, as an adult, I heard some of the other stories of possible abductees winding up somewhere different than the last place they remembered being."

As she learned more about abductees, she recognized connections with her own experiences. X-rays revealed a foreign object in her nasal cavity, which abductees refer to as an alien implant. She went to two dentists who asked a lot of questions, but they were baffled and had no explanation.

Like abductee Diane Fine, Jenny also had a missing pregnancy. "Almost three years after my son was born, I was pregnant, I had every symptom. I took a pregnancy test and it was positive. I've been told you can have a false negative, but not a false positive. So, we told friends and family and started planning. I made my doctor's appointment and completely accepted that we were having our second child. When I went to the appointment, *I was not pregnant.* I didn't have a miscarriage or pain, but I *was not pregnant.*"

Jenny has no recollection of being on an alien vessel or of seeing aliens. Her interpretation of experiences in her life are the sort that skeptics would say were influenced by what she read, was told by others, or watched in movies or on television. Yet, the experiences have continued and one even involved her boyfriend, a skeptic.

About a year and a half ago, the two of them were out at night on a drive when they stopped to look at something overhead. She described it as a glowing, undulating object with iridescent colors flowing silently through the sky. "My boyfriend, the non-believer, jumped out of the car yelling over and over that it was from another world. 'That was a real UFO.

That was not the government!' he shouted. He was in total shock."

What bothers Jenny more than anything—and the main reason she contacted us—is that she suspects her ten-year-old daughter has also been taken. A year earlier, her daughter woke up with lines all over the bottom of her feet. It was as if the first two layers of skin had been removed in patterns. "My first thought was a parasite or flesh-eating bacteria or something terrible. They looked like hieroglyphic writing or symbols. It happened two or three times and she had no idea what it was and it caused no pain."

In the spring of 2012, her daughter complained that something happened to her head. She showed Jenny a spot on the top of her skull where a patch of hair was missing. The bald spot was a nearly perfect circle about the size of a half-dollar. "I asked if she had played with scissors or a razor, and I asked her sister about it. I could tell by their reaction that neither of them had anything to do with it. It was spring break and she had been with me every day. It was so disturbing and puzzling. When I realized my daughter could've possibly been abducted, I felt very angry and violated. I'm overprotective as it is, but when something so out of your control possibly happens to your child…it's an awful feeling."

Interestingly, when we posted Jenny's story on our blog in two separate posts, one of the people who commented was Charles Fontaine, whose encounter we wrote about in *Aliens in the Backyard*. Regarding the hair loss Jenny's daughter experienced, Charles wrote:

"The hair loss reminds me that several days before my own encounter in my backyard, I had noticed that I was losing my hair instantly and profusely day after day. I knew it was abnormal. I thought I would become completely bald. Oddly, after my encounter, I stopped losing my hair."

THE DIVIDE

The views expressed by Darren Rogers and Jenny Adams exemplify the divide in the community of believers—the growing numbers of people who contend *they* are here and in contact. The firsthand witnesses, those who have had encounters, either consider themselves *abductees* or *experiencers*. The abductees describe their encounters as terrifying, debilitating, debasing, humiliating, essentially the worst thing that has ever happened to them; they can't even talk about it without fearing ridicule. They ask, *If these entities are here to help us, why do they take us against our will and do as they please without our permission?*

The experiencers tend to consider their encounters beneficial, even though they may have undergone similar experiences. In the next chapter, we interview Jim O'Connell, an *experiencer* who heads a team of other experiencers to investigate encounters. His group, Xperiencers, is now endorsed by and part of the John E. Mack Institute. Their philosophy is similar to that held by John Mack, that encounters are ultimately positive. They are convinced that alien races are not only here, but want to help us. Many experiencers are abductees who have moved past their fears and say they are in contact with alien beings and await the day when the contact can become open and clear.

To that end, they demand that governments open their files and tell us what they know. Many contend that leaders are blocking disclosure because they fear the changes that would ensue. Meanwhile, the experiencers say those changes would include access to new means of energy and allow us to enter a galactic community.

There are others, like Marshall Vian Summers, author of *The Allies of Humanity,* who take a more cautious view. Summers's two books under the title are "channeled," supposedly dictated by a group of beings that call themselves our allies. They are also disturbing in that they present a bleak picture for the future of humanity unless we assert our rights to those beings who would take them away.

The allies say that we don't know who is visiting our world or why. Governments are not revealing what they know, and most people are still in denial that this phenomenon is even occurring. Furthermore, they say that most of the visitors are intent on integrating into human societies for their own advantage. Since the alien presence consists of small groups, they must rely primarily upon deception and persuasion to achieve their goals.

The allies emphasize that we face a grave danger by accepting and becoming dependent upon technology offered by the visitors, that it will result in our loss of freedom and self-sufficiency. They emphasize that we must pursue Earth-based solutions to our problems. On the bright side, Summers says, we still have a great advantage if we can respond in time.

Summers's books suggest that we have an opportunity to enter a galactic community, and we can do so as either an independent race or one dependent on and beholden to other beings. Of course, before we can take any steps we have to reach a point where there is widespread recognition that *others* are here.

It could be that the continuing denial that exists in government, mainstream science and media serves to protect us from contact. But one day the denials might fall away, just as other secrets have been exposed. That probably won't happen until the visitors make themselves known in a manner that will be undeniable. If and when that does happen, we'll see how well prepared we are to deal with a new cosmic reality.

Chapter 15
XPERIENCERS, SYNCHRONICITY & ENCOUNTERS

Quite often, just writing about encounters triggers synchronicities. As Trish was reading through this material on Xperiencers, she received an e-mail from Katy Walker—whose encounter story was told in chapter 14—that is pertinent to this chapter.

"Our screenplay is a fictional story of two people who realize they have been abducted throughout their lives (they come together through a crazy sync). We want to use a real life practitioner for the film (not an actor) who works with abductees. I'm putting my feelers out."

Jim O'Connell, the Xperiencer we interview in this chapter, works with abductees. We passed on his name and contact information to Katy.

This synchro acted as a confirmation that we should include the interview as a separate chapter. Synchronicity was also involved in how we initially made contact with Jim.

When *Aliens in the Backyard* came out, we e-mailed a number of radio show and podcast hosts as part of our publicity venue for the book. One of them was Joe Montaldo at ICAR. We never heard back from Montaldo, but several weeks later, we received an e-mail from Jim O'Connell of Xperiencers and the John E. Mack Institute.

Dear Trish,

It's come to our attention that you're interested in speaking with knowledgeable alien encounter researchers who may be able to assist you. Our Xperiencers team collaborates on some cases with Joe Montaldo's ICAR group and your case was one that was handed off for evaluation and/or investigation.

Our Xperiencers team is staffed with people that are living with ongoing alien encounters, so we understand what you're going through and know best how to help you find understanding, peace and purpose from your extraterrestrial encounters.

Trish wrote back and explained she was an author, not an abductee, and that she had written Montaldo about Rob and her appearing on ICAR's radio show. Jim and Trish began corresponding and although we never did appear on Montaldo's show, we learned about the Xperiencers and interviewed Jim O'Connell.

Jim started Xperiencers and now has a team composed of individuals who investigate encounters. The group was endorsed by the Mack Institute board of directors, and a contract was generated by Mack's son, Danny, which cemented the two organizations together. They currently have a reality TV show in development. This organization is unique in that the investigators are themselves experiencers. Their philosophy is similar to that of John Mack's. As the Harvard psychiatrist stated in *Abduction*:

"...the guiding or regenerative myth of the abduction phenomenon offers a new story for a world that has survived many holocausts and may yet be deterred from a final cataclysm. The abduction phenomenon, it seems clear, is about what is *yet to come*. It presents, quite literally, visions of alternative futures, but it leaves the choice to us."

Other researchers, such as Dr. Jacobs, believe that encounters are overwhelmingly negative. Budd Hopkins and Mack, who were friends for many years, parted ways over their difference of opinion about the abduction experience.

1) You use the term Xperiencers. Could you explain the range of experiences covered by the term?

Xperiencers is derived from the word experiencers used by Dr. John Mack. I decided to drop the "e" and allow "X" to represent the unknown as is done in solving common equations. The unknown elements that our Xperiencers team will solve can be any of the following:

Missing-time
Unexplained marks, scars or rashes
Hearing voices or messages
Visits from non-human beings
Newly discovered abilities
Time-shifting

Newly developed phobias

Feeling the need to save the planet/human race

Searching for hybrid children

Understanding that there is no government cover-up, but rather an alien cover-up

Sightings of UFOs, glowing orbs, etc.

2) What is your take on the abduction experience? Do you see it as a positive or negative experience or something in between?

The term "alien abduction" reflects the mindset of those people who feel they've been taken against their will and were violated in some fashion by some alien beings. On the other hand, there are those calling themselves "contactees" or "experiencers," which indicates they consider themselves willing participants in the extraterrestrial phenomenon. This second group also believes they may have agreed to their off-world contact before incarnating here on planet Earth and feel they have some important mission to fulfill.

I'm not sure that there is any real difference between the abductees and experiencers except for the way in which they process trauma and difficulty in their lives. Being an optimist or pessimist determines whether your glass is half-full or half-empty, but I do believe that experiencers look at the glass and say, *I know why the glass is there and it's because I wanted something left to drink on my journey.*

Each day I get out of bed and do all I can to understand this mysterious relationship and gauge its impact on my life and those around me. So far, it's made me a better person and exposed me to amazing experiences, so I remain open to contact, no matter what we call it.

3) John Mack seemed to think the abduction experience was ultimately positive. If that's the case, why are so many abductees terrified by their experiences?

Dr. John Mack felt that many of these encounters have been positive, as do I, but there is a primal response to the unknown and unfamiliar and we process that as fear. Humans live in fear all day, every day. We're in fear of losing our jobs, the car breaking down, getting sick, going broke, being divorced, etc., so when something comes into our lives that looks different and comes in the dark to take us, our fear response is cranked up to maximum.

I understand this response, because when I was new to the nighttime encounters, I too was frightened and started thinking I could be losing my mind, but in the light of day, I began to see benefits that indicated there was nothing to fear. If we humans could understand that fear only serves to separate and isolate us from new experiences and new relationships, our world and our universe would expand and richer experiences may await us.

4) In our research, we found that the Grays were by far the most frequent beings involved with encounters or abductions. Have you found that to be the case and what is your opinion on the intent of the Grays?

On the surface it may appear that the "Grays" are most frequently seen during any encounters and we believe it's because they may be a sort of "worker-bee" or "drone" that's utilized in hazardous conditions. Hazardous conditions are defined as those situations in which the Grays are in direct contact with humans who could easily injure these fragile beings. There are also taller female Grays who act as a "queen-bee" and orchestrate the activities of the drones and initiate direct human contact and telepathic communications. I wish I could give you an absolute profile of these beings, but I feel that would be like describing all human beings with one word.

It's best that each experiencer decides for himself or herself what the intent may be with each group of Grays they meet. We wouldn't dare define any race of people in general terms, so why would we paint any new off-world visitors with one broad brush?

5) What other type of beings—besides Grays—have experiencers encountered?

For those involved in ongoing encounters, a diversity of alien beings begins to emerge in the fabric of their contacts. I present a short list:
Reptilian
Short Blues
Bird men
Insect or Mantis
Pleiadian or Nordics
Dog heads or Anubis

6) Have you recalled your experiences consciously or through hypnosis? What is your opinion on hypnosis as a means of recovering memories of encounters?

Everything I know about my own encounters comes from conscious recall and I've never utilized hypnosis to access any of these alien experiences. Many of my most amazing encounters involved other people who were able to corroborate my story, so I was never left alone to wonder if I was seeing things or having psychiatric issues.

The use of hypnotic-regression should be applied to those experiencers who are already comfortable and stable in their contacts because hypnosis allows us to relive the entire encounter and that includes all the images of these alien beings and the procedures they perform on us, which can be very traumatic. This is why they apply hypnotic-blocks in our memories to protect our minds from being overloaded or traumatized from exposure to images truly foreign to us.

7) How does your Xperiencer team investigate an abduction? What does it entail?

First, let me say that we're investigating alien encounters and not all events fall into the abduction category. The process by which our Xperiencers team investigates is very simple, but utilizes gifts given to each team member during their early encounters. You see, I was told by the ET beings, long ago, to "seek out those like myself and then look within."

This leads me to believe that the aliens may have left some piece of information in the subconscious memories of each experiencer. It seems that there is some magical connection between our team and our fellow experiencers that allows us to unlock those important memories and learn from each new case. We do, however, employ a process by which we record information about the experiencer's home or encounter environment that may tell us why they were selected for contact. This is done on arrival at the experiencer's home.

Our Technical Specialist, Bobby Ledford, then sets up a series of detection devices that comprise our A.I.M. system (Alien Incursion Monitoring). This simply provides another way of possibly sensing the presence of our extraterrestrial beings if they choose to be with us during our investigation.

Beyond the technical, we rely on the information we receive from our extraterrestrial visitors by way of the information they send to us directly. Xperiencers team member, Janet Ingham, receives information from her ET counterparts in a real-time fashion that allows her to guide the investigation. In a slightly different way, I am given information by way of an implant inserted into my head years ago that allows me to receive communications at certain times.

So, as you can understand, our team is unlike any other paranormal, ghost or UFO investigation team ever assembled. Our research is truly guided by the very alien beings that everyone is searching for and wants to make contact with. These extraterrestrials are already here and can walk amongst us at will. Yet they seem to operate by something similar to *Star Trek*'s "Prime-Directive," which keeps them from directly interfering with our evolution.

8) How did you become involved with the John E. Mack Institute?

I had been discussing the idea of reaching out to the John Mack Institute to see if we might be able to tap into some of the encounter cases Dr. Mack studied. I knew that my own case file had to be stored in there with all the others. Our lead Investigator, Christina Knowles, then initiated contact with the institute and the next thing I knew, I was on the phone with the institute discussing my alien encounters, the goals of our Xperiencers group, and the reality show we were developing.

During this call, Will Beuche explained that he felt our organization was following in the tradition of Dr. Mack and suggested that it might be possible to get the endorsement of the Mack Institute for our Xperiencers project. Both Christina and I were sort of shocked at this possibility because Will had also mentioned that the institute had been contacted many times before by film, television and research groups which wanted to have this kind of association, but all were denied.

It took a few months, but eventually it all came together. This relationship has given us a greater level of credibility and visibility for our work. Many people were thrilled to see renewed activity from the institute and they believe our work honor's Dr. Mack's legacy.

During a later discussion with the board of directors from the John Mack Institute, we were told that it was Dr. Mack's wish that one day the experiencers themselves would continue his research. We are the Xperiencers.

9) Do experiencers report a deepening of intuitive/psychic abilities? Do they report a greater frequency of synchronicities? If so, what does this mean about the nature of the encounters?

Without a doubt, we've found numerous cases of intuitive/psychic abilities and it just becomes part of who we are. It doesn't make us different in any noticeable way, but it does serve as a layer of protection and additional guidance in our lives.

As for the frequency of synchronicities, there is only one answer, and it's YES. Each experiencer has his or her own level of synchronicities and I feel it's determined by how willing they are to acknowledge the events as they happen. Experiencers are all woven into this extraterrestrial fabric and one thread cannot be pulled without affecting the others.

As for me, my life has become one endless stream of synchronicities that come in the form of mystical, magical or miraculous events. Even after all these years, I still am amazed and thrilled each time it happens. I feel as though I'm on some sort of alien Indiana Jones adventure. I've often described this as a cosmic scavenger hunt, where one clue leads to the next, so we just keep following the trail of alien breadcrumbs.

What does this all mean about the nature of encounters? We're being taught a new language, not of letters and sounds, but rather a language of experiences. Each experience forms a new image and when the images are connected, we understand the conversation. The conversation they're having with me tells me to live my life according to the possibilities rather than the limitations. They've also asked me to be the ringmaster at the big-top and my job is to announce the show and get people into the tent, so they can see the most amazing show on earth.

10) What have your experiences and research revealed about the nature of consciousness?

We've learned that for the most part, humans are asleep and their connection to the cosmos has been severed. Mankind has been conditioned to accept only what they're told and to shut off the inner antennae that receives the most important signals. This is why, in this politically-correct world, the one group it's still okay to assault and humiliate are those claiming close encounters.

Experiencers are people who've abandoned the confines of religion and mainstream politics, to embrace spirituality and karma. We are experiencing an awakening and I believe we're meant to serve as an example for the world to follow.

11) Some abductees report that they have implants. What's the purpose of these implants?

I know without a doubt that my implant allows me to receive communications from these extraterrestrials. In other cases, we believe that the implants are like remote-telemetry devices, sending vital physical data, video, etc. that allows our alien visitors to monitor our environments. I'm certain that these implants are used for other purposes not yet understood.

What I do know is that humans have been radio-tagging endangered species for years to help us understand the ways in which we can help save these animals. So, could our extraterrestrial counterparts be trying to save us?

12) Do you think there's a connection between aliens and the dead?

I have been in contact with Dr. Kenneth Ring in the past and he was studying the similarities between the abduction phenomenon and near-death experiences. I do acknowledge some commonalities in the mechanics of how each may happen, but I think the jury is still out on this issue.

Chapter 16
UFOS AND THE PARANORMAL

BLOWN OPEN

Not surprisingly, synchronicities occur with astonishing frequency during and after UFO sightings, encounters, and abductions. It's as if the experience—whatever its context—blows open an individual's consciousness, forcing it to expand, to recognize patterns that may have eluded the person before.

John E. Mack, writing in *Abduction: Human Encounters with Aliens*, noted that the UFO abduction experience "bears resemblance to other dramatic, transformative experiences undergone by shamans, mystics, and ordinary citizens who have had encounters with the paranormal. In all of these experiential realms, the individual's ordinary consciousness is radically transformed."

Because of what the person experiences, he or she is initiated into what Mack calls a non-ordinary state of being that brings about a "reintegration of the self, an immersion or entrenchment into states and/or knowledge not previously accessible."

Curiously, the U.S. government, which officially has no interest in the subject of UFOs or paranormal phenomena, published a book in 1978—compiled by the Library of Congress—called *UFOs and Related Subjects: An Annotated Bibliography*.

In the preface, senior bibliographer Lynn E. Catoe links UFOs with the paranormal: "A large part of the available UFO literature is closely linked with mysticism and the metaphysical. It deals with subjects like mental telepathy, automatic writing and invisible entities as well as phenomena like poltergeist (ghost) manifestations and possession. Many of the UFO reports now being published in the popular press recount alleged incidents that are strikingly similar to demonic possession and psychic phenomena."

In fact, people who have had UFO encounters often notice that they began developing psychic abilities in the aftermath of their experiences.

PRECOGNITION & ENCOUNTERS

If you've watched any cable channel programs on the Bermuda Triangle over the past two decades, you've probably seen Bruce Gernon of Wellington, Florida. He's a pilot who in December of 1970 experienced the Bermuda Triangle effect—enormous, fast-moving clouds, weightlessness, and apparent teleportation—and lived to tell about it. For years, Gernon has appeared on documentaries and described what he had encountered as a mysterious weather-related phenomenon that he called electronic fog.

Gernon is well aware that UFOs are often linked to the Bermuda Triangle, but for years he avoided connecting the phenomenon with the concept of electronic fog. He felt that what happened to him was strange enough without bringing in UFOs and the concept that the area might be an inter-dimensional portal. Yet, all the while, he was keeping a secret that started coming out in 2005 when he and Rob co-authored *The Fog* about Gernon's Bermuda Triangle experience.

It turns out that in the aftermath of his experience, Gernon not only witnessed numerous UFOs, but developed precognitive abilities that enabled him to predict when and where UFOs would appear. He also had a close encounter.

Barely a month after his Bermuda Triangle experience, he took his girlfriend for a night flight over the South Florida peninsula. The weather was perfect, calm and clear. They left West Palm Beach around nine p.m. and climbed to 10,000 feet so they could have a better view of the city lights. When they were over the Miami Airport, Gernon headed east toward the ocean. A few miles off shore, the Atlantic spread out below them, a vast, black abyss.

When Gernon was near the same area where he had traveled through a tunnel in a massive cloud and escaped the Bermuda Triangle phenomenon, he noticed an orange light to the southeast that was about the size of a planet. It was just above the horizon and seemed to be moving slowly. Suddenly, the light expanded in size, assumed the shape of a disk, and he and his companion watched in amazement as it sped directly toward them.

"Within ten seconds it was right in front of us and it was enormous,"

Gernon recalled. "The disk appeared to be more than a hundred yards wide and thirty yards thick. It was bright amber and filled the entire windshield as it continued toward us. It looked metallic, about three times the size of a Boeing 747. I was sure we would be demolished."

Adrenaline pumped through Gernon, his girlfriend gripped the edges of her seat, braced for impact. Seconds before the craft would hit them, Gernon veered sharply to the left, turning as hard as possible, certain they didn't have a chance of avoiding a collision. But somehow, the huge craft missed them.

When Gernon glanced back, there was no sign of the UFO. He didn't understand how it had disappeared so quickly, or why had it flown directly at them. But he sensed the encounter had something to do with his dramatic experience a month earlier in which a massive, fast-moving cloud seemingly pursued and captured his plane in an enormous donut of moiling thunderheads. That life-and-death scenario is described in detail in *Aliens in the Backyard* and in *The Fog*.

But it wouldn't be long before the Bermuda Triangle phenomenon would haunt him again. A year later, as he flew through the same area on a flight from Andros Island, all three of his passengers suddenly passed out. Fortunately, Gernon remained awake and in control of the plane or another aircraft might've been added to the annals of the Bermuda Triangle. He doesn't know what happened and why it didn't affect him, but it soon became clear he was developing precognitive abilities.

Gernon's first vivid precognitive vision happened three years after his experience in the fog. He was watching a television news program when a report about the Bermuda Triangle appeared. It featured Captain James G. Richardson, a former Navy pilot; a world champion breath-holding diver, Jacques Mayol; and a tall, elderly man named Dr. J. Manson Valentine.

"As Dr. Valentine started talking, the television screen disappeared and I saw another image. My eyes were open and I suddenly felt very excited. It was extraordinary, because I saw Dr. Valentine and myself and both our wives dining together at a waterfront restaurant and we seemed to be friends."

As a result of the vision, Gernon contacted Valentine. They later met at Valentine's house in Miami and afterwards Valentine and his wife Anna took Gernon and his wife Lynn to dinner at a waterfront restaurant—the same one Gernon had seen in his vision.

A year later, in December 1974, Gernon was able to photograph a UFO through the window of a commercial jetliner because he was ready for it. He had sensed it would appear. "We were descending toward Palm Beach International and were fifty miles north over the city of Stuart. We were at about 6,000 feet and three miles inland when we first saw the UFO," he recalled. "I was looking east toward the ocean at 7:45 p.m. when a huge, disk-shaped object appeared at an altitude of 3,000 feet. It was just offshore and flying south. It looked like the UFO that I'd almost collided with four years earlier. It was the same color and it seemed to glow from within, creating a metallic appearance."

At first, it was moving more slowly than the plane, which actually passed it. Gernon snapped several photos of the craft before it abruptly sped away and disappeared. The photo distinctly shows an illuminated craft against the night sky. On the upper portion, a bulge like a cap, similar to a cockpit, is visible. However, just as a photo of a moon is not as impressive as seeing a brilliant full moon, the UFO appears distant in the night sky.

The next night, Gernon told his wife he felt they would see another UFO if they went to the beach. They drove to nearby Delray Beach and brought along binoculars with zoom lenses. The night was clear, visibility more than ten miles. Incredibly, they spotted five UFOs within minutes, one after another, all moving on the same flight path, traveling south. Gernon zoomed in with the binoculars and saw that the crafts were identical in shape and color to the one he'd seen the night before.

The last one flew much closer to shore, perhaps ten miles out. "When it was almost adjacent to us, it made a remarkable maneuver, a high-speed 90-degree turn, with no curvature in its flight path. It headed due west at an altitude of approximately 2,000 feet and within a few seconds passed within half a mile of us. When it reached the mainland, it flashed a blue light several times, then vanished."

A few months later, Gernon met with a friend, Timothy Bogle, to talk about plans for a cruising party on Bogle's sailboat. During their conversation, Gernon sensed a UFO would appear while they were partying on the sailboat. Gernon went on to tell Bogle about his Bermuda Triangle experience and his other UFO sightings. Bogle, an accomplished sea captain, doubted that Gernon had ever seen anything unusual because he'd been sailing for many years and hadn't experienced anything out of the ordinary.

But that Saturday night at the cruising party, a bright light appeared in the distance. As the twelve people on board watched, a beam of light from the UFO moved in a slow circle several times as the object descended lower and lower toward the ocean, then simply disappeared into the sea. Bogle said it was the strangest light he'd ever seen in all his years of sailing and he had no idea what it could've been. After that, whenever the subject came up, Gernon would tease him and say, "Tim saw the light." And Bogle would respond, "Gernon showed me the light."

As Rob was writing the above passage, he called Gernon to confirm the details and synchronicity came into play. When Gernon called back, he seemed surprised, then explained that he'd just had lunch with Bogle—who he rarely sees—a couple of days earlier and they were talking about that sighting three decades ago. The reason they met was because a production company was planning another Bermuda Triangle episode for the H2 Channel, and they wanted to interview someone Gernon had told his story to shortly after it happened.

Gernon's psychic abilities and those of others who have had UFO encounters bear an uncanny resemblance to what some individuals report who have had near-death experiences. During their NDEs, they are shown scenes of their own future, what author and near-death researcher Kenneth Ring calls "personal flashforwards."

One astonishing case Ring wrote about in *Heading Toward Omega*, concerned a ten-year-old boy who had an NDE during surgery in 1941 and was shown specific "memories" of his future. These memories included that he would be married at the age of twenty-eight and would have two children. He was shown his adult self and the house in which he would live, where two young children were playing on the floor. As he looked around the room, he saw something on a wall that he didn't understand, a detail his conscious mind couldn't grasp.

"The memory suddenly became present one day in 1968," he wrote to Ring. He was sitting in a chair, reading, when he glanced over at his children and realized this was the room he'd seen as a boy in 1941. And the strange object on the wall that he hadn't been able to identify decades earlier was a forced-air heater, something not invented at the time of the vision. "This was why I could not grasp what it was; it was not in my sphere of knowledge in 1941."

An encounter blows open human consciousness in the same way that a near-death experience does. Is that what it takes for our psychic abilities to shine forth? Must we first be shaken to the core? That could certainly explain the ability that Martin Caidin developed in the aftermath of an experience similar to Bruce Gernon's.

PSYCHOKINESIS & ENCOUNTERS

Martin Caidin, like Gernon, suspected that a UFO encounter was at the heart of an incident in which he and others were trapped inside an unusual cloud for three hours. In addition to Caidin, several other experienced pilots were on board the Consolidated PBY-6A *Catalina* that day in mid-1986: Captain Art Ward, a U.S. Navy pilot and instrument instructor; Rany Sohn, a captain for Northwest Airlines; and Major General Malcolm Ryan, a test pilot and combat leader. Also on board were the *Catalina's* owner Connie Edwards, his wife Karen, and Caidin's wife, Dee Dee. All three were experienced pilots.

Caidin, who died in 1997, was an aeronautical expert and author of more than fifty books. One of his more unusual books was a non-fiction tome called *Ghosts of the Air*, in which he described mysterious and supernatural encounters while flying, including the 1986 flight.

The *Catalina*, which Caidin described as a large flying boat, was outfitted with state-of-the-art navigational equipment, including two location finders, a radar altimeter and multiple radios. Their navigation systems would let them know if they were so much as a tenth of a mile off the planned course. They were linked to a weather satellite, which allowed them to print out photographs taken from space that showed where they were flying at that moment.

They took off from Bermuda—en route to Jacksonville, Florida—in clear, calm weather, expecting an uneventful flight. Caidin was standing between the two pilot seats watching dolphins through the side window when he shifted his gaze from the right side of the plane to the left. One moment he was looking out over the wing, and the next moment the wing vanished into a thick yellow cloud or fog that had risen up 4,000 feet and engulfed the plane. "Suddenly without a bump or a tremor or any indication that things were different, the outside world was gone," Caidin recalled. "Nothing had changed, except that the airplane now was flying through a huge mass of yellow eggnog."

When the pilots checked their instruments, they were startled to see that all the electronic equipment was malfunctioning. The needle on the magnetic compass swung back and forth and then spun in a blur. The gyroscopic instrument that created an artificial horizon failed. Even the needles on the electronic fuel gauges danced about. "Our intricate navigation gear blinked a few time and then every dial read: 8888888. Then the radio went dead!"

In spite of the fog, they were surprised they could peer through a tunnel above the plane and see a patch of blue sky. They also could look down through a tunnel and glimpse the ocean. It seemed the fog was attached to the plane and moved with them—the phenomenon that Bruce Gernon came to call electronic fog. They continued flying in what they hoped was a westerly direction by aiming the plane toward a bright area above the horizon.

During the hours that they were captured in the fog, they descended as low as twenty to thirty feet above the ocean, but couldn't escape the fog. They went up as high as 8,000 feet but were still engulfed in the "eggnog." About ninety minutes outside of Jacksonville, they suddenly emerged into clear sky. And astonishingly, there was no sign of the fog. "The sky was absolutely clear behind us as far as we could see. Whatever had enveloped us for hours was gone." And all the electronics and the radio, were working again. They landed safely in Jacksonville, probably because of the number of experienced pilots who took turns at the controls.

Gernon was impressed by the similarities between the *Catalina* flight and his own from sixteen year earlier. When he, like Caidin, had escaped a similar fog, it was nowhere to be seen. He now believes that both he and Caidin were caught in space occupied by a UFO that was moving in or out of our world through a temporary inter-dimensional window. He says that would explain why flying through the region known as the Bermuda Triangle is normally uneventful. Yet, the number of planes and boats that have disappeared without a trace suggests there are times when the Bermuda Triangle is a dangerous place to pass through.

Noted Caidin: "The single explanation that appears to make sense is that the *Catalina* flying boat was enveloped or affected by an intense electromagnetic field that dumped the instruments and 'blanked out' the electronic equipment." What that energy field emanated from was a mystery. He added: "Any pilot caught in that 'soup' who lacked experienced flying skills with basic instruments and no outside reference would almost certainly have lost control and crashed in the ocean."

In the aftermath of his experience, Caidin became convinced that he had developed psychokinetic ability. He was tested by parapsychologist Lloyd Auerbach, who vouched for his abilities, and was subjected to tests associated with the University of Florida. We had an opportunity to witness his ability several years after Caidin's Bermuda Triangle experience.

We were at a writers' symposium on censorship in Gainesville, Florida. Science fiction writers Jay and Joe Haldeman were also there, along with Martin Caidin and other writers. Rob had just finished writing his sixth original Indiana Jones novel for Lucasfilm and was signing copies when Caidin, who was sitting at the same table, started talking loudly to anyone who would listen about his ability to move objects with his mind. He turned to Rob and said: "Can Indiana Jones do that?" Trish then challenged Caidin to give us a demonstration of his ability. So he invited us to his house in Gainesville.

When we arrived, Caidin was eager to show us the experiment he'd devised to prove that psychokinesis is not only real and possible, but that he himself was psychokinetic. He believed the electromagnetic field through which they'd flown had somehow re-wired his brain.

The experimental room was on the second floor of his home. At one time, it probably had been a walk-in closet, but Caidin had redesigned it with a large picture window that looked into an elaborate array of "psi wheels," pieces of foil cut in various shapes that were balanced on the tip of prongs. The room resembled a field of miniature weather vanes resting idly on a tabletop.

He explained that the room was specially sealed against currents of air so that nothing but the power of the mind could cause those psi wheels to turn. As the three of us stood at the window, Caidin focused intently on the psi wheels. For several minutes, nothing happened. Then a couple of the psi wheels began to turn, then more of them started turning. They weren't spinning wildly, but they were definitely moving. Curiously, some were moving clockwise, others were moving counter-clockwise. It was as if we were watching some sort of psychic dance.

Auerbach sometimes accompanied Caidin on demonstrations and workshops. In his June 2004 column for *Fate* magazine, he wrote: "Martin Caidin was capable of moving things with his mind."

James Randi offered his rebuttal three months later, saying that in 1994 he had offered to test Caidin's ability, but that "he frantically avoided my challenge by refusing even the simplest proposed controls." Caidin had been dead for seven years when Randi made his comment, and couldn't defend himself. But when he was alive, Caidin said that Randi was evading his offer to demonstrate his psychokinetic ability and claim the $1 million prize that the magician-debunker said he would pay anyone who proved that psychic abilities existed.

The bottom line in any investigation of psi abilities is that it's much more scientific to approach a purported ability with an open mind and test it without the preconceived bias that paranormal phenomena is impossible, therefore it can't be real.

SYNCHRONICITY & THE ORIGAMI BALL

Synchronicity often comes out of the blue, unexpected. For example, as you read an uncommon word or phrase, a voice on television or the radio says that same thing. But is it possible to ask for a synchronicity and get positive results?

That's what Jenean Gilstrap wanted to know when she departed on a long drive from Louisiana to Delaware. To test the question, she put out a request to the universe to see something—anything—unusual. It didn't take long for results to materialize. On the first day, she spotted a white object in the sky. She craned her neck to watch it and after a minute or so, it disappeared. As she drove on, she spotted another one, and it also vanished.

"I remember thinking it was weird because I could see planes in the distance and they didn't disappear. However, unlike the planes, whatever I saw wasn't moving. One instant the white objects were there, the next instant they were gone. But I dismissed them, thinking they might be caused by a reflection of the sunlight."

On the second day of her trip, the weather was again perfect, bright and sunny. Not a cloud in the sky. She was on I-40E near Wytheville, Virginia, when another white object appeared in the sky. It was low enough so she could see that it was circular, pure white, the color of fresh snow.

But what was most fascinating, she said, was the exterior of the object. It seemed to be covered in pyramid shapes. "I've looked and looked for something online that might be similar, but the closest image I found was that of an origami ball."

She was taken aback by the sight and weaved into the other lane of traffic. "I had a sandwich in one hand, was holding onto the steering wheel with my other hand, and was trying to figure out how to take a photo of the object. So I dropped my sandwich and reached down for my phone. As I look up, the object simply disappeared. I looked around and up through my sunroof, but never saw the object again."

Jenean's three sightings were an example of synchronicity occurring in clusters. These synchros frequently relate to the appearance of certain numbers, names, phrases, objects, songs, events, symbols. The number 3 seems to be important for those who have had UFO encounters. Some people report bolting awake at 3 a.m., 3:30 a.m. or 3:33 a.m. Abductees often report the presence of *three* Grays, and many sightings involve lights that form three points of a triangular-shaped craft that is often too dark to see. It appears to be a motif, an archetype endemic to encounters. Esoterically, threes represent the trinity of mind, body, spirit; mother, father, child; intuition, right brain thought, creativity.

Another cluster of numbers that occur with experiencers is 11:11. If you Google that sequence nearly 500 million links show up. Esoterically, the numbers are associated with an expansion of consciousness, heightened awareness, and indicate that you are moving closer to "spirit" or to an "ET consciousness."

Uri Geller, the famous Israeli psychic, devotes a section of his website to 11:11. He claims he began experiencing the 11:11 phenomenon in 1986, when he noticed the numbers on computers, microwave ovens, cars, documents, hotel rooms. When he wrote about it on his website, he was inundated with e-mail from others who were also experiencing the phenomenon. He believes 11:11 represents "a crack between two worlds….a bridge which has the inherent potential of linking together two very different spirals of energy."

TELEPATHY & ENCOUNTERS

Telepathy—mind-to-mind communication—is reportedly one of the most common paranormal experiences related to alien abductions. Professor and author David Jacobs, a prominent researcher in the UFO field, has found in his abduction research that telepathy is the main means of communication between abductees and aliens.

Usually, this communication begins once an abductee is on an examining table in the craft. The abductee typically seems to be paralyzed, and is understandably terrified. One of the beings usually leans in close, its large black eyes boring into those of the abductee, and information is telepathically conveyed.

"The transmission of information from the alien beings to the experiencers appears to be a fundamental aspect of the abduction phenomenon," wrote Mack in *Abduction*. "Information…appears to be transmitted in two ways—by direct, mind-to-mind conveyance, or through depiction of phenomena or events on television-like screens."

Sometimes telepathic messages occur beyond words. For Starbrite A. Sprinkle, a telepathic experience occurred in the form of feelings, images, and desires, as well as words.

"My experience occurred while I was listening to one of the late night radio shows and working on my computer," she wrote. "The subject that evening was exo-politics and disclosure. The guest wanted listeners to post online at a site that President Obama set up to ascertain major policy areas that were important to the public. I typically do not interact, other than listening to the show, but somehow, I was drawn to post on the Citizens Briefing Book site. I look upon this as an experience in alien telepathy and connectivity."

Listening to her inner consciousness, she posted:

I heard a comment on the news today that the government knew terrorists were planning an attack prior to the 9/11 tragedy, but did not disclose the information to us because they were afraid that as a nation we could not handle it. That is, we are not sophisticated enough to be given the facts and be allowed to discern the impact of this on our future.

Such I feel is the way that the government has in the past viewed the extraterrestrial presence in our universe. The government has feared that the country as a whole will not be able to handle the reality of the presence of multidimensional beings or alien life forms. Do not make the mistakes of our past administrations by not being forthright with us and allow the information to be disclosed. You said that you wanted to be the administration of change. You have the opportunity by allowing the truth and disclosure of the alien presence to be a primary objective of this administration. To remain in denial as a nation could in the long run be one of the most costly mistakes this administration could make.

After she submitted her comment, she continued to work on the computer until about 2:30 a.m. Then she walked out of her office, which is behind her house, looked up into the sky and spotted an illuminated craft that was close enough so she could make out its oblong shape. Red lights circled along the outer perimeter and oscillated back and forth at its base.

"What amazed me about this encounter is the synchronicity and symbolism. It appeared for me after I had made public comments on disclosure.

I felt they were communicating with me that they recognized the actions I had just taken were the correct ones and they approved. It was a confirmation and affirmation that this was the right thing for me to do. It was a validation that there is an alien presence in our world, and the move towards disclosure is necessary and desired by them."

PARANORMAL ABILITIES OR ADVANCED TECHNOLOGY?

Those who have recalled encounters with alien beings invariably tell stories of incredible abilities that their captors possessed. Not only are the beings seemingly capable of passing through walls, but they can float their subjects through walls as well. Likewise, they seem to be capable of temporarily paralyzing humans with the power of their minds.

Abductees also report that alien captors have healed their injuries. A San Diego woman, Diane Fine, told us that during an abduction, one of the Grays—short, slender beings with large black eyes—healed a chronic knee injury without any apparent surgery. When she asked them to cure her a more serious condition involving autoimmune deficiencies, she was told telepathically that they couldn't do it, because it was karmic—something she had agreed to experience before she came into this life. Diane was also shown future scenes of the Earth's environment collapsing under the collective activities of humans, but was told this outcome could be avoided.

Psychokinetic and healing abilities, telepathy and precognition are some of the talents exhibited by alien visitors. But are these talents paranormal or the product of highly advanced technologies? Possibly, both are true and intertwined. In other words, the power of the mind to move objects and even pass through objects is no more unusual for these beings than it is for us to flip a switch to turn on a light. Some alien beings, in fact, seem capable of moving between the physical and spirit worlds. We'll take a closer look at that intriguing matter in the next chapter.

Chapter 17
UFOS AND THE DEAD

THE PHOTO

One morning in June 2013, we received an e-mail from Connie J. Cannon, one of the abductees we wrote about in *Aliens in the Backyard*. Her son, Kenny, had taken an extraordinary photograph of a UFO outside his home in Maury County, Tennessee, a rural part of the state. He sent her the photo and a description of what he'd seen.

Around 3:50 a.m. on June 23, Kenny was awakened by a "squealing" in his ears and felt "pulled" to go outside. His wife was sound asleep and didn't wake when he got up. As soon as he was outside, the squealing in his ears stopped.

He saw a V-shaped series of large, glaringly bright lights in the night sky. At first, the lights were in front of what Kenny thought was the moon—and the moon on June 23, 2013, was not only full, it was perigee, the closest it gets to the Earth. He rushed back inside the house to grab his cellphone. He was afraid that if he took the time to remove his good camera from the case, the object would be gone by the time he got back outside. He shouted at his wife to wake up, but she didn't move.

When he ran outside again, the brilliant, elongated light that he thought was the moon was still behind the V. He snapped several photos of it. Then, suddenly, the bright light—what he'd mistaken for the moon—"evaporated." But the V was still visible, made up of interconnected white lights with a dark shadow surrounding them. It moved slowly toward the northwest. During this time, he turned and saw that the moon was actually in a completely different position in the sky and realized it wasn't the source of the brilliant illumination that had been behind the craft's V-shaped lights.

Kenny snapped photos, trailing the object as it moved. He stopped as he came to a nearby ridge that overlooked an old graveyard and saw a "straight red line," like a laser, coming out of the object, and shining on one of the gravestones. Kenny was terrified—not so much by the craft, but by the red beam. It reminded him of the lasers that snipers use on their rifles when pinpointing a target in their sights, and he was afraid it would turn on him. The red beam, however, didn't show up in his photos.

Utter silence surrounded him. He didn't hear any of the typical noises you hear in the South at night—no night birds, no tree frogs, no crickets, no katydids. Just total silence. It spooked him. Even worse, the craft didn't make a sound, either. It took about fifteen minutes before it disappeared behind a distant hill. Kenny desperately wanted to get back to the house, but couldn't move his feet until the V slid completely out of sight.

Kenny, badly shaken, finally returned to the house and fell instantly asleep. His wife didn't wake up. As Connie points out, "He's an abductee and I have a sense he was abducted and that he had just been returned to his bed when he heard the 'squealing' inside his head. The squealing prompted him to go outside."

The next morning when Kenny was in the kitchen, his wife rushed out of the bedroom, and threw her arms around him. He asked her what was wrong, and she sobbed that she'd had a nightmare that he was *gone* and when she woke up and saw his side of the bed empty, she thought it was real and that he was *actually gone*. Connie believes that Kenny's wife may have awakened briefly when he was outside—or perhaps in the midst of an abduction—and then had fallen back to sleep.

The next day, Kenny went to the cemetery to locate the grave the object had targeted. Three people are apparently buried there—J.L. Saunders, a man, in the middle; a stepmother, S. Saunders on the left; and a mother, A.E. Saunders, on the right. In the center of the gravestone is a Masonic symbol and—here's the synchronicity—the bottom part of the symbol resembles the V-shape of the craft in the photo.

We were intrigued by the photo and by the connection to a graveyard and sent it to Whitley Strieber for his take on it. Strieber had it examined by a photo expert, who said he thought it looked like what one might see when a time-lapse photo of the moon is taken with a hand-held camera. A reasonable conclusion. But Kenny's cell phone is an inexpensive throwaway with a "point and shoot" capacity for photographs—no fancy time lapses, no way to change the exposure, none of the bells and whistles of a digital single lens reflex camera. Connie also explained that when Kenny had first gone outside, he thought he was looking at the glowing full moon. Then the object disappeared and the V-shaped lights remained.

Maury County, Tennessee, has known its share of high strangeness. On Dec. 26, 2012, seventeen silent orange orbs floated over the county and were seen by multiple witnesses. On May 16, 2013, there was an incident that involved a military helicopter and a plane chasing an orb. Michele Hood of Spring Hill, Tennessee, reported that she and several other adults had seen the chopper tailing an orange orb followed by an illuminated military cargo plane coming from the west. "The helicopter couldn't seem to catch up with the orb. Also, there was a stalled engine sound during the chase—like nothing any of the four adults watching had ever experienced. We get a lot of weird sky activity out here in rural Maury County."

We also found a case reported by BBC News in 2009 that sounded eerily similar to Kenny's experience. The article was headlined… "UFO fired laser over cemetery," and included a reference to a high-pitched noise "like cats wailing." The sub-heading read: "A UFO was seen hovering over a Cheshire cemetery before firing laser beams, according to a police log released by the government." The case dates back to 1996 and was included in a three-year project to release UFO files by the U.K.'s Ministry of Defense and the National Archives.

If we take Kenny's report at face value, that he's describing what he saw, then the question is: Is there a connection between UFOs and the dead? Between aliens and the dead? If so, what is it? Ufologists tend to back away from this corner of the UFO phenomena just as ghost hunters typically don't want to hear about any connection between the ghosts and aliens. It's like two subcultures that strive to preserve their realms and keep things neat and tidy. Ghosts and graveyards on the one hand, aliens and UFOs, on the other.

But let's expand the possibilities for a moment and see what connections could exist. In Eastern metaphysical philosophy, death is merely the end of our journey in a particular physical body. The spirit continues in another dimension and eventually is reborn. Perhaps aliens—at least some of them—are inter-dimensional beings who don't perceive the dead as dead and can interact with spirits in some way.

But why would UFOs hover over graveyards? Unfortunately, when the idea of aliens and the dead come together, many people tend to think of darkness, evil, Satanic rites, vampires, zombies… You get the idea. But perhaps to the aliens, graveyards act as portals between dimensions, an access point to reach our world.

Once Connie explained the conditions under which the photos were taken, Strieber invited the three of us for an interview on *Dreamland* to explore the connection between aliens and the dead.

EXIT 33

Strieber is a compassionate, yet deft interviewer. He knows his topic and asks the right questions at the right time. He immediately put Connie at ease and she was able to describe her son's sighting in great detail. Strieber was interested in the gravestone that the craft's red laser had pinpointed, specifically the Masonic symbol on the gravestone.

The Masonic symbol was particularly important for Connie. She and her entire family, dating back to the 1700s, are Masons. Connie is a 33rd degree Mason, as were her father, grandfather and great-grandfather. Because of the way her father died in 1959, Connie's first thought was whether the red light on this particular Masonic gravestone was her father's way of communicating with her.

At the age of forty-two, her father was diagnosed with brain cancer. As he lay in a coma at Emory Hospital, he was unable to speak or see. The cancer had destroyed his speech center and olfactory nerves. Yet, moments before he died, he opened his eyes and pointed at the window and said, "There's a big ship over there. I'm going to get on it."

It was medically impossible for him to see, much less speak, and because this medical impossibility was witnessed by medical personnel, his case was described in several medical journals. Connie's contention is that certain groups of aliens are connected to the human afterlife and that her father joined them when he died. "Although my father liked to fish, he always did so from shore. He wasn't interested in boats or boating." So when her father pointed at the window and identified a *big ship*, she believes he meant a big ship in the sky.

Strieber pointed out that in Freemasonry, the number three occurs frequently, just as it does in alien encounters. In the first step of Masonry, the three distinct knocks at the door are symbolic of a closed door that opens in response to the knocks. Threes represent the triune—the trinity. It's the Biblical equivalent of "Ask, and it shall be given you; seek, and ye shall find; knock, and it shall be opened unto you."

One night in the 1980s, when Strieber and his wife, Anne, still lived in their cabin in upstate New York where his encounters and abductions had occurred, he was alone in the living room with one of their cats. The cat suddenly freaked out for no apparent reason and darted into a hiding space. Moments later, there were three loud, booming knocks at the door, a pause, then three more knocks, and another pause followed by three more knocks. Strieber just sat there, stunned, paralyzed with fear, terrified at what he might find if he opened the door—An alien? A spirit? Both? Something else altogether?

When we heard this story, it cast one of our experiences in an entirely different light. In 2006, we spent a week in Cabarete, Dominica Republic, one of the premiere windsurfing spots in the world. We had a second-floor apartment in a building that was right on the beach. But before you could get to the beach, you had to circumvent a graveyard.

We had noticed a grave with a half-buried windsurfing board for a gravestone, so one morning we went into the cemetery to take a closer look. The grave belonged to a young man who had died at the age of twenty-four. His epitaph read: *Wherever the wind blows I'll be there.* As we were about to leave, Rob picked up a smooth stone from the graveyard and took it with him.

On our last night, half an hour after going to bed, we woke to the sound of pounding so hard and loud and insistent it seemed to shake the entire building. BAM-BAM-BAM... pause, then another round of three powerful blows, another pause, and a final three booms that sounded as if a demolition ball was striking the side of the building adjacent to our room. We bolted upright simultaneously—and the noise stopped immediately.

At the time, we connected the pounding to the stone that Rob had picked up in the cemetery—spirit contact—so the next day, Rob tossed the stone back into the graveyard. But when we heard Strieber's story, we were struck by the similarities. We had never connected the three sets of poundings to Freemasonry or alien contact.

The interview with Strieber became a conversation among the four of us that was so deeply strange it was as if we were neighborhood friends sitting around a kitchen table in the middle of the night, discussing the inexplicable, the unimaginable, the unspeakable. But the sideshow that went on before and during the interview was startling. Before we started, there was an unusual and persistent noise in the studio that Strieber said sounded like a truck. He was baffled because the studio is typically very quiet. Then, during the interview, we were disrupted a couple of times by voices. Strieber would stop and erase the interference, mystified by its source. When it happened again, he left it in and explained to his listeners what was happening. The equipment was in perfect condition, he said. Everything was in order. Yet, the glitches continued.

At one point, Trish, Rob, and Connie were talking for several minutes when we realized Strieber hadn't said anything for a long while. Rob hurried into Trish's office with a note: *Where's Whitley?* We quickly realized the connection had failed, so the three of us hung up and Whitley called us back several minutes later.

As it turned out, he could hear us and apparently continued recording, but we couldn't hear him. Our voices were being recorded, but his wasn't. He said he felt as if he were in "another dimension"—able to hear, but not able to comment. Isn't this how the dead must feel when they try to connect with us? They hear us, but can't make themselves heard. They can see us—but we can't see them. They are Patrick Swayze and Demi Moore in *Ghost.* As Strieber put it, "Could it be that we are a larval stage to something greater?"

Once we reconnected, we continued without any problems to the end of the interview. Afterward, Strieber wondered if Connie's father had been around and had caused the EVP—electronic voice phenomena. Strieber had distinctly heard voices on the line that weren't ours, almost as if we were doing the interview over an old-fashioned party line.

The connection between the dead and aliens is like the dark matter in this field, the aspect better left alone, an anomaly among anomalous phenomena. But the question begs to be asked. Does contact with spirits, ghosts and cemeteries somehow facilitate alien contact?

THE QUEBEC CONNECTION

When Charles Fontaine heard about the UFO-graveyard story from Tennessee, he felt vindicated. Like Kenny, he lives near a graveyard and experienced something startling there that he relates to UFOs, even though he didn't see a craft. In his case, a dramatic UFO encounter took place in his backyard days after a frightening experience in the graveyard.

Fontaine's story, which is detailed in our book, *Aliens in the Backyard,* involves a possible abduction in the graveyard that resulted in a trip to the emergency room after his pants filled with blood. A subsequent colonoscopy surprisingly detected nothing unusual and the doctor couldn't explain the blood. Days later, when mysterious beams of light appeared in the field that separated his property from the graveyard, Fontaine and his wife lost their memories of what happened after they spotted a craft approaching them in their backyard.

Prior to his encounter, Fontaine had no interest in UFOs or aliens and thought they were fictional creations. Likewise, if there were ghosts or spirits haunting the nearby graveyard, he was unaware of any such activity and skeptical about the possibility. But after his dual experiences and subsequent synchronicities and hauntings, he became convinced that both existed and were somehow related.

That contention, however, didn't sit well with a long-time French-Canadian ufologist to whom Fontaine explained his story. The researcher dismissed the graveyard event, and insisted the story began with the encounter in the backyard.

UFO researcher Scott Corrales understands that perspective. He noted in an article that, "In an effort to accentuate the positive, we overlook some of these grotesque aspects, mainly because they do not jibe with our concept of an advanced, benevolent, spacefaring, technological civilization—such as one that we may have read about in the books of Larry Niven or Hal Clement. This dark side is raw and primitive, evoking fears that go as far back as the caves, but taking place in our own troubled times. Some of these behaviors suggest—to the discomfiture of many—that the intelligence behind the UFO is far more earthbound than we know, and more closely related to medieval lore than outer space."

Likewise, years ago, when Rob and a prominent ghost hunter were talking about the possibility of co-authoring a book, the man took strong exception to the idea that UFOs and aliens had any connection with the subject. "If I came out with a book that included aliens, I would be ridiculed by my colleagues."

Yet, there are stories.

HIGH-PITCHED SCREECHING

Elk Garden, West Virginia. As of the 2010 census, this community consisted of 232 people. Yet, it has attracted UFOs for more than fifty years, when local residents began to see them in the vicinity of Nethken Hill, whose cemetery contains a number of the small town's most prominent citizens and is adjacent to a Methodist church. The Kalbaugh family, which resides on a farm located a short distance from the cemetery, claims they've seen lights over the cemetery since the late 1960's. They insist that the lights aren't airplanes or helicopters.

According to Bob Teets, author of *West Virginia UFOs: Close Encounters in the Mountain State* (1994), other eyewitnesses agree that the lights were white in color and accompanied by a high-pitched sound. Maybe sound is a key factor in these reports. Typically, those who witness low-flying unidentified crafts say the vessels made no sound at all. But we've noticed that a high-pitched screeching seems to accompany many sightings over and around graveyards.

The most memorable and eerie of the sightings over Nethken Hill took place October 8, 1967, when Reverend Harley DeLeurere and two members of his congregation went up to a promontory from where they had a panoramic view of the cemetery. Intrigued by the stories of sightings, they patiently watched the skies until later that evening when one of the men saw an object described as "a big turtle with lights on it." It appeared over the Nethken Hill and moved deliberately toward the church.

The men were stunned when the luminous turtle-shaped object descended to approximately six feet off the ground and shone its lights at the graveyard. One of the men referred by Teets as "Leonard Jr.," recalled that the object's lights projected into a day-old grave at the cemetery. "It seems like every time there was a new grave, within the next couple of nights, people would see lights up there."

ORANGE LIGHTS

Another case occurred when two sisters, driving along Route 29 in Chillicothe, Illinois, spotted two large orange lights hovering above a cemetery. Simultaneously, the radio station they were listening to abruptly turned to static, according to the report filed with the Mutual UFO Network (MUFON) on June 19, 2011.

The driver immediately pulled into the cemetery and noticed other cars pulling over to the side of the road, supposedly to view the unusual lights. "I watched them for the next few minutes as they just stayed above the cemetery, not moving," the witness said. "The one on the right moved closer to the one on the left, and that's when I saw the top of the larger one."

The object was shaped like a teardrop or an inverted cone. The base of the object glowed an extremely bright orange and numerous long spikes protruded from the top and curved downward. The witness, whose name was not revealed in the public report, said that after a few minutes the smaller craft moved off toward a field behind the cemetery and the larger one followed.

The two sisters returned to their car and started following the objects. When they reached the high school, they noticed a helicopter heading in the direction the UFOs had taken. "We weren't able to make much sense of it, but definitely believe that the helicopter was following in their direction."

ILLUMINATED CLOUD

In 1977, an unusual event occurred in the town of Gerena, Spain, fourteen miles northwest of Seville. It involved UFOs hovering over a cemetery. On October 23, Ana Rumín and Manuel Fernández were walking along a street near the outskirts of town near where they lived. It was a clear night, the sky studded with stars. Rumín drew her companion's attention to a glow above a nearby cemetery. Fernández assured her that the glow was most likely "a cloud illuminated by the town's streetlights." This seemed a reasonable explanation and they continued down the street.

They saw that the 'cloud' above the cemetery had a reddish hue, and cast its light on the tall cypress trees and the mausoleums. An uncanny silence enveloped the area and they realized that something out of the ordinary was taking place. They stopped at a neighbor's house to get a better look at the phenomenon from his rooftop.

By the time Ruperto Muñoz and his wife accompanied the two witnesses to the rooftop, the red cloud had vanished. But the four onlookers were able to see a small, red circular object heading off into the distance. It changed colors from red to green and blinked intermittently before it disappeared in the distance.

Spanish UFO researcher Joaquín Mateos Nogales reported the case and noted that "the area in question offers a wealth of unidentified flying object reports, which we have attested through many years of on-site research."

WHAT'S IT MEAN?

Researchers have offered a number of possible explanations for why UFOs hover over cemeteries. While the reason remains a mystery, possible motives range from the absurd to the grotesque. One researcher wrote that maybe the aliens had seen long lines of cars with lights on during the day turning into cemeteries so they investigated. Besides the fact that the idea assumes the occupants are mostly clueless about life on this planet, the reasoning also overlooks the point that many cars now have automatic daytime lights. Another proposed solution suggests that alien implants are in short supply and that the nighttime graveyard visits are all about removing the devices from the recently deceased. A parallel explanation, one that's a bit more practical, proposes that the implants are being deactivated through sound or light. But if the aliens can monitor or track people from a great distance, it seems they could also deactivate the devices from far away as well.

Then there's also an explanation that sounds like a plot element from a B-grade science fiction movie: the aliens are re-activating the bodies of dead humans and turning them into UFO pilots, who are apparently given time to wander about and frighten people. However, considering the interest in zombies in recent years, it seems this alternative—the un-living, recycled humans mixing with aliens from who-knows-where—is an intriguing option, at least one with possibilities for the world of horror-based entertainment.

Scott Corrales explored this idea in some depths in his article and provided examples:

A man known only as "Mr. Rible" took his daughter to an airstrip near Butler, Pennsylvania, in 1967 to watch for mysterious nocturnal lights known to appear in the area. The father and daughter soon found themselves catching more than a glimpse of the phenomenon when two luminous objects suddenly headed straight for their Volkswagen.

Rather than crashing into the vehicle, the lights abruptly morphed into a half-circle of five humanoid figures "dressed in sloppy green-gray trousers" with their heads covered by flat-topped caps. The exposed skin of their arms and faces was coarse and gave the appearance of being severely burned. Startled by the sight, Rible anxiously turned on the VW's engine and quickly drove around the semicircle of frightening figures.

Corrales wonders if the men-in-black phenomenon, usually related to the early days of the UFO sightings, is connected to the concept of re-animated humans. Stories of encounters with the beings, who typically wear ill-fitting clothes and drive black hearse-like vehicles, are well known not only in North America, but also in South America and Europe. Their men-in-black outfits usually consist of white shirts, black ties and black suits, common clothing for dead men.

The re-animated human—zombie—concept focuses on the idea that the physical remains of humans are of some value to aliens, that they somehow thrive on dead matter. It's clearly a low-life perspective, far from the concept of star people or benevolent ETs.

THE SPIRIT CONNECTION

The supposed presence of aliens remains an enigma. Anyone who tells you differently is guessing. None of us knows the big picture. While there's plenty of anecdotal evidence to suggest *they are here*, everything else—who they are, what they are, and what they are doing—is shrouded in mystery. Likewise, their nature—benevolent, neutral, or antagonistic—is unclear. Most likely it's all of the above. While the Grays seem to be the predominant race, there are stories of other races as well and contact with spiritually enlightened beings.

And why should we assume they are from distant planets? They might be time travelers or inter-dimensional beings. If so, then it could be, as we mentioned earlier, that inter-dimensional travelers are using graveyards as portals and might be in contact with the dead, who seem quite alive from their perspective.

Terence McKenna, a lecturer and writer on human consciousness and metaphysics, believed that UFOs are manifestations of the human soul or collective spirit. He thought they exerted psychological influence over the course of history and they would fill our skies and occupy our minds by 2012. ·

McKenna was off on his dates; a fleet of UFOs has yet to fill the skies. But UFOs do seem to occupy our collective mind. If you enter *UFO videos* in the YouTube search bar, nearly six million hits are returned. When you enter UFOs on Google's search bar, the hits double.

Researcher Hilary Evans, author of *Gods, Spirits, Cosmic Guardians: Encounters with Non-Human Beings* (1987) and *Visions, Apparitions, Alien Visitors: A Complete Study of the Entity Enigma* (1984) concluded that alien entities may have originated in the minds of the experiencers and are connected with paranormal phenomenon.

In 1957, Carl Jung published *Flying Saucers: A Modern Myth of Things Seen in the Sky* and made a convincing case for UFOs as the unfolding of a modern myth. As Barbara Hannah explained in her biographical memoir,

Jung: His Life and Work, Jung wasn't interested in whether UFOs were real. The fact that people all over the world were seeing *round objects* in the sky was what intrigued him. "Roundness is the symbol par excellence for the Self, the totality," Hannah wrote. In other words, these round saucers were *symbolic* of an emerging collective need for wholeness.

In the nearly sixty years since Jung wrote his book on UFOs, crafts of numerous shapes and sizes have been reported, physical evidence has been left behind, and thousands of abductees have come forward with their stories. How is that a myth?

But as Dean Radin pointed out in *Supernormal: Science, Yoga, and the Evidence for Extraordinary Psychic Abilities,* "Jung's use of the term 'myth' does not imply that UFO sightings or for that matter encounters with angels, aliens, fairies, spirits, elves or demons are just fantasies. Rather, it suggests that some of these experiences may literally be psychophysical, a blurring of conventional boundaries between objective and subjective realities." Or, "*mind literally shapes matter,* that the imaginal and the real are not as separate as they seem."

Chapter 18
A CLOSE ENCOUNTER
WITH WHITLEY STRIEBER

One day in the late 1980s, we were headed into a Little Professor Bookstore in Fort Lauderdale, Florida, when we stopped and stared at a display in the front window. A stack of hardcover books faced the door, with one of them upright. The cover depicted an alien with a large, bald head, huge, almond shaped, liquid black eyes, a negligible nose, and a dash for a mouth, an image very close to what we now collectively associate with Grays. The book was *Communion: A True Story* by Whitley Strieber.

We were familiar with the author's fiction—*The Wolfen, The Hunger, Warday, Nature's End*—but hadn't heard about this book. We read the back cover, the inside flap, and bought it. We knew this was the book and author to whom Budd Hopkins had referred nearly a year earlier, when we were covering a UFO conference in Hollywood, Florida, for *OMNI Magazine*.

We had been sitting outside with Budd and Betty Hill to arrange interviews with both of them. The conversation turned to Budd's newest book, *Intruders,* which would be coming out the following year. It was specifically about the sexual experimentation many abductees reported that seemed to be related to reproduction. He had been on a radio show earlier that morning and one of the callers was a woman whose story suggested she had been abducted. Hopkins hoped to regress her, but didn't have any transportation. So we offered to give him a ride.

During that forty-three-mile trip to Lake Worth, he mentioned he had been working with a famous writer whose abduction experiences spanned many years. "I'm telling you, when this book is published, it'll be explosive."

We pressed Budd for the name of the writer, but he refused to tell us. When we saw *Communion* on that display case, we suddenly *knew*. And Budd was right. The book *was* explosive. After all, in 1987, not much was known about the alien abduction experience. In fact, a dozen publishers rejected *Communion* and one editor advised Strieber not to publish it because it would ruin his career. In the end, William Morrow not only bought the book, they paid a seven-figure advance for it.

Communion quickly hit the top slot on the *New York Times* bestseller list for nonfiction and went on to sell several million copies in hardback and paperback. It was followed by a movie starring Christopher Walken and became a worldwide success. *Communion,* coupled with the publication of Hopkins's book *Intruders*, helped the abduction phenomenon to reach a tipping point in public awareness. Strieber's skills as a writer, his ability to delve into the emotional horror and esoteric confusion his experiences triggered, and the stunning cover gave the aliens a face that is now embedded in our collective consciousness.

At the time, the abduction phenomenon was so far outside mainstream thought that the repercussions of the book's success were both a curse and blessing for Strieber. Accused of writing fiction as though it were true, reviled by skeptics and comedians who ridiculed his description of rectal probes, his fiction career suffered. He and his wife, Anne, eventually lost their home in upstate New York, where the abductions had occurred. *Communion* had led to literary ex-communication.

Some writers might have given up at this point. But Strieber not only persevered, he continued to publish both fiction and nonfiction. *Communion* was followed by *Transformation* and *Breakthrough*, the three books detailing his experiences between 1985 and 1994. He went on to write *The Coming Global Superstorm*, a nonfiction book co-authored with popular radio show host Art Bell, which was turned into a movie, *The Day After Tomorrow*. His subsequent novels, like *Hybrid*, certainly reflect his experiences and questions about his abductions. He wrote *The Key* in 2001, which describes a 45-minute lecture on spirituality, the environment and other issues by a stranger, who walked into his hotel room in the middle of the night.

Now, more than twenty-five years after the publication of *Communion*, Strieber has one of the best websites about UFOs, the paranormal and everything alternative and mysterious (unknowncountry.com). He also hosts a popular podcast, *Dreamland,* which features shows on cutting edge ideas about the nature of reality. He remains baffled by how so many people still think that *Communion* was fiction and that after all these years he's still somehow keeping up the ploy, living the lie.

We asked Strieber for an interview, and decided upon written questions that would allow him to expound in detail. He agreed to our plan and we submitted a dozen questions.

1) You've expressed opinions about the Grays that seem to indicate they are neither benevolent nor malicious Whether or not that remains your opinion, could you explain in more detail what you think about these beings?

I don't know what they are. The evidence is just too sketchy. They are certainly something, but if they are aliens, why is it that so many people, me included, report seeing their dead friends and relatives during close encounters? If they are indeed aliens, they are certainly radically different from us. I will say that it's obvious that somebody is shooting at something, so there is a material reality involved that the Air Force, at least, does not like. But is it an alien presence or simply something that they do not understand, but which appears to violate air space they are duty-bound to protect? Without more information, I think that it's premature to come to conclusions about benevolence or maliciousness.

2) You have never stated that you were abducted by aliens. You refer to them as visitors. So what can you say about the nature of their reality? Are these entities us, from the future? Are they the dead in another form? Are they inter-dimensional? Are the Grays robotic as some have suggested?

Once again, I have not drawn any conclusions. In my life, the Grays were very far from robotic. They were, in fact, filled with complex emotions, mercurial and volcanic, like people might be if they had no way of concealing their raw feelings from the society around them. As to the nature of their reality, being with them for even a few minutes while in full consciousness is devastatingly powerful. When I was with them once, I went forward in time or into a parallel universe, and found myself when I returned unable to understand the English language for about half an hour. When I tried to navigate streets I had known all my life, I could not find my way.

To enter their reality is to enter oneself in ways that have always been hidden, but which seem entirely appropriate at the time. Since they so often appear with the dead, I have to say that there is some connection there. Perhaps, in their reality, there is no veil between the living and the dead. If so, then their entire approach to reality is entirely different from ours.

3) David Jacobs and others believe that we are essentially "farm animals" to the Grays who are using us for a breeding program. Do you agree with

that? If not, what do you think is actually going on? Is genetic material being harvested?

My genetic material has been harvested. I have been face to face with a very strange man who I think must have been either some sort of genetic experiment or a sport of nature or even a hybrid. But what was being hybridized I do not know. I do know this: the close encounter experience penetrates us at the very deepest levels, intellectually, emotionally, spiritually and physically.

4) Stephen Greer has said he thinks the Grays are man-made creatures, controlled by the military, and that the real aliens are benevolent. Do you agree? Have you ever encountered any beings that you would consider benevolent?

I have no idea if any of these entities are man-made, elements of nature, or even physical beings as we understand that phrase. When I went into the forest in early 1986, my experience changed from one of being treated like a lab animal to one of being treated like a student. I was given a phenomenal eleven-year education that transformed what I had thought of as myth and wishful thinking, into a reality I can no longer deny. I live in a soul-blind world, but I know for certain that there is a soul, and that it bears reference to a much larger world than this one, and lives by rules we do not remember in the hurly-burly of physical life, except at moments of great beauty and great mystery, and when we face the dark.

5) As a result of the massive numbers of letters you have received from abductees after writing *Communion*, you have estimated that millions of people have undergone the alien abduction experience. A Roper Organization poll in 1999 said that 33 million people fit the profile for abductees. If that's the case, why haven't there been more witnesses? Why isn't the FBI investigating these serial crimes involving so many people?

The government is not alone. Whatever it does arises from a level of control that is higher than anything we can see. As far as the close encounter experience is concerned, it is part of life and probably has been from time immemorial. What has changed is us, not the experience, in the sense that we now see it not in terms of demons, angels and other mythological beings, but as something more objectively real. Our first stab at explaining the fact that it is objectively real is to call it an encounter with aliens. But that's only the beginning. As we go further down the road, we will inevitably discover that we live inside a much larger reality. Its nature and dimensions we do not yet know.

6) What is the most important thing that you learned from your encounters and abduction experiences?

How to be rigorous about the question.

7) You've written about implants and have said that you have one in your body that doctors haven't been able to remove. What's the purpose of these implants? Do you feel you're "monitored?"

I don't know their purpose, but the one in my ear is a constant issue with me. I dearly wish the doctor had been able to remove it, but it moved away from his scalpel and he closed the incision. It was put there by people, and I do not think it necessarily has a good purpose. I feel that, at the least, it is an invasion of my privacy. Living with it has been very difficult.

8) When you say "it was put there by people," I'm assuming you're referring to humans, not aliens. If that's the case, do you think the "people" actually could've been Grays who had shape shifted? Have you experienced any such shape shifting behavior among them?

As far as I'm concerned, it was put in by two people. They were not aliens and the person directing them from outside spoke clear English in a male voice. As I woke up, he said "condition red," and they rushed to the bedside and overcame me by unknown means. I could hear and feel, but not move.
    Shape shifting? I didn't get any impression like that at all.

9) Do you think disclosure is coming soon? What impact would it have on the consensus worldview if we learned that our government and others have been aware of an alien presence for decades?

I don't think that anything can be initiated from our side of the fence. There's nobody in any government with the power to disclose anything.

If such a thing were to happen, it would be in the context of a profound change in the whole nature of human experience, and it would be initiated from the other side, would be my best guess. I have known many people in the U.S. government who had knowledge of strange things, but nobody who could say for certain that the presence they were dealing with was "alien." Whatever they are, they enforce the secrecy. They could obviously show up in a moment, but they don't. Therefore, the secrecy is their choice, not ours.

10) From your books, we have a sense of how your abduction experiences sculpted your professional life. But what impact did they have on you personally? On your personal relationships with your wife and son?

My writings on this subject marginalized me and ruined my life. However, I am happy to say that my family life was full of love always, and remains so, and I have lost none of the old friends who know me well. But I have been tuned out by the literary community, the public, the press and just about every institution of voice that we have. While I probably have one of the most important stories to tell that has ever been brought forth, I am ignored or derided. I reached the edge of the world and saw beyond. The result? I'm laughed at as the "rectal probe" man.

11) The entire abduction scenario begs the question: what's the nature of our reality? What is the true nature of consciousness?

Consciousness is a leaf on a tree.

12) In addition to your extensive website and radio show, *Dreamland*, what are your current projects?

I am working on a new book series called *Alien Hunter*, which is also a project with the SyFy network. It is a fictional series that is designed to both be fun to read and also offer a sense of empowerment.
   Alien Hunter was published in August, 2013.

Chapter 19
THE FEARLESS JOURNEY

During the writing of this book, we reached several points where we weren't sure about its structure and direction or if we had enough of the right kinds of stories. So we would set it aside for a few days and, invariably, a synchronicity would occur that infused the project with new energy, new stories. Then we would fine-tune the structure, adjust our compass, and move forward again.

Even though these topics are gaining more mainstream acceptance, they still don't fit into the existing paradigm of how the universe—and everything else—works. In a room filled with strangers, you can probably talk about some aspects of the paranormal—telepathy, for instance, or precognition—and the people you're talking to may chime in with one of their own experiences. The same is true for meaningful coincidence. But in that same room, if you mention alien contact and encounters, you probably risk ridicule or, at the very least, some strange looks.

Then again, because the existing paradigm is in flux, there could be someone in that room who has experienced missing time. Or someone like Martin Caidin who claimed to have psychokinetic powers. Or there could be an abductee who believes he or she is psychic as a result of alien contact. It's understandable that abductees would want to remain silent, yet more and more are speaking out. And perhaps as the paradigm shifts, our collective fear of ridicule is losing its hold on us.

In decades past, if the mainstream media reported at all on sightings or encounters, the report was facetious, the newscasters snickering. The implied message was, *Wink, wink, we know it's silly, don't we?* Recently, though, local TV affiliates are beginning to report on sightings without that snickering.

On August 5, 2013, an NBC affiliate in upscale Naples, Florida, reported on "a mystery over the skies of Collier County." Strange lights were captured on security surveillance cameras at a condominium complex. As newscaster Rick Ritter reported, "Whatever the showing of lights was, it came and hovered over this (swimming) pool behind me for nearly thirty minutes. Residents said they've never seen anything like it."

The images the cameras captured are like something out of the movie *Cocoon* or perhaps out of *Abyss*. Video shows strange lights sweeping in over the pool, then the lights sink down toward the pool and expand like a web. The newscaster noted that his affiliate sent the video off to MUFON in Ohio. The organization was in the process of analyzing it, but didn't think it was a hoax. The station also showed the video to a biologist at the Conservancy of Southwest Florida to see if the images captured on video might be those of an animal. The biologist didn't believe it was.

"Meanwhile," Ritter continued, "officials at MUFON tell me this is one of the most fascinating videos they've seen in a while. And, *coincidentally,* this pool is closed for the next few days for some maintenance."

Ritter delivered all this without any hint of derision, a straight news story. And he noted the apparent coincidence that the pool was closed for maintenance.

News coverage like this, even if it's mostly by local network affiliates, suggests that the existing paradigm is fraying at the seams. As more of us speak up about our experiences with synchronicity, the paranormal, alien contact and everything else that goes bump in the night, the unraveling of the existing paradigm will continue.

"If the transformation of human consciousness is the goal of evolution," wrote Rupert Sheldrake in *Science Set Free,* "then why do there need to be a billion stars besides our sun in our galaxy and billions of other galaxies beyond it? Is human consciousness unique? Or is consciousness developing throughout the universe? And will our consciousness ultimately make contact with those other minds?"

Perhaps synchronicity is one of the brightest beacons in the evolution of our consciousness, a kind of twilight zone of magic, a bridge that connects the unconscious to the conscious mind, the present to the past and to the future. Jung believed that the more frequently you experience synchronicity, the less fragmented you are as a human being.

For centuries, man has recognized signs and symbols as meaningful. In the fourth century B.C., Greek philosopher Heraclitus saw all things as interrelated or following cosmic reason. He believed that events were not isolated happenings, but had repercussions across the entire fabric of existence, that all things were linked by a web of organization created by Logos.

Hippocrates, born twenty years after Heraclitus died, expressed similar thoughts. "There is one common flow, a common breathing. Everything is in sympathy. The whole organism and each one of its parts are working together for the same purpose. The great principle extends to the most extreme part, and from the extremest part returns again to the great principle."

The Roman scholar Agrippa referred to a Fifth Essence, something beyond earth, air, fire and water that held existence together. He also called it the World Soul, which penetrates all things and is a thing in itself. Agrippa's contemporary, Plotinus, wrote, "Chance has no place in life, but only harmony and order reign therein."

In the Middle Ages, this idea was known as the *unus mundus*, one world, and referred to a collective knowledge that exists independently of us, yet is available to us. In this cosmology, the source of meaningful coincidence is separate from our conscious awareness and egos, but it's where our psyche and the external world touch.

For physicist and writer F. David Peat, synchronicity is a bridge between mind and matter: "Synchronicities open the floodgates of the deeper levels of consciousness and matter which, for a creative instant, sweep over the mind and heal the division between the internal and the external."

Physicist David Bohm referred to this inner world as the implicate order. "Every action starts from an intention in the implicate order," he wrote. "The imagination is already the creation of the form." In other words, imagination and reality are ultimately indistinguishable. Bohm called our external reality the explicate order because it unfolds from this deeper order of existence. In Bohm's view of the universe, everything is part of a continuum.

Robert Lanza, an M.D. and professor at Wake Forrest University School of Medicine, goes even farther than Bohm in his book *Biocentrism*. Lanza makes a convincing argument that consciousness is everything. Remember the koan? If a tree falls in a forest and nobody is there to hear it, does it make a sound? According to Lanza, it doesn't. In his cosmology, neither the tree nor the forest exists if a consciousness isn't perceiving it.

This isn't New Age happy talk about the unity of man and the universe. It's science that begins at the quantum level. So where do UFOs, aliens and encounters belong in these cosmologies? Well, in Lanza's worldview, if you open that door in your consciousness, then these entities and experiences exist for you.

In the Jungian worldview, these experiences symbolize archetypes that have become active in our psyche. "If (flying saucers are) a rumor, the apparition of discs must be a symbol produced by the unconscious.... If (they are) a hard and concrete fact, we are surely confronted with something thoroughly out of the way....The phenomenon of the saucers might even be both, rumor as well as fact," Jung wrote in a letter.

In Bohm's worldview, these mysterious objects may be a holographic phenomenon. Astrophysicist Jacques Vallee, one of the world's most respected UFO researchers and the model for the character Lacombe in *Close Encounters of the Third Kind*, seems to agree. He said the behavior of UFOs is the behavior of an image, or a holographic projection.

Yet, as Michael Talbot addresses in *The Holographic Universe*, UFOs and aliens can't be just psychic projections of the unconscious, not with all the physical evidence left behind—like the scars and incision marks of abductees. "Given that quantum physics has shown us that mind and matter are inextricably linked, I suggest that UFOs and related phenomena are further evidence of this ultimate lack of division between the psychological and physical worlds. They are indeed a product of the collective human psyche, but they are also quite real." He theorized that the phenomenon isn't subjective or objective, but "omnijective," something humans haven't yet learned to comprehend properly.

Physician and near-death researcher Kenneth Ring recognizes parallels between NDEs, abduction experiences, and the mythic realities through which shamans journey. Again, this is not a New Age belief system. It's science, the study of consciousness and the nature of reality.

Whitley Strieber once said that encounters "may be our first true quantum discovery in the large-scale world: The very act of observing it may be creating it as a concrete actuality, with sense, definition, and a consciousness of its own."

All that said, mainstream science still labels all coincidence as random events, mere curiosities, but ultimately meaningless. At the other extreme, some people are trapped in a fear of the unknown and say that synchronicities can't be trusted, that such experiences are manipulated by malignant forces that are controlling you and everything else in the universe. Or they say that aliens or the shadow people or some other hidden, terrifying forces are running the show.

Fear and divisiveness have always been the favored weapons of petty tyrants. And there are plenty of tyrants still struggling to hold the exhausted paradigm in place. Don't fall for it. We write our scripts from the inside out, from the fabrics of our consciousness, from the fundamental tenets of our belief systems, whatever they are.

By remaining open to the unknown, the unseen, the uncharted, you're inviting synchronicity into your experience, and it may be the best and most reliable beacon we have to venture into the enfoldment of this new paradigm, whatever it may be.

Resources

Bair, Deirdre. *Jung: A Biography*. New York: Little, Brown, 2003.

Cameron, Grant and Crain, T. Scott. *UFOs, Area 51, and Government Informants, A Report on Government Involvement in UFO Crash Retrievals*. Rochester, New York: Keyhole Publishing, 1991, 2013.

Combs, Allan and Holland, Mark. *Synchronicity, Science, Myth and the Trickster*. New York: Marlowe and Company, 1989.

Goodchild Veronica. *Songlines of the Soul: Pathways to a New Vision for a New Century*. Lake Worth, Florida: Nicholas-Hays, Inc., 2012.

Grasse, Ray. *The Waking Dream: Unlocking the Symbolic Language of Our Lives*. Wheaton, Illinois: Theosophical Publishing House/Quest Books, 1996.

Harner, Michael. *Cave and Cosmos: Shamanic Encounters with Another Reality*. Berkley: North Atlantic Books, 2013.

Hennacy, Diane. *The ESP Enigma: The Scientific Case for Psychic Phenomena*. New York: Walker & Company, 2008.

Hopcke, Robert. *There Are No Accidents: Synchronicity and the Stories of Our Lives*. New York. Riverhead Books, 1997.

Hopkins, Budd. *Art, Life, and UFOs, A Memoir*. San Antonio, New York: Anomalist Books, 2009.

Jacobs, David. *Secret Life: Firsthand Documented Accounts of UFO Abductions*. New York: Touchstone. 1993.

Ingerman, Sandra, Wesselman, Hank. *Awakening to the Spirit World: The Shamanic Path of Direct Revelation*. Louisville, CO: Sounds True, Inc. 2010.

Jung, Carl. *Memories, Dreams, Reflections*. Translated by Richard Winston and Clara Winston. New York: Vintage Books, 1961.

Lanza, Robert and Berman, Bob. *Biocentrism: How Life and Consciousness Are the Keys to Understanding the True Nature of the Universe*. New York: BenBella Books. 2009.

MacGregor, Trish & Rob. *Aliens in the Backyard: UFO Encounters, Abductions & Synchronicity.* Crossroad Press, Hertford, N.C., 2013.

MacGregor, Trish & Rob. *The 7 Secrets of Synchronicity: Your Guide to Finding Meaning in Signs Big and Small.* Adams Media, Avon, MA, 2011.

MacGregor, Trish & Rob. *Synchronicity & the Other Side: Your Guide to Meaningful Connections with the Afterlife.* Adams Media, Avon, MA, 2012.

Martini, Richard. *Flipside: A Tourist's Guide on How to Navigate the Afterlife.* Los Angeles: Premier Digital Publishing, 2011.

McMoneagle, Joe and Tart, Charles. *Mind Trek: Exploring Consciousness, Time and Space Through Remote Viewing.* Charlottesville, Virginia: Hampton Roads. 1997.

McMoneagle, Joe. *The Stargate Chronicles, Memoirs of a Psychic Spy.* Charlottesville, Virginia: Hampton Roads. 2002.

Miller, Arthur I. *Deciphering the Cosmic Number: The Strange Friendship of Wolfgang Pauli and Carl Jung.* New York: Norton, 2009.

Monroe, Robert. *Journeys Out of the Body.* New York: Broadway Books, 1977.

Radin, Dean. *Supernormal: Science, Yoga, and the Evidence for Extraordinary Psychic Abilities.* Crown Publishing, New York, 2013.

Ring, Kenneth. *Heading Toward Omega.* Harper Perennial, New York, 1985.

Sheldrake, Rupert. *Dogs That Know When Their Owners Are Coming Home and Other Unexplained Powers of Animals.* New York: Three Rivers Press, 1999, 2011.

Sheldrake, Rupert. *Science Set Free: 10 Paths of New Discovery.* New York: Crown Publishing, 2012.

Strieber, Whitley. *Solving the Communion Enigma.* New York: Tarcher/Penguin, 2011.

Talbot, Michael. *The Holographic Universe.* New York: Harper Collins, 1991.

Tarnas, Richard. *Cosmo and Psyche: Intimation of a New World View.* New York: Plume, 2007.

Wilson, Colin. *Mysteries: An Investigation into the Occult, the Paranormal, & the Supernatural.* Watkins, London, 2006.

About the Authors

ROB & TRISH MACGREGOR reside in South Florida. They write fiction and non-fiction. Both have won the Mystery Writers of America Edgar Allan Poe Award. Trish's latest novel is *Apparition*. Rob's latest novel is *Time Catcher*. Their most recent non-fiction books are *The 7 Secrets of Synchronicity*, *Synchronicity and the Other Side*, and *Aliens in the Backyard*. They also co-authored *The Everything Dream Book* and *The Lotus & the Stars: The Way of Astro-Yoga*. Trish is also the author of *Power Tarot* and Rob is the author of *Psychic Power* and co-author of *The Fog* (with Bruce Gernon).

Curious about other Crossroad Press books?
Stop by our site:
http://store.crossroadpress.com
We offer quality writing
in digital, audio, and print formats.

Enter the code FIRSTBOOK
to get 20% off your first order from our store!
Stop by today!

Made in the USA
Las Vegas, NV
29 September 2024